MASS
AWAKENING

SHOSHI HERSCU

BALBOA.
PRESS

A DIVISION OF HAY HOUSE

Balboa Press books may be ordered through booksellers or by contacting:

Balboa Press
A Division of Hay House
1663 Liberty Drive
Bloomington, IN 47403
www.balboapress.com
1 (877) 407-4847

Because of the dynamic nature of the Internet, any web addresses or links contained in this book may have changed since publication and may no longer be valid. The views expressed in this work are solely those of the author and do not necessarily reflect the views of the publisher, and the publisher hereby disclaims any responsibility for them.

The author of this book does not dispense medical advice or prescribe the use of any technique as a form of treatment for physical, emotional, or medical problems without the advice of a physician, either directly or indirectly. The intent of the author is only to offer information of a general nature to help you in your quest for emotional and spiritual well-being. In the event you use any of the information in this book for yourself, which is your constitutional right, the author and the publisher assume no responsibility for your actions.

This book is a work of non-fiction. Unless otherwise noted, the author and the publisher make no explicit guarantees as to the accuracy of the information contained in this book and in some cases, names of people and places have been altered to protect their privacy.

Print information available on the last page.

ISBN: 978-1-9822-0855-4 (sc)
ISBN: 978-1-9822-0856-1 (e)

Balboa Press rev. date: 07/25/2018

Dedicating the Book to Liz Halevy, my best friend ever and like a surrogate mother to me

First, I would like to express my sadness and gratitude for one of my best friends, if not the best, since the age of thirteen until her passing three years ago. Someone who is unfortunately gone, will not see this manuscript, and would probably be ecstatic about it, the late Liz Halevy R.I.P. You were more like a wonderful second mom, more than a friend was. I love you and miss you so much. I wish you were here to see this. I will never ever forget your kindness, your wit, and amazing tomato soup. You were the best!!!!

CONTENTS

ACKNOWLEDGEMENTS

John Nelson, my editor, who guided me through the process of writing this book and made it possible… from an idea to a complete manuscript… a miracle

My amazing 93-year-old auntie Mali Malbina Meshulam (Mali for us in the family) who always believed in me when I wrote the book and saw me as successful even when there was no proof for it and I was just beginning writing this manuscript. I'm so grateful for her presence in my life and uplifting my spirits when I need it badly.

My friends and lightworkers and other independent journalists worldwide who also research the truth about our reality. Nir (alias, not his real name), who helped me discern vast amounts of information, taught me how to do so, helped me connect the dots, provided evidence for his conclusions, and most importantly, has so much patience in replying my endless questions on these topics (especially on geo-politics and finances topics). Thank you, Hector Guerra, my friend and a brother from a different mom in Latin America for providing me support and having faith in me in writing this book. Your patience with me is invaluable.

Justin Nexus Booth you gave me a glimpse as to what six degrees of separation is about. We started talking about people that we both admire and found out that you're a close friend of few of them (as Michael Tellinger, the founder of the Ubuntu Liberation Movement). Thank you for the great information that you provided me and the amazing shift in consciousness that you embody in all the activities that you're involved in.

His moving words:

my pleasure to be connected and help each other grow my dear
It's much more
we are all creating New Earth together
I'm doing it by words, research and speaking you're doing it your
way which is amazing too
I'm thrilled and excited to be part of this huge global movement
this is sort of like our umbrella conscious corporation that assists us
in sharing information with the masses
your heart and your minds eye will take/guide you exactly where
you need to be when you need to be there
everything happens in divine timing my soul sista

My friends who are always there for me….. Dorit Scheter, who is my friend since we've been 11 years old in Africa and my big sister from a different mom (although she was born 3 months after me), my very dear cousin and friend Iris Tyroler, you are my rock whenever I feel in turbulent waters (which is quite often), Matt Polani who makes me laugh when I'm concerned and sad and always believing in me; and sincere flattery always helps, of course.

I'm grateful for my parents who provided me support throughout the last "lean" years. I couldn't make it without you. Thank you very much Adela and Nathan Herscu.

I would also like to mention my source of inspiration Lisa Nichols (featured in the Secret movie and the CEO of Motivating the Masses). I admire your courage, perseverance, and kindness – I still keep your emails. For me, you're an incredible role model for what you managed to do in your life, for saving the lives of so many youths (from committing suicide) and their parents too and for the life that you created for you and your son Jelani. You're unforgettable. You're my Shero, Lisa. Your truly big fan from Israel.

Nicu Constantin who sent me invaluable information; especially on the protests in France. Brilliant man and highly spiritual. Thanks, my friend.

Tory Smith (R.I.P), who was abused as a child, continued to

suffer from such abuse into adulthood and in spite of his suffering he chose to expose the crimes of the elite and other entities war/agenda against humanity and earth. I mention him here as he was the one who revealed to me what is going on in regards to perhaps the most horrifying crime against humanity: ritual sacrifices and the related subject of human trafficking, especially children. Thank you, Tory for your fearless struggle against these inhumane atrocities that you suffered so much.

INTRODUCTION

My name is Shoshi Herscu, a 47-year-old woman and an independent journalist from Haifa, Israel, who survived a childhood growing up in three different countries: Romania, Israel, and the Ivory Coast where my father relocated us as he worked as a construction engineer for the "Sonitra" company. Growing up in such varied countries and cultures imbued me with an appreciation for their great diversity and an abhorrence for the mono-culture that is being "engineered" in today's world, especially in the West. And although, like most of us, I came to trust my parents and their surrogates—education, church, and government—I sensed at an early age that I was being sold "a bill of goods," or a certain life perspective and wanted to choose my own.

Living in Africa with its earthy population more in touch with primal instincts allowed me to develop and trust my intuition about people and agendas. After returning from Africa, I travelled extensively with my parents in Europe at a time when traditional cultures were giving away to the Americanization of the world. I was a very curious child in general, reading a lot (a real bookworm) and developing a different perspective from the people around me. I just love learning about new places, tasting new cuisines, and meeting new and different people from all over the world all the time. I'm just intrigued by the diversity and new experiences to have.

It was for this reason that after my undergraduate studies in Israel and my release from military service, I chose to obtain my MBA in England (1994-1995). I was interested in international business, and I wanted a more global perspective. After I graduated, I traveled the world and got as far as Australia. I enjoyed the atmosphere there, the great diversity of its landscape, but on the other hand, I noticed the large number of surveillance cameras in all its cities. I didn't know back then that it was one of the "5-Eye Nations." To me it was strange, as Australia is supposed to be a democracy. So I asked others why there were so many surveillance cameras here? People told me that it's for "security reasons," but Australia wasn't exactly a terrorist hotspot. While I wasn't convinced by this explanation, I didn't investigate further.

When I was traveling there, the then Israeli Prime Minister, Itzhak Rabin, was assassinated. I was so shocked that I didn't want to return to Israel. I felt that if an Israeli prime minister, one of most protected people in the world, could be assassinated in Tel Aviv by a radicalized student, it was no longer a democracy and I didn't want to live in such a country. I cried for two days, even though I disagreed with his views, and was ashamed to leave the house with my swollen eyes. I did return to Israel at the beginning of 1996.

I worked as a content editor and the Webmaster of Infotour. co.il, a site covering tourism in Israel, including attractions and events, which was sponsored by the Ministry of Tourism. Seeing the commercial need, I became a Hebrew-English translator in 2005. I've been a social activist over the years and an independent journalist writing about these topics in my blogs. Between 2012-15, I worked at for pCon, a computers and technology magazine in Israel after applying for a job as a reporter and writing an investigative report on encryption in the corporate world. Learning about how people and companies used encrypted messages via email to hide information and activities, I got my first glimpse into how pervasive the control of information had become. I assumed this was a reaction to government surveillance. I then discovered that a discrete mailing service (encrypted) was shut off by the government, despite the business success of this service.[1] I realized that the "Big Brother" wants to know everything about us and wouldn't allow any "slips".

I followed this lead in other investigations and saw how information was being managed and in many cases hidden from the public by the government. From this job and others in the technology sector, I became an avid researcher able to analyze masses of information and to find the truth about our real reality and connecting the dots.

In 2013, I started seeing news alerts on covert topics such as Geoengineering, Chemtrails, and Solar Radiation Management (SRM), which I ignored for months. I just didn't give any thought to these alerts. They appeared too farfetched. My mind was, in the parlance of technology, just turned off to these indications. Then something struck me. I looked up at the sky one day and saw that there were strange cloud shapes like cobwebs; some were spread across one part of the sky but not in another, and there was no uniformity in their shapes. I also noticed white tracer lines that started "swelling" in the middle of the summer where in Israel we're supposed to have blue cloudless skies for at least half a year, and definitely during the summer. I started taking pictures when I came upon pink clouds. Yes, pink. One day I was so shocked that it was dark at noon in midsummer that I was speechless. I took endless photos as evidence for my followers on Facebook, who apparently weren't aware of this phenomenon because it wasn't being reported—or was it being suppressed?

I finally realized that something very strange was happening. So I started paying closer attention to this growing phenomenon. I searched for relevant information in Hebrew newspapers and magazines and online sites, but couldn't find any commentary. I used to write for a popular alternative news site which was called (it doesn't exist anymore) "Israeli Patrioti" (Patriot Israeli). Shaul Cohen, the owner of the site didn't believe me at first, but I wrote an article for him entitled: "The Connection between Chemtrails and Agenda 21." This is a plan devised by the UN and signed by 178 countries at the Rio, Brazil Earth Summit in 1992. Agenda 21 promotes world "depopulation" by employing many means, among them Chemtrails (although this term is not mentioned in this plan)—the spraying of heavy metals, pathogens, and viruses carried out by unmarked military aircrafts and passenger airplanes (normal contrails from airplanes dissipate very quickly but not these).

I found so much proof for this phenomenon, including an extensive list of patents (for "Geoengineering," the euphemism of Chemtrails) created by many companies[2], along with testimonies from workers involved in these industries, as well as those employed in intelligence agencies like whistleblower Ted Gunderson. This former head of the Los Angeles FBI tried to warn us about such hidden government agendas and was assassinated. You can check out the excellent Italian documentary entitled "Chemtrails the Secret War"[3] or "What in the World Are They Spraying?"[4] Other evidence includes lab test results[5] of water samples in areas spotted to be sprayed (in the USA, Germany, Israel and other places too), and Guardian Newspaper published a map of "Geoengineering Projects" around the world[6]. I provided this editor with so much hard evidence that he started following the news on this topic himself.

One day he even told me "Shoshi, you were right about this. Here, read this article!"[7] Since then, over 20,000 people have read my online articles that were posted both on Israeli Patrioti, the defunct alternative news website, and my personal blog on Cafethemarker. com.

I asked one of my brilliant friends, the very brave activist and an independent journalist, Shabtay Avigal, how is that despite all this immense manipulative brainwashing and propaganda from Main Stream Media (MSM), such as claiming that Chemtrails are simply "normal" contrails and that no one is dumping toxic heavy metals into the atmosphere, people like us are awakening from this false reality? His reply was that some of us are beginning to think "outside the box." But I believe there are few reasons why I was able to awaken while others are not seeing these signs at all. I intuitively stopped watching TV (tell-lie-vision is the more appropriate description), reading newspapers, listening to the radio and mainstream music for a few years (except for Coldplay which I love!). These medias are not intended to inform or entertain the public, but are aimed at brainwashing (actual subliminal mind control) and distracting the populace from the truth of this massive control. These are the forces that keep them in ignorance.

I think that most of us live in denial because what we think we see is so hard even to imagine, not less believe. I mean, I had days that I was numb with pain, disbelief, and total shock from my discoveries of over 800 FEMA (Federal Emergency Management Agency)[8] Camps in the US, which are unmarked concentration camps. I could see a guillotine with Google Earth and Americans started asking on Facebook why the army purchased 30,000 guillotines![9] (Of course Wikipedia dismisses such reports as conspiracy theories). I found testimonies of soup agents, including Ted Gunderson (who I mentioned earlier), about guillotines in the US[10].

Moreover, I was overwhelmed by constantly finding more information about the hidden depopulation agenda (See Georgia Guidestones: "The Georgia Guidestones is a mysterious monument on which are carved ten "commandments" for a "New Age of Reason."). The first commandment: Maintaining the world population under 500 million people."[11] Governments worldwide are reducing the population on earth by all means possible and impossible, including vaccines, fluoridation, GMOs, smart meters and the list goes on. I could only cry at these revelations after a while.

This book is mainly written for those who want to understand why this world is becoming so crazy even more than usual. Today, there's a lot of information mixed in with disinformation (intentionally misleading information) such as the global warming hoax, which can't be maintained as scientists say that earth is actually cooling, so they changed it to climate change (but climate always changes)[12]. This misinformation (unintentional spreading of misleading information) is pervasive, as uninformed bloggers unintentionally repeat the disinformation they hear on TV or other mainstream media outlets.

This disinformation campaign is a desperate effort to distract the populace from signs of a mass awakening of human consciousness and its dire consequences for these controllers. Human consciousness is rising, people are awakening to the truth of their connection to the greater whole of life and to each other and the self-empowerment that brings. As a consequence, our eyes are being open and we are demanding the full disclosure of these programs of control, which will lead the Global Elites' demise. Thus, the 1% of this world's population—probably much less—will be unable to rule the awakened populace anymore. They will lose their power; they know it, and they're fighting back. This shift in consciousness will bring world peace and a higher standard of living for everyone, because those who perpetrate the wars and their reigns of terror, who gobble up our food and energy resources, will have their day of reckoning. So there will be peace on earth, as the unshackled mainstream media starts broadcasting the truth about the hidden technologies withheld from us that can be used for the benefit of humanity and elimination of poverty and hunger worldwide.

This book intends to discuss both the concealed and the revealed aspects of this huge shift in human consciousness occurring today worldwide. Most people are not even aware of this awakening, benumbed by media distortions and the constant "terror" alerts that send them into a fear-based state and cut them off from higher aspects of themselves. I will partly describe some of my own experiences of awakening to the higher aspects of myself, which allowed me to see through the distortion and how it allowed me to see the truth of these hidden agendas. For instance, I found out that the vaccines, given to children and even "flu" shots to adults, contain Thimerosal, 49% mercury by weight, which can cause "mild to severe mental retardation" in infants and problems in adults[13]. This is but one example of how the medical establishment is being used in this agenda. I'll share documentation of the revealed and concealed information about the ongoing "shift of the ages" occurring worldwide when it's relevant.

I write this for those who are very unaware of these government agendas and want to know what is going with our world, which seems to becoming crazier by the day, where it's all heading, and how to spot the signs for this shift from their own experiences and the data they received. I will share my experience with you and will give you some pointers on how to adapt to the changes both spiritually and physically (like grounding daily by walking barefoot on the beach or on grass to discharge the static buildup of electricity, sunbathing, eating cilantro and wheatgrass, and taking natural dietary supplements like spirulina and chlorella to help the body remove the toxins, daily exercise, and meditations often twice a day).

I will share my own experience hopefully to make this adaptation for you less trying. I want to inspire the readers to step forward and embrace this great changeover, to understand what is transpiring while providing a grand vision of the upcoming Golden Age, to provide strength and to encourage you not to be afraid of what's coming. Yes, it's difficult to believe . . . I know. I had a hard time believing some of this myself. I'm not a natural optimist; the opposite is true. But as I mentioned earlier, I can't ignore the evidence coming from soft disclosure and recent events. I needed a lot of hard evidence to believe this myself.

We are in the midst of a peaceful revolution worldwide in all the areas of our lives, including finances, medicine, education, political systems, society, food, and technology, and we must become aware of our "real" reality worldwide. As I've said, while it's hard to believe, we're heading to a massive positive shift and transformation worldwide. It seems, even to me, that things are deteriorating in many areas, but at the same time, positive things happen simultaneously. There are recently increasingly more false flags attacks (especially in the UK), while at the same time pedophilia rings are being exposed and thousands of these criminals are arrested (87,000 in one of the largest busts in the last month in Germany)[14]. There's a massive struggle going on behind the scenes. The negative and positive occur at the same time. However, before we see a reversal of these trends, it's going to get worse, as you can already see.

There's a war going on behind the scene (in-fighting within countries, within organizations) between "dark hats" (the "Powers that Be" who will become the "Powers that Were") and the "white hats" (the good guys worldwide who are involved in dismantling this power structure). It is a very coordinated effort underway, and has been for years, to remove the dark forces from this world and that they want to get humanity out of this mess that we currently experience.[15] As the saying goes, "it's darkest before dawn."

We're now living right before the dawn of this mass awakening, although there is no definite date when we will see a breakthrough in this process which is called "The Event." There are many groups involved worldwide in bringing on this "Event" and its changeover to fruition. "It will be a moment of breakthrough for the planet, which will be physical and nonphysical. On the nonphysical plane, there will be a *'big wave or flash of Divine energy and light coming from the Galactic Central sun going towards the surface of the planet.'* This energy will "permeate the earth and humanity, raising the frequencies of all living entities on the planet."[15]

"It will calm humanity in the light of love energy and end duality. It's a magnificent energy not seen or felt before on Earth. Everyone on Earth will feel and know something has happened. It will be a surprise as to when it will happen, even for us. It's never happened before. It will not be a major shock event, it will be a positive event." [15]

"On the physical plane there will be:

- The arrest of the Cabal (already started).
- The reset of the Financial Systems.
- Disclosure—the release of ET information.
- The beginning of a new, fairer financial system with prosperity funds for all humanity.
- NEW Government/Political system, Education system, Healthcare system, etc.

- Awakening of humanity slowly and gradually to the existence of positive non-terrestrial races and our galactic connections.
- Introduction of new advanced technologies.
- The release of spiritual growth and healing for every human being on the planet.
- The Event is actually many things at the same moment. *It is when the light forces take over the mass media and release intel about ET involvement, about the crimes of the Cabal, about the advanced technologies, so FULL disclosure.* This is part of it.
- *The other part of it is the mass arrest of the Cabal.*
- *The other part of it is Financial reset* that the Eastern alliance has been preparing for quite a long time.
- *And of course we have been gradually going toward the first contact, which is an actual official contact between the earth civilization and other positive ET races that exist throughout the galaxy.* And the Event is a trigger point which begins that process.
- That's the short overview of what the Event is. *And of course we have the pulse from the galactic central sun.* The galactic central sun is a living entity, and it times the pulse of energy according to our global awareness and the level of that awareness and the level of the awakening. And when we have this compression breakthrough the level of awakening is high enough for humanity to receive that pulse of increased energy from the galactic center." [15]

We, those who follow and investigate these topics for years, see the acceleration in soft disclosures like pedophilia, which is rampant at the top echelon of society in Western countries (though not only), as well as other signs which cause us to believe that the "Event" is very close. This breakthrough will lead to Full Disclosure and mass-arrests, which are going to be devastating to all, including those who actively investigate our reality (me included) . . . There's even a movement entitled "Full Disclosure Now". This is a global grassroots movement which intention is to serve as the people's conduit for Full Disclosure[16].

"In light of whistleblowers coming forward over the past decades such as Edward Snowden, Julian Assange, Corey Goode, Chelsea Manning, Philip Sneider, Bob Lazar, Mike Ruppert and others [like Tory Smith]; it has become apparent to anyone listening that humanity is living a lie within a lie within a lie. The complexities of which NOT ONE single group is aware of completely, a compartmentalized self-perpetuating enigma growing more complicated and reckless with each day. With the understanding that fossil fuels are not needed, religious institutions are spiritually bankrupt, and our governments are morally corrupt networks of self-serving occult bloodlines and criminal syndicates hell bent on power and control, how can humanity reclaim it's free will?"[17]

"It is our time now, our time to ask for and accept the truth buried within each of us. We must exclaim to ourselves that "I am ready to know the truth," and embrace each other as we take one step closer each day toward Full Disclosure Now! These are people from all over the world demanding that the whole truth about our reality to be fully exposed"[17] (The Event Chronicle site).

This information on the war behind the scenes, this ongoing transformation, and our "real" reality will be vital for the general populace worldwide after the shift, as many people (those totally unaware of this hidden reality) will feel that their entire world has collapsed due to these drastic changes in all areas of our lives and the extremely hard-to-take revelations. These disclosures are going to shock everyone. We're fast approaching a total science-fiction reality, or as Corey Goode (a whistleblower who worked twenty years in the secret space program) termed it: a "Star-Trek society." These technologies are already in use in secret space programs (such as replicators to produce food as on the Enterprise spaceships on the *Star Trek* TV series) or in DUMBS—deep underground military bases—that after full disclosure these technologies will become available to humanity. That's the reason it is so important that as many people become aware of these topics now to prepare them.

What Are the Signs Indicating that We're Heading This Shift?

You can see that the arrests of pedophiles have accelerated recently in the U.S. (about or over 3000 since January 2017, since Donald Trump's inauguration)[18]. This is Trump's policy to "drain the swamp" of pedophiles and human trafficking, which is rampant at the top echelon of politics and that's the reason why he's so hated on mainstream media which is controlled by "Team Dark" or the "controllers." Moreover, soft disclosure has also been accelerated, including on those training and funding Daesh (ISIS), and terrorist attacks discovered to be false flag attacks, staged attacks by the government. It doesn't mean it's fake and people don't die. In some, they do die like the 3,000 victims in the 9/11 attack (I'm sending my sincere condolences to the families of the victims), but in others, it's not certain if the casualty toll like "Sandy Hook" or the "Manchester Terror Attack" at the Ariana Grande concert in Manchester are accurate. "The term **false flag** describes covert operations that are designed to deceive in such a way that activities appear as though they are being carried out by entities, groups, or nations other than those who actually planned and executed them."[19] (Wikipedia).

People are becoming more aware worldwide of what is really happening in our reality. They are very suspicious about false flag attacks and search for signs indicating it's such an attack immediately after it occurs, and they sharing online the evidence. For example, it took me 1 ½ hours to find out the truth about the Nice Attack after talking with a friend who lives there, and just a little longer to scope out the last "fixed" elections in France. I can also add as a sign the accelerated rate of soft-disclosures about pedophilia and ritual sacrifices, which is the Elite Controllers' Achilles Heel. People are awakening en-mass worldwide and demanding their rights back (major provisions of 2001 Patriot Act in the U.S. were recently extended to 2019)[20], eager to know the truth and demanding it worldwide. Take the case of Edward Snowden, who uncovered the massive U.S. gov. surveillance worldwide; Seth Rich—Wikileaks' source; and Rep. Steve Scalise, who was actively seeking to stop pedophilia and whose shooter was killed on-site—people demand the truth and don't believe the official "story."

Free energy technology cannot be suppressed anymore[21], like Nicola Tesla's inventions[22] that threaten the moneyed elite by making electricity much more affordable. His inventions gathered energy from natural sources, such as from the heat of ambient air, which he called "a self-acting engine" and could run indefinitely from the solar energy stored in the air. His most famous attempt to provide free energy to all points on the globe was his World Power System (his WardenClyffe Tower), which is a method of broadcasting electrical energy wirelessly through the ground (http://free-energy.ws/nikola-tesla/). Keshe and many others (let's remember Wilhelm Reich—orgone energy or orgonites—who like Nikola Tesla, if less famous, died in jail to suppress his inventions/discoveries). Recently we watched how free energy means became mainstream when "Israel's Prime Minister Benjamin Netanyahu took his Indian counterpart Narendra Modi out on a drive on the Olga beach in the Gal-Mobile. The Gal-Mobile is an independent mobile integrated water desalination and purification vehicle that turns seawater into safe and high-quality drinking water. It can purify up to 20,000 liters of sea water a day."[23] The seawater fuels the car and the byproduct is desalination.

Moreover, new economic models like Ubuntu Liberation movement led by Michael Tellinger are becoming more widespread worldwide. The Ubuntu Movement creates "a totally new system that turns competition into collaboration," a philosophy known as Contributionism. There is no use of money but "working together to create towns, cities, countries and lives overflowing with abundance, food, arts, music, sports, technology, health, leisure and infinite variety." "The first stage of the 'One Small Town' initiative is to create food and income generating projects within a community, all run by the power of the community members. In the beginning stages these funds are funneled back into more produce and income generating projects, until eventually the town is self-sustaining & generating a sizable income through external sales.

This money is then split between the further advancement of the town, the business owners, and the community members themselves. The members of the community are rewarded for their efforts with free products and services, and an ever-growing income as more and more money generating projects are formed."[24]

The tribunals being established for the purpose of prosecuting the Elite (for committing crimes against humanity), who cannot be prosecuted right now under the current legal system (the top echelon is above the law under the current legal system). These tribunals are: the International Tribunal for Natural Justice (https://www.itnj.org/), Judicial Commission of Inquiry into Human Trafficking and Child Sex Abuse, and the International Tribunal into Crimes of Church and State (or ITCCS) (http://itccs.org/) established by Kevin Annett. Their purpose is "to lawfully prosecute those people and institutions responsible for the exploitation, trafficking, torture and murder of children, past and present, and (2) To stop these and other criminal actions by church and state, including by disestablishing those same institutions."

I will systematically explore all the information brought forth in this introduction in more detail with documented proof.

FOOTNOTES:

[1] https://en.wikipedia.org/wiki/Lavabit

[2] http://www.geoengineeringwatch.org/links-to-geoengineering-patents/

[3] "Chemtrails the Secret War" https://www.youtube.com/watch?v=U-5VnMIiKPY

[4] "What in the World Are They Spraying?" https://www.youtube.com/watch?v=jf0khstYDLA

[5] Lab test results (in Germany can be understood even if you don't know German) http://www.nwo-rebell.de/chemtrails-fallout-analyse-zusammensetzung/

[6] A map of "Geoengineering Projects" around the world, the Guardian https://www.theguardian.com/environment/graphic/2012/jul/17/geoengineering-world-map

[7] http://beforeitsnews.com/alternative/2010/09/us-reported-in-panic-after-chemtrail-planes-forced-down-in-india-nigeria-171044.html

[8] FEMA Camps in the US http://www.disclose.tv/news/List_Of_All_Fema_Concentration_Camps_In_America_Revealed/86674

[8] https://wwFw.linkedin.com/pulse/america-2017-concentration-camps-lists-citizens-guillotines-holt

[9] Video about the US government purchasing 30,000 guillotines https://www.youtube.com/watch?v=v6jDYgt4M40

[10] Ted Gunderson testimony on the US government purchasing guillotines http://www.thecommonsenseshow.com/2013/06/29/why-does-the-government-need-guillotines/

[10] Testimony from military on the run for refusing to collaborate with the agenda of killing innocent Americans by guillotines https://www.youtube.com/watch?v=lDUvwhTboSE

[10] https://truth11.com/2016/03/20/30000-guillotines-800-fema-camps-and-15000-russian-troops-whats-going-on-obamacare-code-icd9e978-execution-by-guillotine-666-mark-of-the-beast/

11 https://vigilantcitizen.com/sinistersites/sinister-sites-the-georgia-guidestones/

12 https://realclimatescience.com/2017/01/earth-cooling-at-the-fastest-rate-on-record/

12 https://www.sciencenews.org/article/earth-mantle-cooling-faster-expected

12 http://www.express.co.uk/news/science/723481/Earth-ICE-AGE-big-freeze-solar-activity

13 http://www.whale.to/vaccines/thimerosal.htm

14 http://yournewswire.com/police-politicians-pedophile/

14 http://victuruslibertas.com/2017/07/high-level-politicians-arrested-in-huge-pedophile-sting/

15 Prepareforchangeleadrship.org http://prepareforchangeleadership.org/home/

16 The Full Disclosure Now Facebook page https://www.facebook.com/groups/1759064740995644/

17 The Event Chronicle site http://www.theeventchronicle.com/editors-pick/full-disclosure-now-11-11-16-1111-ampm-get-involved/#

18 http://anonhq.com/former-navy-seal-exposes-3000-high-level-elite-pedophiles-media-silent/

19 https://en.wikipedia.org/wiki/False_flag

20 https://www.comparitech.com/blog/vpn-privacy/a-breakdown-of-the-patriot-act-freedom-act-and-fisa/

21 Here's an example of free energy device that is supposed to be sold already. http://www.dailymail.co.uk/sciencetech/article-3462885/The-electricity-generator-pedal-Free-Electric-bike-create-24-hours-electricity-just-hour-exercise.html

22 http://www.nuenergy.org/nikola-tesla-radiant-energy-system/

23 https://auto.ndtv.com/news/prime-minister-modis-drive-with-pm-netanyahu-in-israels-gal-mobile-1721709

24 https://ubuntuplanet.org/

REFERENCES:

1. The article "Chemtrails and the Connection to Agenda 21" published by Shoshi Herscu in Israeli Patriot (Patriot Israeli) in Hebrew on September 5th, 2013.

2. The article "We Fund Our Own Genocide by Chemtrails – by Secret Budget" published by Shoshi Herscu in Israeli Patriot (Patriot Israeli) in Hebrew on April 17, 2014.

3. http://beforeitsnews.com/alternative/2010/09/us-reported-in-panic-after-chemtrail-planes-forced-down-in-india-nigeria-171044.html

4. http://www.geoengineeringwatch.org/the-budget-obama-didnt-want-you-to-know-about/

5. **True or False! Did the U.S. Gov Purchase 30,000 Guillotines?** https://www.youtube.com/watch?v=v6jDYgt4M40

6. http://www.thecommonsenseshow.com/2016/01/28/fema-camps-are-open-guillotines-are-in-place-isis-executioners-await-your-arrival/

7. "Confirmation for Chemtrails Being Sprayed Worldwide" posted by Shoshi Herscu on Cafethemarker.com in Hebrew on September 5, 2013. http://cafe.themarker.com/post/2979165/

8. "You Thought You Were in Danger for Chemical Attack by Asad or the Rebels? Think Again. We're Being Sprayed to Death by Chemtrails – with Evidence" published by Shoshi Herscu in the blog on Cafethemarker.com in Hebrew on September 18, 2013. http://cafe.themarker.com/post/2986318/

9. "Do You Want a Cellular Antenna at Home? Refuse Dangerous and Polluting Smart Meters". Published by Shoshi Herscu in the blog on Cafethemarker.com in Hebrew on October 3, 2013. http://cafe.themarker.com/post/2993936/

10. "If You Don't Want a Cellular Antenna at Home, Reject Smart Meters – Dangerous and Conducting Surveillance 24/7". Published by Shoshi Herscu in the blog on Cafethemarker.com in Hebrew on November 6, 2013. http://cafe.themarker.com/post/3011213/

11. "We Are Being Manipulated/Duped – The Israel Electric Company PR Offense in Favor of Smart Meters – Carcinogenic, Cause Fires, and Conduct Surveillance 24/7". Published by Shoshi Herscu in the blog on Cafethemarker.com in Hebrew on January 4, 2014. http://cafe.themarker.com/post/3039644/

12. "More and More Whistleblowers/Insiders Expose Chemtrails, the Spraying of Chemicals Worldwide, to Annihilated Humanity". Published by Shoshi Herscu in the blog on Cafethemarker.com in Hebrew on April 17, 2014. http://cafe.themarker.com/post/3088285/

13. "The Carcinogenic, Highly-inflamable Smart Meters "the Big Brother" Are Quickly Installed Across Israel without Citizens' Concent". Published by Shoshi Herscu in the blog on Cafethemarker.com in Hebrew on August 21, 2015. http://cafe.themarker.com/post/3250423/

14. "Do You Want a Cellular Antenna at Home? Resist Smart Meters". Published by Shoshi Herscu in the blog on Cafethemarker.com in Hebrew on January 8, 2016. http://cafe.themarker.com/post/3284773/

15. "Litzman, Leave My Water Clean" (Video). Published on March 27, 2016 on Youtube and Cafethemarker.com: http://cafe.themarker.com/post/3302029/; https://www.youtube.com/watch?v=k1WQydvUOsg&feature=youtu.be

16. "Say No to Smart Meters in the Cities Modiin, Tel Aviv, Beer Sheva, and Jerusalem." Published on October 30, 2016 on Cafethemarker.com http://cafe.themarker.com/post/3346926/

17. The UN United Nations, *Agenda 21 Earth Summit The United Nations Programme of Action from Rio*, city of publication?, Createspace Independent Publishing Platform, 2013. https://www.alibris.com/search/books/isbn/9781482672770?bookbin=11638915634&gclid=EAIaIQobChMIj-fJ4fK52QIVz73tCh05_wVJEAQYAyABEgJI9fD_BwE

PART I

THE AGENDA

CHAPTER ONE

THE DEPOPULATION OF PLANET EARTH

I first became aware of this deadly population decimation and control agenda for humanity a few years ago after finding information about chemtrails, smart meters, and the orchestrated emigration from Africa to Israel and from the Mideast to Western countries. For a long time, I had no idea that there was any connection between these diverse topics. I was overwhelmed even learning about each of them separately. The most difficult experience during this time was feeling so alone. No one in my surroundings would listen to me—definitely not my family or friends. Actually, when I mentioned to my best friends about the phenomenon of "chemtrails," I was ridiculed. However, over time they realized what was happening, and one day I even overheard a friend explaining to someone else about chemtrails. I felt that this phenomenon was so crazy, and it made me sad and depressed. I didn't share much about these topics at the beginning. I just couldn't. I first had to absorb this information and make sense of it. Everything in my reality looked upside down; from that time on, I began to interpret my reality through these filters.

However, after a year or two I began to write about these topics for an Israeli alternative news site and on my blog, and started getting feedback from many people in Israel—negative, positive, and inquisitive inquiries too. As there was no information about these topics in Hebrew, people were eager to become informed on the subjects. Then somehow, I found people who had been researching these topics and we started to discuss them, to connect the dots, share information and our emotional outrage with each other, so that we all felt less isolated in general. It was interesting that more people came forward who felt the same as I do—whether in Israel or other countries—on Facebook or in real life, even on the train, at supermarket or out on the town. In Israel, it's very common for people to strike spontaneous conversations everywhere, so it made discussing these topics a little easier.

So, let me start by presenting a little background on this depopulation agenda:

The Population Explosion over the Last 200 Years

First of all, the world's human population has exploded over the last two hundred years. According to UN estimates[1], we only numbered one billion people in 1850, while today there over seven billion humans living on Earth! This is a staggering fact considering that for thousands of years, the population of the world increased very slowly. However, in the last century, it has grown exponentially from 1.5 to 6.1 billion between 1900 and 2000! Yet, despite these steady increases, recent studies show that this pattern has changed and that population growth is actually seemingly declining "naturally." It decreased from a peak of a 2.1 percent per year in 1962 to almost 1.05 percent in 2017.

So, in the last half century, the population growth rate has declined steadily, and the UN projections show that this seemingly natural decline will continue in the next decades, with an estimated projections of a 0.1% annual rate of growth by 2100. However, this population growth is uneven, with a great disparity between different countries worldwide. The Clio Infra project's cross-country analysis[1] of total population by country in the last five centuries shows substantial differences. It reveals that while in the period 1800-2000 the population in France doubled, the U.S. population increased almost 50-fold. Moreover, there is also a great difference between regions. Asia is and has been throughout history the most densely populated region in the world, especially India that its population increased 5-fold, while China's population grew by over 4-fold during this period of time (the data from the History Database of the Global Environment (HYDE)).

Negative Natural Population Growth

Today there are even some countries in the world, which display a slightly negative natural population growth: the death rate exceeds the annual birth rate. According to research, this is a new phenomenon. There were no countries with negative natural population growth until the 1970s. Furthermore, the UN projections show that this decline in growth rate is evident worldwide across all countries and regions, despite the difference in this growth rate between the "developed countries" and the "less developed countries."

Fertility

Fertility is the most evident indicator of population growth. The number of births per woman measures the overall fertility rate. Up to the 1960s, fertility rates were stable worldwide with few differences between the "developing" and the "developed" countries. However, after this period, fertility rates started declining around the world.

Some countries considerably reduced their fertility rates until 1975-1980. China's fertility fell to 3 from just over 6 with their one-child-per-family quota; India's fertility rate fell to a 4.9 from just under 6, while other countries still maintained a very high fertility rate, with 8.6 children per woman in Yemen. Today, the average global fertility rate is 2.5, which is barely higher than the replacement rate at which the population size remains steady. Countries with the highest fertility in the 1950s show a significant reduction in the number of children per woman. This seemingly natural decline in fertility is seen worldwide in the last 50 years. The (causal) correlation which emerges is that increased infant survival leads to parents' decreased demand for children.[2]

Strain of Population Explosion Placing on Our Global Resources

The exponential growth in the human population has put immense pressure on our environmental resources, including air, food, and water, as well as medicine, biodiversity, and habitats. The increasing pressure to grow and compete economically, whether it's developed countries or developing countries, continues to deplete and pollute the environment and diminish its resources, while threatening the future of life on earth.

That said, forests worldwide are being destroyed at a devastating rate just to support the population increase. There is also an unrestrained use of energy and fuel to the depletion of non-renewable resources. Yet, many regions across the globe still suffer from a lack of such basic living essentials as food and water. The production of increased waste by the growing population and the destruction of natural habitat, such as land and soil degradation (leading to more scarcity of food and water), are serious concerns.[3]

Environment Degradation

The relentless uptick in global population leads to an increase in the use of (depleting) resources and drives up energy prices and over-high oil prices. The largest increase in the population growth rate is seen in the developing countries, where the use of energy also rises at the fastest rate. Not only does this phenomenon foster greater worldwide demand for fossil fuels, such as coal, natural gas and oil, they also diminish vital fresh-water supplies. Consequently, this leads to a constant decrease in land available for agricultural produce while food prices soar. So this trend of a lower birth rate could reduce the increasing pressure on the world's supply of arable land, fresh water, and fossil fuels. Moreover, it would decrease the destruction of rain forests, extinction of animal species and plants and the continued pollution of air and water caused by population growth.[4]

As is projected, the developing countries are expected to continue contributing the most population growth. The earnings of the people in these countries are also expected to double, which will lead to increased daily spending from 1.8 billion to 4.8 billion. Therefore, there will be a rise in demand for fuel, which has shown a decline since 2007.[5] This puts additional strain on food production which will be required to double; especially, in the developing countries and an investment of $100 billion per year (excluding the infrastructure required for such increase in production to implement and support it).[6]

"Today humanity uses the equivalent of 1.5 planets to provide the resources we use and absorb our waste. This means it now takes the Earth one year and six months to regenerate what we use in a year." (Global Footprint Network) **This is an alarming situation, and it seems that the governments of the world have been aware of this threat to our existence for some time, but their response is frightening.**

Agenda 21

Before I started to do research on this plan, I thought that the UN was totally insincere in many areas, but I could hardly believe what my research revealed: that the UN is downright evil to have devised such a well-planned agenda to depopulate the planet. It looked too farfetched to grasp at that time. However, I started investigating it and sharing information with the group entitled "Israel Against Agenda 21"[7] on Facebook (I noticed it in 2013). There were so many topics that I wasn't even slightly aware of, such as the orchestrated immigration from Africa to Israel. I started reflecting about how people who barely earn 300 USD per year could afford a journey that costs (according to some immigrants' testimonies) $3000 USD. Then I started thinking about what we aren't being told about this massive population migration to Israel. At the beginning, the Israeli mainstream media called them "refugees." However, after the UN representatives had checked their status, they pointed out that only 6 percent of them were real refugees. This required the mainstream media to change its terminology in regard to them as "asylum seekers."

To understand its significance, refugees cross one border with their families and wait until it's safe to return back to their own homes. Here, we've seen a massive wave of mostly young men as immigrants. (The "refugees" from Syria into Europe also mostly comprised young men). I read about May Golan (and then contacted her), an activist living in the "conquered" area of south Tel Aviv, where her mom and she are being terrorized by these infiltrators on a daily basis. She told me how the NGOs (Non- Government Organizations) involved in this mass immigration are protecting them, while the local Israeli population is afraid of leaving their homes and feel abandoned by their government. I searched for information and read what Alon Dahan, PhD has written about Agenda 21 in Hebrew and its connection to the NGOs, which are replacing the government's agencies and their role in managing the problem these infiltrators present. I started investigating this particular topic in Israel, but found out that it's a global phenomenon.

Many NGOs (funded by foreign governments and foundations) are doing everything in their power to maintain these immigrants, who terrorize the local Jewish population in Israel and maintain their status by utilizing the court system. The local Israeli populace have become refugees in their own country (as Oslo, Norway became the rape capital of Europe after a massive emigration from Africa and the Middle East), and are often required to vacate their houses in Southern Tel Aviv. The areas overtaken by these infiltrators actually became "extraterritorial" where Israelis, including the media, cannot enter. I surmise that this is an orchestrated immigration to Israel, resembling that from Syria and Africa to Europe and the U.S., is to destroy the Western countries and those aligned with them from within. Again, Agenda 21 is carried out by NGOs funded by foreign countries. They are funded by many foundations and even by Muslim countries with the intentions, I surmise, to destroy Israel from within like with other Western countries.[8, 9, 10]

One thing led to another and I found detailed information about Agenda 21 from speeches and lectures given by Rosa Koire and other whistleblowers, who verified this information that NGOs are pushing Agenda 21 locally together with the cooperation of municipalities (by ICLEI).

What Is Agenda 21?

Agenda 21 is a plan to depopulate 95 percent of the world population by 2030[11]. It has already begun and we can see the outcome worldwide. There are many means implemented to achieve this goal, including vaccines, irradiated food, GMOs (Codex Alimentarius), and other means, which all sound great when they are termed the "sustainable development" under Agenda 21.

According to the UN's own website, this is a "comprehensive plan of action to be taken globally, nationally and locally by organizations of the United Nations system, governments and major groups, in every area in which human impacts on the environment."[12]

According to Rosa Koire (the executive director of the Post Sustainability Institute), the question that should be asked about UN Agenda 21's "sustainable development" program is what it is not. It is in fact a plan that is involved with every aspect of our lives. "It is the blueprint[;] it is the action plan, to inventory and control all land, all water, all plants, all minerals, all construction, all animals, all means of production, all energy, all information and all the human beings in the world. It is a completely comprehensive plan[;] it's global and it's implemented locally. . . It is in every single town all across the United States and across the world."[13] Impacting every aspect of our lives, UN Agenda 21's Sustainable Development agenda is a corporate manipulation using the Green Mask of environmental concern to forward a globalist plan." (www.openmindconference.com)

How Is It Implemented?

It is run by the United Nations via an NGO called "International Council for Local Environmental Initiatives," commonly known as **ICLEI** (pronounced Ik-lee). It is implemented locally by municipalities of major cities worldwide, including London, Berlin, Rome. From my research, in 2008 fifteen cities in Israel joined this NGO.[14]

This is paid for by you, taxpayers worldwide (not only in the U.S.), without your knowledge or consent, as none of us was informed of it and obviously, you didn't have had a vote on its implementation. This UN Agenda 21 is responsible for the building programs you are not aware of in your area, behind the mass engineered immigration in the West and heavy population surveillance everywhere (as with "smart meters").

According to ICLEI's official website, this NGO comprises "12 mega-cities, 100 super-cities and urban regions, 450 large cities as well as 450 medium-sized cities and towns in 84 countries."[15] This NGOs stated goals is that "By 2050, a third of all humans will be living in cities."[15]

All these programs are means-to-one-end discovered from Rosa Koire and the research of others: It is intended to wreck nations and their identities and create a world government.

Is It Legal?

As this plan is covertly implemented in the name of UN Agenda 21 by an NGO called ICLEI, none of us had been informed about it or have voted for it in any way; it basically leads to the loss of personal freedom and sovereignty worldwide. This is a deceit of humanity rooted in darkness and our complicit ignorance, which allows the UN to implement this treacherous plan. This is totally undemocratic "and it relies on our passive, ill-informed acceptance of 'authorities'."[13]

How I Discovered Codex Alimentarius?

I watched a lecture on Youtube in Hebrew called "What Is Codex Alimentarius? First Lecture in Israel.[16] This lecture discusses the food laws and regulations that were written and ratified in 2009. It discusses the connection between IG Farben (former BAYER, BASF, HOECHST) and the food laws and regulations ratified by the UN. It raises many important questions such as: How are these regulations connected to the depopulation agenda? And why is our food filled with toxins and elements that risk our health? Are there really too many people on earth? Is the World Health Organization interested in our general wellbeing?

I found out that Nazis like Fritz ter Meer, a former executive member of IG Farben (which produced and supplied the cyclone B to the death camps during the Second World War), who was incarcerated for fifteen years in prison after being convicted in the Nuremberg War Crimes Tribunal, was employed by the UN after being released. He was part of the committee designed to plan the food resources for humanity that devised the Codex Alimentarius. (This is an UN-sponsored global food standards body, which **criminalizes** the production of healthy nutrition both commercially and at your home, whether it's organic food, your dietary supplements, or even your organic garden). Dr. Rima Laibow talks about these regulations, which has determined that vitamins are toxins and therefore to be limited in consumption to ineffective dosages, and which includes irradiating the food supply to destroy all nutrients in our food, and to switch to the GMO foods to be consumed by the masses. This alone will lead to the death of three billion people worldwide in the next few decades according to Dr. Rima Laibow.[11] The World Health Organization confirms these estimates.[17]

Here is more explanation on those behind the outlining of this plan:

Several companies who were convicted only fifteen years before in the Nuremberg War Crimes Tribunal again devised the next major human rights offences. They established the Codex Alimentarius Commission In 1962 (Remark made by the Dr. Rath Health Foundation) (http://www4.dr-rath-foundation.org/PHARMACEUTICAL_BUSINESS/history_of_the_pharmaceutical_industry.htm).

In 2015, I worked as the content manager of the Israeli Agriculture Portal (israelagri.com) and accidently found out that all fresh produce being imported to Israel is irradiated at the Soreq nuclear plant, as part of the international trade agreements that Israel signed and is also part of Codex Alimentarius (UN depopulation agenda). I interviewed someone "in the know" and asked him off record if this is true. I just wanted to verify this information, which sounded farfetched even to me. He confirmed my suspicions, but as he is part of the system and heavily brainwashed, he believed that it was a good thing to kill the "bugs" (and all its nutritious value as a result). I contacted the Ministry of Economy concerning this topic and asked the respective person about it. Of course, he denied everything. At this period of time, Monsanto was brought to Israel, while so many countries banned this company. GMO ingredients are prevalent in food of popular brands (Big Food in Israel); especially, snacks and food for children.

What Is Agenda 2030?

In 2015, agenda 2030 was approved by two hundred world leaders aiming to depopulate 95% of the world population by 2030.[11] I found out that this plan attempts to reduce the population from a little over 7 billion people on Earth to fewer than half a billion. If you think this is just a conspiracy theory, think again. They state their intentions very vaguely couched in high-minded rhetoric. You have to look at the implementation of this plan rather than to the slogans they use. Depopulation is considered as the method used to decrease environmental degradation and instability according to the UN, the initiator of this plan. This plan is comprised of seventeen goals that they promote as beneficial for everyone. What can be bad about ending poverty or hunger? The answer is in its implementation. The vocabulary used is very vague, which leaves a lot to be interpreted, but the method is mass genocide to achieve their goals. If you want to see these plans for your city, simply type in Google: Agenda 21 and the name of your city, and you'll receive all the data on it. You can also find information on FEMA Camps internment camps spread across the U.S.[18]

I did it and found the plans to be implemented in Haifa for Agenda 21. But no one talks about it. I've never heard anything about this agenda in the news or from the municipality. There is a cloak of complete silence, but it's something that affects all of us. The UN states that they will raise $400 billion annually to finance "development needs" to implement Agenda 21 by calling for an international tax for a global government, which would have elicited outrage if humanity was informed about it. However, no one is being informed about this plan. We, the citizens of this world, are forced to cough out this money that we haven't been informed about or voted for.[19] This is only one example of how the UN finances these plans, including Agenda 21 and Agenda 2030, without our consent but with our taxes.

Why Don't People Hear About This Plan?

Most people use mainstream media, including TV, newspapers, radios and other means to keep informed, which suppresses this information; those in power control mainstream media and don't want you to be aware of this plan. This media has denied the existence of such a plan for years, despite the existence of a book entitled "Agenda 21" (350 pages) published by the UN. So if you don't rely on alternative media coverage, it's improbable that you'll find information about this vast global plan and all of its goals.[13] If the public worldwide had known of such a plan, they would immediately rise up against it and stop its implementation, which is definitely something "the powers that be" don't want. So they have introduced this plan incrementally by using appealing terminology like "sustainable development" or some other "green"-sounding term so people would gladly accept it (as fascist regimes have always done). However, it is not about environmental sustainability at all. It's true goals are implemented by deception, concealing its real aim to take over the entire planet and all its assets by a handful of people.

If you don't know who these people are and this is a new topic to you, they include royalty (as can be seen in his speech 'The New Environmental Agenda'[20]), top politicians like Obama, who addressed the UN General Assembly on September 27, 2015 and stated that the UN blueprint "is one of the smartest investments we can make in our own future."[21] Bureaucrats, CEOs and the top of international banks and corporations like the CEO of an agri business company said, "This place is getting busier and more crowded. As long as you've got money in your back pocket and you drive your station wagon to the supermarket on weekends, then it's out of sight, out of mind, so far."[22] According to Forbes[23], a U.N. policymaker, clearly stated that the real goal of Agenda 21 is to eliminate the middle class, as "it is not sustainable." This is from his opening remarks in the first U.N. Earth Climate Summit (1992) in Rio de Janeiro, Brazil which he organized and where Agenda 21 was signed by 178 governments. Here he said, "We may get to the point where the only way of saving the world will be for industrialized civilization to collapse. Isn't it our responsibility to bring this about?"

The lifestyle of the "global elite" with their private trains and jets, fleets of cars, and palaces and their businesses are excluded

12

from this plan and continue to be considered sustainable. Lord Christopher Monckton[24,] the third viscount of Benchley, advisor to former Prime Minister Margaret Thatcher, gave a speech on March 18, 2012 to supporters of the "International Free Press Society, Canada" at Windermere Manor in London, Ontario. The topics of his speech included the Agenda 21, Marxism, environmentalism, and "sustainable development". He exposes Agenda 21 as a communist plan that will reduce the lives of people to ones more resembling past centuries. He asked, "Just imagine how many people would have to die to bring about the myth of 'sustainable development' and let's start with the number of people dying already because of the myth of sustainable development." And now if any of you agree with this statement: that the world needs to be much less populated, then simply ask yourself if you would volunteer to have you and your children sterilized or be the first to die.[13]

How Do They Depopulate the World?

Dr. Rima Laibow exposed documents showing that these people actively worked to reduce the world population by utilizing Codex Alimentarius, which according to her, only by implementing part of its directives could lead to the death of three billion people worldwide.[11]

Chemtrails

In 2013, after finding out that "chemtrails" do exist, I started writing to prominent activists on this topic like Dane Winington (geoengineeringwatch.org site); especially, after feeling distraught and helpless about it. I was sick, my throat hurt, and there was no one I could turn to except for those activists reporting and sharing health tips on how to maintain our health and sanity when all this insane information comes out.

First, after realizing this phenomenon, I took a lot of pictures and then one day I notice two airplanes spraying and leaving these white trails behind them that other planes didn't leave. I tried to take a video, but my excitement got the best of me and my hands shook so it wasn't clear (it was also on the most basic cell phone). This occurred so many times that a friend and I just watched these planes. She also took some usable photos and videos and posted them on Facebook. I started feeling helpless and hopeless seeing these unmarked airplanes spraying and being unable to do anything except to watch them spraying their poison.

Later on, I also found out that not only do they spray from airplanes, but they also use underwater jet streams in the seas and oceans aimed at our beaches where it's possible.

The founder of this site Geoengineering Watch (http://www.geoengineeringwatch.org/), Dane Winington, together with others filed a lawsuit against the authorities (the regime), who are supposedly behind this crime against humanity stating that HAARP is being used as a weapon that induces climate change.[25]

I found out about a patent for H.A.A.R.P (High Frequency Active Auroral Research Program)[26] that it has installations worldwide, which together with chemtrails they can actually create earthquakes, tsunamis, and other "natural" disasters. Cobra (the resistance movement) also calls it ionosphere heaters[27] (the most famous one is located in Alaska, but such facilities can be found worldwide) and they posted a respective map.[28]

I watched videos that people worldwide uploaded on Youtube showing strange colorful "clouds" half an hour before a "natural" disaster occurred.

I also started investigating why does it feel that we're almost being "fried" in Israel during the summer, and discovered that in 2016 around one hundred Indians died in a massive heat wave, and why there was such a heavy draught in West U.S., while the rest of the U.S. didn't experience the same. I thought that perhaps there's a connection. I found out an article written by Dane Winington entitled "Climate Engineering and Microwaved Skies,"[29] where he actually explains in detail how this "climate change" is all related.

U.S Black Budget to Spray the Populace like Roaches

I found out that a secret "black" budget of a former President of the U.S. sponsoring our own demise; shockingly, I discovered that we unknowingly finance our own genocide (Secret Presidential Chemtrail Budget Uncovered—Congress Exceeds Billions To Spray Populace Like Roaches[30]) and that it goes on for decades.[31] Here's the words of Dane Winington on the ongoing chemtrails and Geoengineering: "Historical records prove beyond doubt that climate engineering has been fully deployed on a substantial scale for over 65 years (hurricane suppression for over 53 years), so why do major publications continue to lie about this blatant reality? Because that is what they are paid to do. Once global populations fully grasp the gravity of the biosphere collapse that is rapidly unfolding around them (further exacerbated by Geoengineering), our paradigm will overturn. The power structure is trying desperately to hide this reality for as long as possible. Unfortunately, most environmental groups and organizations are major participants in Geoengineering denial. I and several other activists just attended a global warming presentation with standing room only, we made sure that the Geoengineering subject was not omitted from this event." (http://www.geoengineeringwatch.org/2015/10/)

Pharmaceuticals/Big Pharma

I come from a family with relatives, even very close ones, who are retired now from health care-related professions (nurses and hospital lab professionals), so I never gave it a second thought to the legitimacy of vaccinations or pharmaceuticals. I was vaccinated as a child and in the army without questioning its credibility. Moreover, I always approach an MD first if I experience any health issues.

But finding out about how many holistic health practitioners have died in recent years made me start asking questions—I especially became alarmed in 2015 when twenty-nine such practitioners died during a conference. However, there were so many others that it made me think what is going on.[32]

I found out that it's been twenty years since the FDA allowed prescription drug ads on television and they are now in just about every TV program. I watched, to my amazement, ads sponsored by the UN that show elderly people with the actors saying "I have lived a good life"[33]; namely, I lived enough and it's my turn to go for good to make room for the younger generation, which I associated with Agenda 21 depopulation agenda. So, I figured out that perhaps allowing prescription drug ads on TV might be also part of the depopulation plan and are tainted.[34] Some other disturbing findings that I found was that the number of deaths caused by drugs or wrong diagnosis and surgeries. For instance, the number three reason of death in the U.S. is the healthcare system according to the Journal of American Medical Association.[35] The Americans ranked favorably compared to other industrialized nations in the consumption of alcohol or smoking, and yet their health care system is causing more deaths than in other developed countries. So what is the difference? Over 70 percent of Americans are on one or more pharmaceutical drugs, which often has adverse side-effects. And the Americans are not alone in this bleak statistics. According to Dr. Mercola, death by prescription drugs is the 21st century's epidemic worldwide termed 'Pharmageddon', as medicines produce more ill-health than health today.[36]

I also started to obtain a lot of information on Facebook, both in Hebrew and in English, on vaccination injuries which couldn't only be attributed to genetic reasons. Then I found out that parents report on healthy toddlers who became autistic after vaccinations. One family had three healthy boys who all became autistic after vaccinations which couldn't be ruled as caused by their genetics.[37]

I started asking questions on Facebook of vaccine skeptics

in Israel and why boys are being administered a vaccine which purpose is to prevent cervical cancer. I asked why the vaccine was administered when they don't have uterus at all? This seemed very strange to me. So I looked up for reasons and found that this vaccine caused so much injury, paralysis and death of young healthy women that in Ireland the pharmaceutical company is being sued for damages.[38] In connection to Agenda 21 and the depopulation agenda mentioned earlier, doctors in Kenya discovered a depopulation experiment by foundations that provide extra funding for many vaccination programs after they became suspicious of a sudden increasing infertility rates. They looked for the reason and found anti-fertility drugs in Tetanus vaccines that had been given to millions of African women as part of such a foundation program.[39] Moreover, I found information on vaccines, given to children and even "flu" shots to adults, which contain Thimerosal, 49% mercury by weight, which can cause "mild to severe mental retardation" in infants and problems in adults (the documentary Trace Amounts http://traceamounts.com/).

I even found out that an organization which alleged purpose is to prevent diseases in America, and is supposed to be a branch of the government, is actually a commercially-driven company.[40] Moreover, I found out that the process of approving new drugs and vaccines is heavily influenced by lobbyists and close connections between the pharmaceutical companies and state health policymakers.[41] I was quite shocked by this revelation as you should be. I can't see needless suffering without investigating it. Another topic, which arose during this investigation, was that nurses in Israel are being rewarded on each vaccine given (with memos from the different health maintenance organizations called Kupot Holim).

Fluoridation

When Did I Discover that the Water in Israel Is Fluoridated?

I remember that there was an investigative TV program years ago discussing that fuel from the gas stations penetrated the water that we drink in Israel. Since then, I've asked myself how can I cope with this? I started looking for information on different water filtration systems and I wasn't sure about their effectiveness, and some were very expensive like reverse osmosis systems. However, five or six years ago I decided that my health is more important. I then started collecting more information on the pollution of the water in Israel in general—before I was aware that it is being polluted intentionally and not by mistake. This was simply unthinkable. However, I started investigating and found out that fluoridation of city water is taking place and that fluoride is not the ingredient that prevents dental cavities, but is an extremely lethal neurotoxin. It is a waste product from the phosphate industry—a byproduct of phosphate fertilizer manufacture—that is being added to our water called hydrofluoric acid[42]. To my amazement, I found out that 6,000 tons of this poisonous toxin is added yearly to our water supply in Israel[43], whether it's tap water, for agricultural purposes or showering. It means that even if we do have a filtration system at home, we're still getting fluoridated food and agricultural produce.

At the end of 2014, the then minister of health, Yael German (a woman), signed new regulations which abolished this practice at the end of her term. Despite this brave move, which was aggressively fought against by the top officials of the Ministry of Health, the fluoridation continues as usual. Lab tests by the national water company of Israel (in Hebrew), [44, 45, 46] before and after her move to ban fluoridation, showed there was no change in the actual policy. You can see that after 2015 the water contains detergents, arsenic, nickel, lead, barium, and . . . cyanide. Yes, this reminds of very bad collective memories that hit close to home in Israel.

What Are the Consequences of Fluoridation in Israel?

The cancer rates in Israel doubled since 1998 when they started fluoridating the water; especially, bone cancer which is typical to fluoridation[47]. From 12,000 new patients every year a decade ago, this number spiked to 25,000 new patients each year. However, in those adjacent areas to the polluting facilities, there is a patient or someone who died of cancer in almost each household.[48]

What Is Fluoridation?

According to Dr. Edward Group, "Fluoride is one of the most toxic substances known to man, yet based on its inclusion in virtually every brand of toothpaste, the American Dental Association believes it's okay to use fluoride for preventative dental care. Other products, such as bottled water, infant formulas, and even vitamin supplements, now contain fluoride!"[49] (https://www.globalhealingcenter.com/natural-health/how-safe-is-fluoride/) "Fluorides are more toxic than lead and only slightly less poisonous than arsenic . . . and these toxins can enter your body from brushing your teeth or rinsing with many popular dental care products!" Fluoride was also classified as developmental neurotoxin with lead and arsenic by Lancet Medical Journal. The research comprising 27 cross-sectional studies of children in China, who were exposed to raised fluoride concentrations in drinking water, which suggested an average IQ decrement of about seven points[50].

I found that there is much confusion between the fluoride (hydrofluoric acid) that is being added to water and is toxic waste from industry, and the fluoride that can be found naturally in spring water in small amounts. However, being a component found in nature doesn't make it safe to consumption, although it's not the toxic waste source mentioned herein.

What Steps Were Taken in Israel to Stop This Practice?

Activists pressed charges at local police stations across Israel against Benjamin Netanyahu, the prime minister, and the Yaakov Litzman, the minister of health to stop fluoridating the water in Israel in 2015[51]—despite the fact that the former minister of health, Yael German, cancelled the regulations implementing mandatory fluoridation of city water. Other lawsuits were filed against this practice in the Supreme Court. However, it still continues according to water lab tests from 2015 when it was supposed to stop (as mentioned above).

I wrote to the Israeli water company, and the reply wasn't even signed by any particular person, as they are afraid of being sued by the citizens. I wrote to the company that supplies the water to Haifa, and the only reply I received was from their lawyer who was unable to reply my "activists'" questions.

Moreover, Yael German sued the government over the continued practice of fluoridation in the Israeli Supreme Court (as it is a form of forced medication for the entire population of Israel), despite her abolishing this practice at the end of her tenure as the Minister of Health in 2014.

It should be mentioned that part of the Israeli "mineral" bottled water (certain brands) are fluoridated too without the people's awareness of this. Moreover, I found out that fluoride is an active ingredient in Prozac. Why?

Where Was It Implemented First?

The most unsettling information that I uncovered was that fluoridation was used for the first time in concentration camps by the Nazis to pacify the inmates and make them easier to control.

I wanted to verify this, so I started looking for more information and found it. In the 1930s Hitler and his Nazi cohorts sought a far-reaching plan for the control of their population and used mass medication of the drinking water supply to cause sterility in women, reduce individual stamina to resist social domination, and to slowly poison parts of the brain to make people submissive to authority. Sodium fluoride was a major component in their plans.[52] I found out that sodium fluoride was in fact added to drinking water in the German Ghettos in the 1930s and 1940s, and then in Nazi concentration camps.[53]

FOOTNOTES

[1] World Population Growth by Max Roser and Esteban Ortiz-Ospinahttps://ourworldindata.org/world-population-growth/

[2] https://ourworldindata.org/fertility/ by Max Roser

[3] Rahul Mittal May 2013 IMPACT OF POPULATION EXPLOSION ON ENVIRONMENT https://www.researchgate.net/publication/237771340_IMPACT_OF_POPULATION_EXPLOSION_ON_ENVIRONMENT

[4] http://www2.ljworld.com/news/2008/jun/23/population_growth_strains_global_resources/

[5] http://www.nbcnews.com/business/global-leaders-tackle-growing-strain-natural-resources-4B11241410

[6] https://www.potatopro.com/news/2016/effect-population-growth-efficiency-food-production

[7] https://www.facebook.com/IsraelAgainstAgenda21/

[8] https://www.algemeiner.com/2016/09/28/george-soros-israel-hatred-spills-out-into-the-open/

[9] http://www.express.co.uk/news/uk/597254/ISIS-Map-Europe-Terror-Organisation-Andrew-Hosken-Caliphate-Abu-Musab-al-Zarqawi

[10] http://www.zerohedge.com/news/2016-12-04/something-strange-taking-place-mediterranean

[11] How The Elite Plan To Kill 3 Billion in 30 years, Vinny Eastwood with Rima E. Laibow MD 15June2013 – The Dr Rima Truth Report 15 June 2013 https://www.youtube.com/watch?v=r8_NL_kC1Nc

[12] https://sustainabledevelopment.un.org/outcomedocuments/agenda21

[13] http://www.endagenda21.com/

[14] http://www.ynetnews.com/articles/0,7340,L-3501178,00.html

[15] https://archive.li/H5Iz0

[16] "What Is Codex Alimentarius?" First Lecture in Israel https://www.youtube.com/watch?v=IYCd9q_7bNg

[17] http://presscore.ca/un-ordered-depopulation-of-3-billion-people-by-food-malnutrition-has-started

[18] http://beforeitsnews.com/agenda-21/2015/02/agenda-21-exposed-american-concentration-camps-222015-video-1242.html

[19] http://www.un.org/en/development/desa/news/policy/wess2012.html

[20] http://www.endagenda21.com/uploads/1/2/5/4/12545535/prince_charles_agenda_21_speech.pdf

[21] https://www.thenewamerican.com/tech/environment/item/22267-un-agenda-2030-a-recipe-for-global-socialism

[22] http://www.seattleorganicrestaurants.com/vegan-whole-food/Monsantos-CEO-calls-GMO-activists-elitist.php

[23] https://www.forbes.com/sites/larrybell/2013/01/22/the-u-n-s-global-warming-war-on-capitalism-an-important-history-lesson-2/#43b9f67029be

[24] http://www.dailymotion.com/video/xq55q9

[25] http://www.veteranstoday.com/2014/07/08/american-people-targeted-by-weapons-of-climate-engineering-warfare/

[26] https://www.google.com/patents/US4686605

[27] https://en.wikipedia.org/wiki/Ionospheric_heater

[28] http://worldtruth.tv/elf-gwen-towers-and-haarp-connection/

[29] http://www.geoengineeringwatch.org/climate-engineering-and-microwaved-skies/

[30] https://www.intellihub.com/secret-presidential-chemtrail-budget-uncovered-exceeds-billions-to-spray-populations-like-roaches/

[31] https://chemtrailsplanet.net/2017/04/25/no-conspiracy-theory-u-s-government-engaged-in-weather-modification-since-1953/

[32] https://www.davidwolfe.com/breaking-29-holistic-doctorspractitioners-found-poisoned-some-nearly-dead-another-attack-on-alternative-medicine/

[33] https://standupforthetruth.com/2012/11/time-to-die-u-n-ads-promote-killing-off-the-elderly/

[34] http://www.washingtontimes.com/news/2017/feb/8/drug-ads-on-tv-should-be-banned/

35 http://www.health-care-reform.net/causedeath.htm

36 http://articles.mercola.com/sites/articles/archive/2011/10/26/prescription-drugs-number-one-cause-preventable-death-in-us.aspx

37 http://thinkingmomsrevolution.com/vaccines-caused-sons-autism/

38 http://www.irishexaminer.com/ireland/families-look-to-sue-over-vaccine-against-cervical-cancer-374796.html

39 http://www.theunknownbutnothidden.com/abortion-drugs-discovered-bill-gates-vaccines/

40 http://www.naturalnews.com/2017-02-16-cdc-is-a-vaccine-company-owns-56-vaccines-sells-4-1b-of-vaccines-a-year.html

41 https://www.ncbi.nlm.nih.gov/pmc/articles/PMC3483914/

42 https://en.wikipedia.org/wiki/Hydrofluoric_acid

43 Emet Aheret site (Alternative Truth, in Hebrew) 6,000 tons of hydrofluoric acid are added to the water in Israel annually http://www.emetaheret.org.il/2012/06/25/%D7%A2%D7%A6%D7%95%D7%9E%D7%94-%D7%97%D7%93%D7%A9%D7%94-%D7%A0%D7%92%D7%93-%D7%94%D7%95%D7%A1%D7%A4%D7%AA-%D7%A4%D7%9C%D7%95%D7%90%D7%95%D7%A8%D7%99%D7%93-%D7%9C%D7%9E%D7%99%D7%9D/

44 Testing chemical parameters in the water in Netanya on March 15, 2012, the Ministry of Health, the National Public Health Laboratory Tel Aviv https://drive.google.com/file/d/0B_QWnbQROAudSlh2anVESWpzbmdUVlZCbFNFUTNDZFJ5ZDNz/view?pref=2&pli=1

45 Water chemistry supply in different areas/regions in Israel (the F stands for Fluoride), January 1- March 31, 2014. https://drive.google.com/file/d/0B_QWnbQROAud

NTNNVEFkZlBLNkVIazM3ZWtCdk1ST09hVElV/
view?pref=2&pli=1

[46] Mekorot Water Company Ltd, the national water company of Israel, chemical lab tests July 1 – September 30, 2015. The 'F' stands for Fluoride.
https://drive.google.com/file/d/0B_QWnbQROAudcXQ0
TEJHSTFRTDJnNVlzMW15Zzh2SEU5YzNn/
view?pref=2&pli=1

[47] http://www.webmd.com/cancer/news/20060406/
does-fluoridation-up-bone-cancer-risk#1

[48] http://meshanim.com/haflara/

[49] https://www.globalhealingcenter.com/natural-health/
how-safe-is-fluoride/

[50] https://www.thenewamerican.com/usnews/health-care/
item/18324-top-medical-journal-labels-fluoride-a-neurotoxin

[51] http://www.mako.co.il/news-israel/health-q3_2015/Article-
a1ca92e9cb22f41004.htm

[52] http://rense.com/general79/hd3.htm

[53] http://www.wakingtimes.com/2014/08/22/
fluoride-affects-consciousness-will-act/

REFERENCES

1. Alon Dahan PhD On Agenda 21

   https://www.articles.co.il/article/157532
   /%D7%90%D7%92'%D7%A0%D7%93%D7%94%20
   21%20%D7%95%D7%94'%D7%A7%D7%95%D7%9E%
   D7%95%D7%A4%D7%90%D7%A9%D7%99%D7%
   96%D7%9D'%20%D7%94%D7%97%D7%93%D7%A9

2. Rahman Sigalit, Kayamut Mekomit – Sviva Ve'hevra (Local Sustainability – Environment and Society), 2010, the Ministry of Environment Protection, the Department of Environmental Policy (sigalitr@sviva.gov.il), the State of Israel

3. https://www.amazon.com/Behind-Green-Mask-U-N-Agenda/dp/0615494544

4. https://sustainabledevelopment.un.org/outcomedocuments/agenda21

5. http://www.forum15.org.il/uploaded_files/documents/iclei_report_2009_U4526.pdf

6. Total fertility, 1950-2010 and projections until 2100 (UN Population Division estimates and forecasts for medium fertility variant) http://www.un.org/en/development/desa/population/publications/pdf/trends/WPP2010/WPP2010_Volume-I_Comprehensive-Tables.pdf

7. http://www.globaltruth.net/agenda-21-working-sperm-counts-halved-in-40-years/

8. http://www.nova.org.au/earth-environment/population-environment

9. https://www.foe.co.uk/what_we_do/about_us/changing_diets_future_food_demand_41432

10. http://news.nationalgeographic.com/news/2014/09/140920-population-11billion-demographics-anthropocene/

11. http://mida.org.il/2017/03/13/%D7%93%D7%A8%D7%95%D7%9D-%D7%AA%D7%9C-%D7%90%D7%91%D7%99%D7%91-%D7%A7%D7%95%D7%A8%D7%A1%D7%AA-%D7%94%D7%9E%D7%A1%D7%AA%D7%A0%D7%A0%D7%99%D7%9D-%D7%94%D7%A4%D7%9B%D7%95-%D7%9C%D7%A8%D7%95%D7%91-62/

12. https://spectator.org/raw-exposure-leftwing-islamic-alliance-fabricated-europes-migration-crisis/

13. https://www.rt.com/op-edge/361376-george-soros-investing-forced-immigration/

14. http://www.frontpagemag.com/fpm/263873/george-soross-open-border-foundations-joseph-klein

15. https://gefira.org/en/2016/12/04/ngos-are-smuggling-immigrants-into-europe-on-an-industrial-scale/

16. http://www.zerohedge.com/news/2016-12-04/something-strange-taking-place-mediterranean

17. http://www.antinewsnetwork.com/vatican-calls-meeting-discuss-global-depopulation-agenda-new-world-order/

18. http://www.democratsagainstunagenda21.com/

19. https://www.infowars.com/msnbc-in-cover-up-of-manifestly-provable-population-control-plan/

20. http://www.postsustainabilityinstitute.org/what-is-un-agenda-21.html

21. https://en.wikipedia.org/wiki/ICLEI

22. http://www.iclei.org/compactofmayors.html

23. https://www.youtube.com/watch?v=7ykELwj1Ta8

24. Census shows big U.S. cities continue to grow

   https://www.usatoday.com/story/news/2016/05/19/census-shows-big-us-cities-continue-grow/84552378/

25. Agenda 21 whistleblower

   https://www.youtube.com/watch?v=K2o82bi3oMc

26. Another whistleblower on Agenda 21

   https://www.youtube.com/watch?v=fBp2ARF4cWI

27. http://www.theblaze.com/news/2012/11/19/what-is-agenda-21-after-watching-this-you-may-not-want-to-know/

28. https://www.haaretz.co.il/magazine/.premium-1.2219437

29. http://www.fao.org/docrep/008/y7867e/y7867e00.htm

30. http://drrimatruthreports.com/codex-alimentarius/

31. Alon Dahan PhD On Agenda 21

https://www.articles.co.il/article/157532/%
D7%90%D7%92'%D7%A0%D7%93%D7%94%2021%20%
D7%95%D7%94'%D7%A7%D7%95%D7%9E%D7%95%
D7%A4%D7%90%D7%A9%D7%99%D7%96%D7
%9D'%20%D7%94%D7%97%D7%93%D7%A9

31. http://www4.dr-rath-foundation.org/PHARMACEUTICAL_
    BUSINESS/history_of_the_pharmaceutical_industry.htm

32. http://www.disclose.tv/news/agenda_21_the_plan_to_depopulate
    _95_of_the_world_by_2030/138071

33. Implementing Agenda 21 in Israel http://www.un.org/esa/
    agenda21/natlinfo/countr/israel/natur.htm

34. http://www.globaltruth.net/un-agenda-2030-global-plan-for-
    sustainable-development/

35. United Nations Official Document

    http://www.un.org/ga/search/view_doc.asp?symbol=A/
    RES/70/1&Lang=E%20The%202030%20Agenda%20for%20
    Sustainable%20Development

36. https://climateviewer.com/2014/10/18/ionospheric-heaters-how
    -haarp-really-works/

37. https://climateviewer.com/haarp/

38. http://www.nature.com/news/2008/080423/full/452930a.html

39. https://en.wikipedia.org/wiki/High_Frequency_Active_Auroral
    _Research_Program

40. http://www.geoengineeringwatch.org/category/haarp-2/

41. 30 mins before the 2008 Sichuan earthquake in China

   https://www.youtube.com/watch?v=KKMTSDzU1Z4

42. Very Strange Phenomenon before the 2014 Yunnan earthquake in China

   https://www.youtube.com/watch?v=FTZvIwtBe_4

43. Did "Earthquake Clouds" Predict the Japanese Earthquakes?

   https://www.youtube.com/watch?v=_pERlNiXsrw

44. Earthquake lights in the sky – Argentina

   https://www.youtube.com/watch?v=K1iWmoHWNmQ

45. http://www.alternativenewsnetwork.net/top-government-scientists-refuse-vaccinate-children/

46. http://www.neonnettle.com/news/2505-world-famous-holistic-author-who-exposed-big-pharma-found-dead

47. http://vaxxedthemovie.com/

48. http://articles.mercola.com/sites/articles/archive/2012/01/24/hpv-vaccine-victim-sues-merck.aspx

49. http://anhinternational.org/2017/01/18/official-hpv-vaccine-vaccine-dangerous-yet/

50. http://www.globalresearch.ca/the-toxic-science-of-flu-vaccines/5554257

51. http://galacticconnection.com/aluminum-is-toxic-to-all-life-forms-so-why-is-it-used-in-vaccines/

52. What vaccine researcher say about vaccines? http://www.searchforthetruth.co.uk/vaccinations

53. Lobbyists boosted vaccine program | Toronto Star

https://www.thestar.com/news/2007/08/16/lobbyists_boosted_vaccine_program.html

54. https://aim4truth.org/2017/03/26/5663/

55. http://www.newstarget.com/2016-09-08-top-7-noticeable-signs-of-anti-health-sabotage-indicating-the-depopulation-agenda.html

56. http://www.sheeple.news/2017-01-20-adhd-medication-side-effects-harm-children-big-pharma-profits.html

57. https://www.scientificamerican.com/article/hidden-side-effects-medical-studies-often-leave-out-adverse-outcomes/

58. http://www.globalresearch.ca/the-evils-of-big-pharma-exposed/5425382

59. https://envirowatchrangitikei.wordpress.com/2017/02/24/there-have-been-31741-adverse-effects-including-6248-permanent-injuries-and-144-deaths-recorded-following-gardasil-vaccines/

60. https://blogs.scientificamerican.com/cross-check/psychiatrists-must-face-possibility-that-medications-hurt-more-than-they-help/

61. https://envirowatchrangitikei.wordpress.com/tag/pharmaceuticals/

62. http://www.activistpost.com/2013/09/22-medical-studies-that-show-vaccines.html

63. https://avscientificsupportarsenal.wordpress.com/2015/04/29/vaccines-do-cause-autism-undeniable-scientific-proof/

64. http://www.surviveunagenda21depopulation.com/

65. http://www4.dr-rath-foundation.org/PHARMACEUTICAL_BUSINESS/history_of_the_pharmaceutical_industry.htm

66. Total fertility, 1950-2010 and projections until 2100 (UN Population Division estimates and forecasts for medium fertility variant) http://www.un.org/en/development/desa/population/publications/pdf/trends/WPP2010/WPP2010_Volume-I_Comprehensive-Tables.pdf

67. http://anhinternational.org/2017/01/18/official-hpv-vaccine-vaccine-dangerous-yet/

68. Countries that fluoridate their water http://fluoridealert.org/content/bfs-2012/

69. The reasons to end water fluoridation http://fluoridealert.org/issues/water/

70. Ten Facts about Fluoridation http://articles.mercola.com/sites/articles/archive/2013/04/30/water-fluoridation-facts.aspx

71. 50 Reasons to Oppose Fluoridation http://fluoridealert.org/articles/50-reasons/

72. http://www.healthy-holistic-living.com/fluoride-officially-classified-neurotoxin-worlds-prestigious-medical-journal.html

69. fluoridation is medication without consent and feeding babies with fluoridated water is bad idea https://www.youtube.com/watch?v=914lSW7dw0E

73. https://thelittleshamanhealing.wordpress.com/2015/10/05/does-prozac-contain-fluoride/

74. http://www.abc.net.au/news/2017-08-24/melbourne-doctors-investigated-over-anti-vaccination-allegations/8837554

75. http://www.thinktwice.com/autism.htm

76. https://askmarion.wordpress.com/2011/03/29/un-ordered-depopulation-of-3-billion-people-by-food-malnutrition-has-started-pbspecial-report/

77. http://www.newdawnmagazine.com/articles/microwave-towers-faster-downloads-the-hidden-health-impact-of-wireless-communications

78. http://www.latimes.com/business/la-fi-cellphone-5g-health-20160808-snap-story.html

79. http://whatis5g.info/health-safety/

80. https://www.counterpunch.org/2016/11/02/living-in-a-5g-world-wireless-pollution-is-getting-out-of-control/

81. http://www.saferemr.com/2017/08/5g-wireless-technology-millimeter-wave.html

82. http://www.theecologist.org/News/news_analysis/2988266/wireless_pollution_out_of_control_as_corporate_race_for_5g_gears_up.html

83. http://www.odwyerpr.com/story/public/7841/2016-11-03/fcc-may-force-powerful-5g-wi-fi-communities.html

84. more about Smart Meters, the independent documentary "Take Back Your Power" https://takebackyourpower.net/

85. https://americanpolicy.org/2016/05/10/six-issues-agenda-21/

CHAPTER TWO

ELECTRONIC POLLUTION IS KILLING US

Wi-Fi and Electronic Pollution

We live in an increasingly irradiated environment (radiation soup) with all the smartphones, tablets, Wi-Fi networks, and cell towers and their microwave transmissions. People are dying of cancer in buildings where they allowed these providers to install these antennas on buildings for a fee. I remember that a few years ago my ear would burn from the heat emitted from my mobile phone in just a few minutes. I also got a serious headache when I pressed the device to my head. I didn't know back then that there are so many health problems associated with the use of mobile phones in general. Therefore, immediately after purchasing a simple mobile phone (not a smartphone), I returned to the mobile services provider that I bought this phone from and asked them to replace it with a device that "won't give me severe headaches in less than 5 minutes of talking on the phone." Needless to say, they didn't have such a cell phone.

This microwave radiation surrounds us and leads to decrease in fertility (sperm count decrease), which seemingly may be related to the depopulation agenda. It was discovered that sperm is damaged even from very low radiation rate at 0.00034- 0.07 micro-watt per centimeter.[1] Prof. Martin Pall, an expert on human effects of RF radiation, warns that humanity is approaching extinction due to infertility with the level of radiation we're exposed to these days:

"DNA damage known to be produced by these EMFs occur in human sperm and may also occur in human eggs, leading to large increases in mutation in any children born. It is thought that an increase in mutation frequency of 2.5 to 3-fold will lead to extinction because of accumulation of large numbers of damaging mutations. We may already be over this level, and if so, simply continuing our current exposures will lead to eventual extinction. Further increases in exposures will be more rapidly self-destructive."[2]

How Did I Become Aware of This Risk?

From my chemtrails research, I picked up the topic of smart meters[3] that are being installed in many countries, including in Israel. They conduct surveillance within our homes (like detecting how many, if any, people are in the house at any given time), store vast amounts of information on our habits (when you shower or wash the dishes from the water delivered by electricity), and emit radiation 24/7, although the utility companies say that they transmit signals only twice a day.[3]

I found out that a "shadowy" committee in Israel had gathered together without informing the public about it in 2013, passed a reform concerning the Israeli energy economy that enforces the installation of smart meters across Israel without the public's knowledge or consent.[4] I became proactive in the relevant Facebook Israeli pages, writing to members of the Knesset, ministers, to the mainstream media, including newspapers and national television companies and others. To this day, I have received replies from only one member of these committee members. I did receive some replies from members of the Knesset and few ministers. At the beginning, the journalists that I talked with were really interested in investigating this topic (even a successful anchor in one of the main channels in Israel found it interesting), but after a while they dropped their inquiry. This topic was totally suppressed here, and some activists were aggressively intimidated and were even afraid to speak with me about their investigation into the forced installation of smart meters. There would be no hiding from it. In Israel, Jerusalem was chosen to become the first "smart" city in Israel[5], and this is promoted as a big step in line with other "advanced" smart cities around the world, as if this were a positive development in their town. No one tells them that home surveillance and radiation levels will increase ten-fold or more.

What Is a Smart City?

According to Dr. Cindy Russell (*The Bulleting* January/February 2017)[6] Smart Cities "have comprehensive digital connectivity by installing a massive wireless sensor network of almost invisible small cell antennae on light posts, utility poles, homes and businesses throughout neighborhoods and towns in order to integrate IoT with IT." Internet of things (IoT) "is the inter-networking of physical devices, vehicles (also referred to as "connected devices" and "smart devices"), buildings, and other items embedded with electronics, software, sensors, actuators, and network connectivity which enable these objects to collect and exchange data. The IoT allows objects to be sensed or controlled remotely across existing network infrastructure,[4] creating opportunities for more direct integration of the physical world into computer-based systems, and resulting in improved efficiency, accuracy and economic benefit in addition to reduced human intervention.[5][6][7][8] When IoT is augmented with sensors and actuators, the technology becomes an instance of the more general class of cyber-physical systems, which also encompasses technologies such as smart grids, virtual power plants, smart homes, intelligent transportation and smart cities. Each thing is uniquely identifiable through its embedded computing system but is able to interoperate within the existing <u>Internet</u> infrastructure." (Wikipedia). Businesses claim that this "will improve services, the economy and quality of life."[6] However, it also poses serious health risks, as it will create "an expanded electromagnetic microwave blanket above each city."[6] Increasing number of people from all professions, ages, and walks of life from around the world have come down with similar symptoms due to the presence of mobile and wireless devices. The FCC recently extended its current policy of involuntary irradiation of the public without adequately studying the potential health impact on everyone, especially, those most vulnerable to exposure to radiofrequency radiation. These vulnerable populations include pregnant women, young children, unborn children, the elderly, teenagers, men of reproductive age, the chronically ill, and the disabled (Ronald Powell, PhD, Letter to FCC on 5G expansion).

Dr. Scott Eberle, a well-respected Petaluma hospice physician, eloquently described his development of electro-sensitivity in the November 2016 issue of the SCCMA Bulletin. He goes to great lengths to continue his profession, interact with his colleagues and maintain a healthy existence.[61] More and more Israelis, including children, report various aches and medical conditions, which emerge when they are in the presence of mobile phones, Wi-Fi routers or cell towers.[7]

I found out that this is a topic (smart meters and everything that the word "smart" is attached to) connected to a global tyrannical agenda called the New World Order that have so many of our "leaders" repeating this term (like Bush junior and senior).

What Is 5G?

According to Dr. Josh Axe, "5G, also known as 5th generation mobile networks or wireless systems, is considered the next phase in mobile technology. These wireless systems are the transmitters that carry signals to our cell phones and other wireless devices. While the public isn't operating on 5G yet, it's anticipated that over the next decade, most wireless carriers in the U.S. will shift to 5G technology. This transition is expected to bring better coverage, lower battery consumption, faster Internet connection speeds, and the ability to support a growing market of products *other* than phones and tablets that feature wireless integration."[8] This sounds so wonderful. So what is the problem with this network or new technology? 5G requires many more cell towers than those used today. Our exposure to this already dangerous radiation is going to increase exponentially and pose even greater challenge to our health. Dr. Axe writes that from 200,000 cell phone towers around the U.S. (4G LTE technology), the number of cell phone towers is going to increase to millions of towers, as 5G requires a much denser network.[9] As these technologies have never been proven safe, the growing scientific evidence suggesting immense health risks to death arising around wireless technology is a cause for concern.[8]

How Is 5G Wireless Technology Connected to "Smart Cities"?

Accenture states on its site that, "The next generation of wireless network infrastructure will be built using small-cell networks employing 5G wireless technology. The Smart City applications currently leveraging today's wireless networks are already showing significant benefits to communities, and are expected to transform local economies."[10]

This 5th generation of Wi-Fi is coming, and no one warns us of our exposure to its massive hazardous, deadly radiation. This is harmful to all human beings, not only those that are "highly sensitive to radiation" (EHS - Electromagnetic Hyper Sensitivity), and it would be impossible for us to protect ourselves as its coverage would be everywhere we go. It should be noted that it's often a constant exposure, and each new technology adds on another level on the existing ones.[11]

Evidence for the Harmful Effects and Confronting This Problem

Recorded adverse symptoms of this overreaching Wi-Fi radiation included, according to a 1981 NASA report, "headaches, eyestrain, fatigue, dizziness, disturbed sleep at night, sleepiness in daytime, moodiness, irritability, unsociability, hypochondriac reactions, feelings of fear, nervous tension, mental depression, memory impairment, pulling sensation in the scalp and brow, loss of hair, pain in muscles and heart region, breathing difficulties, increased perspiration of extremities."[4] Two hundred scientists appealed to the UN and the World Health Organization, stating that the exposure standard (to radiation) that applies to all the (generations of) wireless technologies does not protect the public. This International Electromagnetic Field Scientist Appeal was signed by 224 scientists from 41 nations.[12] Moreover, the IARC Monographs (the International Cancer Research, which is part of World Health Organization) classified all wireless technologies as possible human carcinogens[13] with other potential pollutants, such as lead in category B2.[14] Doctors from the Indian Spinal Injuries Centre also say that smartphones could be the main cause for the development of brain tumors. "In 2011, the World Health Organization (WHO) had classified cell phone radiation as a possible 2B carcinogen. Tissues nearest to the cell phone antenna absorb the wireless energy, which can result in several types of neurological issues including neoplasm, acoustic neuroma, and increase the risk of various types of cancers," said Dr. A. K. Sahani, Head of Department, Neurology, Indian Spinal Injuries Centre."[15]

"Smart" Devices Are Spying on Us 24/7

I found out that when the word "smart" is attached to a title of a device, it indicates that it emits radiation and conducts surveillance. These tools include "smartphones", "smart meters", "smart TVs" or smart home devices in general that connect to the Internet. Smart televisions hooked up to the Internet can be used as surveillance tools. One advanced electronics company even warns customers in its SmartTV privacy policy that they shouldn't speak private matters too close to their TV.[16] This is the disturbing phrase caught in the misnamed "privacy" policy, which allows this company to share this information with any party it sees fit: 'Please be aware that if your spoken words include personal or other sensitive information, that information will be among the data captured and transmitted to a third party through your use of voice recognition.'[17] If you think that surveillance ends in your home, think again! New cars contain emergency GPS and Help-calling systems since 2015 that can track car movements for days, informing them exactly of where your past movements.[18] Do you want to track a car by using a cell phone? Here are the instructions how to do it

https://www.techwalla.com/articles/
how-to-track-a-car-using-a-cell-phone

Violent Media to Disconnect People from Their Higher Sources

Years ago, I realized that despite having TV and so many channels, I was bored with it and barely watched anything. After a few weeks of not watching anything on television, I decided to try the VOD option. I did and couldn't find any movie that I like, so I canceled my subscription with the cable TV. I've always preferred to go to the cinema to watch movies. Even when I still watched TV, I intuitively felt that the mainstream media is alarmist. I had no idea why I felt this way. I noticed that it constantly broadcasted news on terror, wars, natural disasters, or economic crises. I started questioning myself how's that there aren't good news. Years ago I started thinking that, perhaps more than the boredom and revulsion I felt toward the mainstream media content, they are intended to keep people distracted from their higher connection and perspective.

I didn't know what to think about this topic and didn't further investigated it until five years ago.

However, in recent years after investigating many topics concerning the agendas of the "controllers" or Team Dark, such as Agenda 21 and Agenda 2030, I noticed so many movies that depict a brutish vision of humanity's future[19] (the outcome of successfully implementing the agendas listed here), sexualize children with famous children's movies[20], and use mind control techniques to hypnotize all watching this media to affect society. This is revealed in the documentary "The TV Mind Control"[21] and MK Ultra inspired movies.[22]

What Is MK Ultra (Monarch) Project?

According to Wikipedia[23] "**Project MKUltra**, also called the **CIA's mind control program**, is the code name given to a program of experiments on human subjects, at times illegal, designed and undertaken by the United States Central Intelligence Agency. Experiments on humans were intended to identify and develop drugs and procedures to be used in interrogations and torture, in order to weaken the individual to force confessions through mind control. Organized through the Scientific Intelligence Division of the CIA, the project coordinated with the Special Operations Division of the U.S. Army's Chemical Corps.[]" "The operation began in the early 1950s, was officially sanctioned in 1953, was reduced in scope in 1964, further curtailed in 1967, and officially halted in 1973.[3]"[23] Yet testimonies from recent years like Cathy O'Brien's[24], Ken Kesey[25] show that its technologies are in broad use today, as "Many of the programming techniques perfected in these experiments are applied on a mass scale through mass media. Mainstream news, movies, music videos, advertisements and television shows are conceived using the most advanced data on human behavior ever compiled. A lot of this comes from Monarch programming."[26] The deception of the mainstream media and Hollywood entertainment, posing as providers of objective information and family entertainment, while serving as a mind control, brainwashing tool for the hidden elite, is alarming. Thus, these TV networks are called FNN—fake news networks.

"MKUltra used numerous methodologies to manipulate people's mental states and alter brain functions, including the surreptitious administration of drugs (especially <u>LSD</u>) and other chemicals, <u>hypnosis</u>, <u>sensory deprivation</u>, isolation and <u>verbal</u> abuse, as well as other forms of psychological <u>torture</u>."[23] "The scope of Project MKUltra was broad, with research undertaken at 80 institutions, including 44 colleges and universities, as well as hospitals, prisons, and pharmaceutical companies.[12] The CIA operated through these institutions using <u>front organizations</u>, although sometimes top officials at these institutions were aware of the CIA's involvement. [13] As the <u>US Supreme Court</u> later noted in CIA v. Sims 471 U.S. 159 (1985) [14] MKULTRA was: concerned with the research and development of chemical, biological, and radiological materials capable of employment in clandestine operations to control human behavior. The program consisted of some 149 subprojects, which the Agency contracted out to various universities, research foundations, and similar institutions. At least 80 institutions and 185 private researchers participated. Because the Agency funded MKUltra indirectly, many of the participating individuals were unaware that they were dealing with the Agency.[15]"[23]

Subliminal Media

Movies like Dan Brown's *Inferno* and the depopulation scheme of sci-fi series like *The 12 Monkeys*, where a religious cult release a virus that kills off 99% of the world population, all reveal the "controllers" agenda and are no doubt supported by it. This is depopulation of this planet and its plans to accomplish this objective, which are detailed in Agenda 21 and Agenda 2030. It is often said that the "truth is hidden in plain sight."

All this media represents a concerted effort to utilize human creativity and the forces of the subconscious mind for degrading rather than uplifting the human spirit. Scientists tell us that the subconscious views film and television dramas as though it is actually happening.[27]. And "the average child will watch 8,000 murders on TV before finishing elementary school. By age eighteen, the average American has seen 200,000 acts of violence on TV, including 40,000 murders."[28]. Not just watch, but witness them. Can you imagine the impact on our sensitivity for the reverence of life and how that is degraded? This is not to mention the all the violent video games children and adults watch with the same effect.

In 1996, I read *The Power of Your Subconscious Mind* by Joseph Murphy MD. After reading it about eight times and only then, I finally understood the principle and was able to heal myself from a recurring health condition that was being treated by antibiotics and made me extremely weak during my studies in the UK. It was the only time when I cured myself without taking any medicine, only by applying the principles that Joseph Murphy discusses. It was also the last time that I experienced this condition to my amazement and joy. But this same principle is used to the detriment of humanity, to create a hellish version of our world. People unconsciously are being manipulated into creating a horrifying reality without being aware of this inducement. They are being mind-controlled and brainwashed into thinking that their thoughts, words, and actions have no impact on the collective reality being created, while the opposite is true. Thus, no responsibility is taken as to what media content to watch, read or listen to (yes, popular and mainstream music has subliminals inserted in them, as do movies and other entertainment venues).

"The controllers" (the powers that be, or team dark) harness this same collective psychic energy and direct for their own agendas. The means include global TV, movies, radio, and Internet, and the collective effect is unprecedented in history.[29] The question it raises is, "Is it possible the aggregated effect generated by untold hundreds of millions of human brains could be consciously tapped by unseen controllers to generate certain effects, phenomenon or circumstances that fit their agendas? Could such a subtle effect even be used to materialize ideas and events and thus [be] used to influence worldly matters?"[29] "What an irony if they were to use *our* own minds . . . to enslave us to *their* objectives and needs! In other words, can the Collective Psyche be harnessed to (mis)lead Man onto paths of social, political, cultural, economic and intellectual destruction? A lot of this is happening today, as any student of PsyOps and PsyWar well knows."[29] "That's called Personal Sovereignty, which is the very first step towards collective sovereignty for entire nations and continents."[29]

Social Media—Engineered Society by These Means

Today these social media networks are used by over three billion people worldwide daily, whether it's Facebook, Twitter, local social media, or Youtube, WhatsApp or Instagram.[30] From my own experience, Israelis are very heavy users of social media and 90% use WhatsApp[31], while Facebook is the leading social media worldwide.[32]

I joined Facebook in 2008 for business promotion purposes. As Facebook does not enable creating a business page without a personal profile, I created my profile. I admit that for years I didn't understand the excitement around it, barely accessed it, and even deactivated my account several times. I became active again, following my few friends and barely approving new ones. Then the alerts on these topics raised here started to appear, and I became a vocal activist in the Israeli relevant pages. I started to get info that some of the founders of these agenda pages or members are actually paid "trolls" and agents, whose aim is to preserve the general population's ignorance on these topics, as well as spying on those who are the most vocal and influential.[33] I didn't really take heed until I met a brilliant guy who helped me analyze the masses of information and find the few bits of truth, as well as teaching me how to connect the dots between these seemingly unrelated subjects.

One day I received a warning from someone I didn't approve as a Facebook friend to not post about "chemtrails." This was very disconcerting to me, as I monitor my contacts very closely. So, I asked my friend and another activist "what shall I do?" They both told me to stay low for two weeks. I also asked brilliant Nir (an alias) if he has some safety social media guidelines, because I'm not a person who is easily silenced but I was concerned. He gave me few excellent ones that I unfortunately never adhered to until recently. One day, before I stopped active participation on this social media platform, I read an article which was posted on one of my friends' walls. It discussed how you can find out if you're being spied after by the "alphabet soup agents—CIA, NSA, etc." I followed the instructions, including going to the list of blocked people and typing in the search box the words "security" and then "security in Hebrew." I found out that I was being followed by no less than fourteen agents!

This was definitely a wakeup call for me about social networking sites being a huge surveillance tool, which I had partly ignored, and now realized it was true. I made screen shots and posted them with inscriptions both in Hebrew and in English. I also thought that other Israeli activists should know about this surveillance and shared this information with them. Only one of them checked it out, and she (outspoken and much more influential than me) found out that she's being followed by forty-two soup agents! The mass surveillance online (by the leading social networking sites and search engines) added up to what I've already started noticing elsewhere: the massive surveillance of the populace outside the Internet (street cameras everywhere, smartphones, tablets, backdoor access to most computer operating systems.)

So, I started to question whether it's true that these social networking platforms and search engines are indeed a hidden arm of a global security network: both security agencies in Israel and worldwide and other more hidden soup agencies. I also found that the *U.S. intelligence community funded and incubated the development of a search engine as part of a drive to dominate the world through control of information. Seed-funded by the security services, this search engine was merely the first among a plethora of private sector start-ups co-opted by US intelligence to retain their 'information superiority.*[34] (Researching this led me to incredible findings: that social media networks performed notorious 'experiments' in 'emotional contagion' and political herding become even more sinister when placed in their rightful context. Despite their chummy image and branding, a founder of such a social media platform has made it clear in numerous interviews that he desires to mold a future of what can only be described as pure techno-totalitarianism. Consumers' every action and thought is mediated through the 'safe' interface of social media platforms—always stalked, surveilled, and tabulated—available to corporations and intelligence agencies at all times. Physical interactions are considered dangerous; they are minimized and discouraged.[35]

Moreover, the owners of highly popular alternative news pages on Facebook (both from the US and Israel) reported that the "numbers on their pages were manipulated"[36], including the number of "shares" and "likes." Greg Prescot from IN5D reported that the number of likes of a particular post was reduced to 60 from 600! After he complained about it to Facebook, they "returned" these likes to that post . . .

Has this Surveillance Started in Recent Years?

People who read this account about this pervasive surveillance may erroneously assume that it began only with the emergence of social media. Nevertheless, it's an old practice of intelligence agencies in the modern era. David Wilcock discusses Operation Mockingbird,[37] which preceded this practice decades ago. He states that "Operation Mockingbird was openly admitted in Congressional hearings in the 1970s. It is no different in the modern Internet age than it was back then.[…] This is called a "limited hangout." A certain amount of truthful information is revealed, while other key facts are completely fabricated or distorted.[…] These lies are commonly known as "disinformation." They serve the purpose of confusing the public, so it becomes very difficult to know what the truth is."[38] He goes on informing that, "For some time now, insiders have told me that certain public figures in our UFO conspiracy community are actually paid, planted 'assets.'"[38] You may ask how does David Wilcock know all this? He says that he was actually "invited" to become a paid asset in July 2017.

Suppression of Information on the Internet

Recently a leading search engine increased its attack against alternative media sources labeling them as controversial and literally blocking access to them with a red banner and a caption: controversial content. It seems as though they are afraid people will actually discover the truth. Moreover, they changed their algorithm so that the conventional mainstream media sources would appear first in the relevant search results, while it's almost impossible to find the alternative media sources, which they now label as "fake news." I had to go to great lengths on Google to find "real" information and had to search seek out pages even 8, 9, 10 in some search results!

Search engines' news-rating guidelines seem like they are out of *1984* written by George Orwell[39], censoring all content that "doesn't follow 'well-established' scientific, medical, or historical "facts".[40]" It simply eradicates any information which is not approved by the establishment controllers. To understand the degree of censoring (Google's search results are definitely not "information choices"), please read this: "On one page, it refers to "Expertise, Authoritativeness, and Trustworthiness (EAT)" regarding on what constitutes "expertise" on a topic in the eyes of Google, then proceeds to link to the BBC and USA Today as "high quality news sources".[40]

Of course, "The guide also specifically mentions giving the lowest rankings to what they deem "conspiracy theories"."[40]

Cult Agendas Like the Georgia Guidestones

What Is the Georgia Guidestones?

This is a huge granite monument of five massive stone slabs engraved in eight modern languages that "[on] the common capstone are 10 Guides, or commandments. That monument is alternately referred to as The Georgia Guidestones, or the American Stonehenge. Though relatively unknown to most people, it is an important link to the Occult Hierarchy that dominates the world in which we live."[41] "The messages engraved on the Georgia Guidestones deal with four major fields: (1) Governance and the establishment of a world government, (2) Population and reproduction control, (3) The environment and man's relationship to nature, and (4) Spirituality."[41] According to Dr. Stanley Monteith of Radio Liberty, he found a book in the public library in Elberton, GA that was written by the man who called himself R.C. Christian. He discovered "that the monument he commissioned had been erected in recognition of Thomas Paine and the occult philosophy he espoused. Indeed, the Georgia Guidestones are used for occult ceremonies and mystic celebrations to this very day. Tragically, only one religious leader in the area had the courage to speak out against the American Stonehenge, and he has recently relocated his ministry."[41]

What Is the Message Engraved in It?

The following are the 10 "commandments" engraved on the Georgia Guidestones[41]:

1. Maintain humanity under 500,000,000 in perpetual balance with nature.

2. Guide reproduction wisely - improving fitness and diversity.
3. Unite humanity with a living new language.
4. Rule passion - faith - tradition - and all things with tempered reason.
5. Protect people and nations with fair laws and just courts.
6. Let all nations rule internally resolving external disputes in a world court.
7. Avoid petty laws and useless officials.
8. Balance personal rights with social duties.
9. Prize truth - beauty - love - seeking harmony with the infinite.
10. 10.Be not a cancer on the earth - Leave room for nature - Leave room for nature.
11. No one knows who was really commissioned to erect this monument.

How Is It Connected to Agenda 21?

When you read these commandments, you will immediately notice the eerie resemblance between the depopulation agenda detailed in Agenda 21 (and later the Agenda 2030) and the first commandments stated in this monument. "This motif was perpetuated by the Georgia Guide Stones which, clearly outline that the population needs to be at 500 million to co-exist with nature, or something to that effect."[42]

FOOTNOTES

[1] http://www.bioinitiative.org/conclusions/

[2] http://electromagnetichealth.org/wp-content/uploads/2017/08/
Pall-Letter-to-CalLegis-FINAL-8-7-17.pdf

[3] http://www.smartmetereducationnetwork.com/smart-meters-
what-they-are-and-what-they-do.php

[4] http://energy.gov.il/Subjects/Electricity/Pages/
GxmsMniElectricityCommitee.aspx

[5] https://cityncountrybranding.
com/2015/09/05/%D7%9E%D7%99-
%D7%AA%D7%94%D7%99%D7%94-
%D7%94%D7%A2%D7%99%D7%A8-
%D7%94%D7%97%D7%9B%D7%9E%D7%94-%D7%94
%D7%A8%D7%90%D7%A9%D7%95%D7%A0%D7%94-
%D7%91%D7%99%D7%A9%D7%A8%D7%90%D7
%9C-%D7%95%D7%9E%D7%94-%D7%96/

[6] A 5G Wireless Future, Will It Give Us A Smart Nation Or
Contribute To An Unhealthy One? Dr. Cindy Russell, The
Bulletin January / February 2017 (www.sccma-mcms.org Santa
Clara County Medical Association).

[7] Does Radiation Hurt? Israel Hayom Newspaper, December 26,
2014. http://www.israelhayom.co.il/article/244397

[8] https://draxe.com/5g-health-effects/

[9] https://www.cio.com/article/3117705/cellular-networks/5g-could-
require-cell-towers-on-every-street-corner.html

[10] https://www.accenture.com/ie-en/insight-smart-cities

[11] Innovations in the Wireless Technologies and Public's Health by
Iris Atzmon ((2017, EatWell – the Portal for Healthy Nutrition
http://eatwell.co.il/%D7%98%D7%9B%D7%A0%D7%95%
D7%9C%D7%95%D7%92%D7%99%D7%94-%D7%95%D
7%91%D7%A8%D7%99%D7%90%D7%95%D7%AA-%D7
%94%D7%A6%D7%99%D7%91%D7%95%D7%A8/

[12] International Electromagnetic Field Scientist Appeal with 224 signatures from 41 nations https://www.emfscientist.org

[13] https://www.spandidos-publications.com/ijo/46/5/1865

[14] The list of agents classified as possible carcinogen category 2B according to IARC Monographs http://monographs.iarc.fr/ENG/Classification/ClassificationsGroupOrder.pdf

[15] http://www.dnaindia.com/delhi/report-smartphones-could-help-cause-brain-tumours-say-doctors-2466327

[16] https://www.theguardian.com/commentisfree/2016/feb/09/internet-of-things-smart-devices-spying-surveillance-us-government

[17] http://www.dailymail.co.uk/sciencetech/article-2950081/It-s-not-just-smart-TVs-home-gadgets-spy-internet-giants-collecting-personal-data-high-tech-devices.html

[18] https://www.driving.co.uk/news/how-your-cars-gadgets-can-be-used-to-track-your-movements/

[19] https://wakeup-world.com/2014/08/05/agenda-21-the-plan-for-a-global-fascist-dictatorship/

[20] http://www.therichest.com/rich-list/most-shocking/14-childrens-films-with-sexual-innuendos-you-never-noticed/

[21] https://globalelite.tv/2015/05/01/the-tv-mind-control-movie/

[22] https://www.inverse.com/article/18521-stranger-things-inspired-by-mk-ultra-the-manchurian-candidate-x-files

[23] https://en.wikipedia.org/wiki/Project_MKUltra

[24] http://www.theeventchronicle.com/editors-pick/interview-whistleblower-cathy-obrien-mkultra-mind-control-target-deep-state/#

[25] http://listverse.com/2015/05/28/10-real-victims-of-the-cias-mkultra-program/

[26] https://vigilantcitizen.com/hidden-knowledge/origins-and-techniques-of-monarch-mind-control/

[27] http://drdavidhamilton.com/does-your-brain-distinguish-real-from-imaginary/

[28] https://www.csun.edu/science/health/docs/tv&health.html

[29] http://www.newdawnmagazine.com/articles/
mind-control-its-all-around-you

[30] http://mashable.
com/2017/08/07/3-billion-global-social-media-users/

[31] http://www.ynet.co.il/articles/0,7340,L-4889555,00.html

[32] http://www.smartinsights.com/social-media-marketing/
social-media-strategy/new-global-social-media-research/

[33] https://www.entitymag.
com/11-creepy-ways-facebook-spying-right-now/

[34] https://medium.com/insurge-intelligence/
how-the-cia-made-google-e836451a959e

[35] http://www.newdawnmagazine.com/articles/
poisoned-mind-social-media-in-the-21st-century

[36] https://www.forbes.com/sites/kashmirhill/2014/06/28/
facebook-manipulated-689003-users-emotions-for-
science/#569123e9197c

[37] https://en.wikipedia.org/wiki/Operation_Mockingbird

[38] http://divinecosmos.com/start-here/
davids-blog/1217-dark-alliance?showall=&start=1

[39] http://www.stillnessinthestorm.com/2017/08/googles-new-
policies-are-straight-out-of-orwells-1984.html

[40] https://static.googleusercontent.com/media/www.
google.com/en//insidesearch/howsearchworks/assets/
searchqualityevaluatorguidelines.pdf

[41] http://www.radioliberty.com/stones.htm

[42] http://www.paranoiamagazine.com/2014/04/
agenda-21-the-population-bomb-and-the-georgia-guide-stones/

REFERENCES

1. http://divinecosmos.com/start-here/davids-blog/1217-dark-alliance

2. https://en.wikipedia.org/wiki/Georgia_Guidestones

3. http://allnewspipeline.com/Secrets_Of_Georgia_Guidestones.php

4. http://www.exposingsatanism.org/georgia-guide-stones/

5. https://www.wired.com/2009/04/ff-guidestones/

CHAPTER THREE

EDUCATED IDIOTS

Dumbing Down Humanity to Control the Masses

If you want to control humanity, you need to control education and start it as young as possible with children. This is what my blogger friend Shabtay Avigal thought when the Israeli parliament (the Knesset) tried to pass the compulsory education law starting from the age of three[1]. While the vote on this law had failed, a Member of Knesset responsible for promoting the law in the Trajtenberg Committee, managed to move the area of responsibility from the Ministry of Economy to the Ministry of Welfare and the Social Services.[2] This attempted intrusion does not stop here. A foundation called "Anu" ("we" in Hebrew) with ties to a foreign NGO checked reporters' reactions in newspaper articles to the idea that the state is responsible for children from birth to age three[3]. (At three months working mothers often have to return to work and place their infants in childcare.)

Avigal explains that from his experience, and that of psychologists, "the first years are all about [the] subconscious . . . Each second during these years creates the foundation of the person that you become. Therefore, controlling the [brain] receptors specialized in detecting conscious and subconscious sensory information establishes control over the person's unconscious mind . . . "[4] His basic assumption, as is mine, is that "the establishment's objective is never to benefit the citizens and those steps that are seemingly promoted as beneficial to them, are meant to imprison them [the citizens] more and more."[4] It's not about making parents' lives easier.

Avigal mentions Rauni-Leena Luukanen-Kilde, https://en.wikipedia.org/wiki/Rauni-Leena_Luukanen-Kilde a Finnish physician who wrote and lectured on parapsychology and mind control (Wikipedia), expounded in a fascinating interview[5] about the CIA's plan for mind control, which was developed in the 1940s-1950s (mentioned previously) called MK-Ultra. This program's goal was to find a doorway to human mind's programming. The establishment (or "the controllers"), Avigal states, realized that it can't implement MK-Ultra on such a large scale of seven billion people (it was implemented individually), so they decided that they need to start programming children at the youngest age as possible[4]. Charlotte Iserbyt in her book entitled *The Deliberate Dumbing Down of America*[6], which is also applicable to the rest of the world, presents the "controllers" or "globalists" agenda as shaping a future intended to produce servile automatons ruled over by a fully educated, aware elite class[7].

Suzanne Meier in her book *Becoming Human Again* delves into the issue of dumbing down humanity by using a wide range of methods to distract us from what's really happening in the world. Thus, we are unaware of and can't resist any part of their agenda (like Agenda 21) implemented by these "powers that be." She shows that the dumbing down of Americans is well-planned and implemented by both corporations and the government. Its dulling effects from chemical pollution and the use of electronic gadgets can be seen clearly everywhere, from chemtrails laced with aluminum, food chemicals, pollutants and hormones in the environment, to our "gadget addiction" and mass media manipulation. This is breaking down our intellect and maiming our human spirit—as we daily encounter ignorance, apathy, and sheer stupidity in today's society.

Penetrating knowledge and intelligence, or being aware of our social manipulation and the political shenanigans implementing it, is making those who speak out targets. For instance, according to a Gallup poll done in 2008, the percentage of Americans who could not locate the US on a map of the world was around 36 percent.[8]

Meier claims that this dumbing down has been a long-term process ongoing for decades "as the media, the school system, culture and the [political] system have dumbed everyone down; dopiness is widely accepted and even thought as cool."[8] She goes on exploring the disastrous results on the mind of outcome-based-education (OBE), which "is a dumbed-down uncensored scheme that smothers the individual's potential for brilliance and attainment by holding the whole class hostage to a level of learning achievable by every child . . . High schools and universities have adapted to the outcome-based educational model . . . resulting in the unadulterated destruction of absolute values of right and wrong—the very foundation that is essential for stable, free societies."[8] How does this serve the agenda of the controllers? The obvious answer is that the "undereducated . . . ask no questions and blindly trust whatever the current governmental administration decrees is best for the nation. Outcome-based education produces followers, making it easier for those in power to control the masses."[8]

It's easy to implement whatever agenda they have in mind (depopulation agenda 21) with no resistance and with impunity when people are so desensitized and dumbed down. "Common core curriculum" is yet another tool designed to dumb down children according to Peter Wood, president of the National Association of Scholars and the co-author of the book entitled *Drilling Through the Core: Why Common Core is Bad for American Education*.[9] The major criticism comes from the scholars stating that it lowered standards in both English language arts and math in the US, "The two parts of the K-12 curriculum that the Common Core covers," Wood told CNSNews.com. It was supposed to be compatible "as high or higher than the highest standards found around the world . . . But the math standards are set way below all of the Asian nations, and the U.S. language arts standards are not matched to international standards," Wood pointed out."[10]

Medicating children by apparently inventing conditions such as ADHD is another way of dumbing down our children. Alan Schwarz recently published his book *ADHD Nation,* a term he coined to describe the widespread mishandling and misdiagnosis of the disorder. In the book he cites statistics from the Centers for Disease Control and Prevention (CDC), that approximately 11% of children between the ages of 4 and 17 have been diagnosed with A.D.H.D. as of 2011. However, if you ask the American Psychiatric Association, they maintain that even though only 5% of American children suffer from the disorder, the diagnosis is actually given to around 15% of American children. Schwarz identifies two main themes involved with this misdiagnosis: the pharmaceutical industry's role in pushing A.D.H.D. drugs, and doctors failing to identify the root cause of children's behavioral issues. It's easy for people to believe this misguided information when it's affiliated with well-known universities like Harvard and Johns Hopkins. Many people don't even realize that these studies are funded by the very companies that profit from the drugs' sale because that relationship is hidden in small print.[11]

Lisa Cosgrove, an American psychologist and others "investigated financial ties between the Diagnostic and Statistical Manual of Mental Disorders (DSM) panel members and the pharmaceutical industry. Their findings showed that, of the 170 DSM panel members, 95 (56%) had one or more financial associations with companies in the pharmaceutical industry, and 100% of the members of the panels on 'mood disorders' and 'schizophrenia and other psychotic disorders' had financial ties to drug companies."[12] Furthermore, Dr. Richard Saul says that ADHD does not exist at all. "But regardless of the label, we have been giving patients different variants of stimulant medication to cover up the symptoms."[13] If you look up the subjective DSM criteria of ADHD that "only requires one to exhibit five of 18 possible symptoms to qualify for an ADHD diagnosis . . . Under these subjective criteria, the entire U.S. population could potentially qualify. We've all had these moments, and in moderate amounts they're a normal part of the human condition."[13] What are the consequences and dangers associated with feeding amphetamines to children? Here is a list of part of the health risks exhibited in children medicated with Amphetamine class drugs:

- Heart problems
- Mania and psychosis
- Hallucinations
- Depression and anxiety
- Violence, hostility and aggression
- Seizures
- Suicide attempts
- Homicidal ideation
- Death[14]

It's not only education that is dumbing down children and adults alike. Television induces its viewers into a hypnotic state by switching the brain's function from the left side to the right side. This is very significant, as the brain's left side is associated with intellectual skills for understand language in general, while the right side does not discern any incoming content, whether it contains words, images, or subliminal messages, which can be used to influence our subconscious concealed as "neutral" entertainment. This is the most effective tool to program the mind. "By age eighteen, children will have witnessed an average of forty-thousand murders and two-hundred-thousand violent acts on TV. Long-term studies show that viewing TV violence causes aggression later in life . . . Surveys show that the average American daily spends more than eight hours in front of screens—televisions, computer monitors, cell phones, gaming consoles—[and] have become passive consumers of canned media content. Excessive TV watching has produced people who have lost the ability to think, reason, and just *be*."[8]

Meier adds that more violence and profanity are introduced year after year, as we become desensitized by the huge amounts of information and media overload that keeps us trapped in a deep slumber. This type of indoctrination into our culture and society that we all undergo as children, whether in the US, Israel, France or any other country, disconnects us from our higher sources. It is our culture, as well as governments and corporations, that propagate constant propaganda about how to behave, sleep, eat, show, think, work, meditate, and talk. It is as though we are totally the creation of someone else; as though we are all copycats of "the way we should live and be" and not human. It seems that no one is living a unique life, connected to a higher source or self. We just follow commands and not even being aware of this; as though we're living on an "autopilot." It is sad to see that children are being dragged out into the real world, taken away from play earlier and earlier. Thus, Meier assumes that, "Perhaps the powers that be are afraid of 'activated' humans, with antennas that can decipher [the] truth of world manipulation. Turned-on humans would not succumb to mind games and infotainment, but demand answers and truth . . . Keeping us on a leash' ensures the system so carefully built runs smoothly and those in control stay there."[8] Moreover, it's not only the system that stays as is, but the 'controllers' or the powers that be can continue implementing their genocidal agenda towards humanity and earth unabated.

Now you may think that if the mainstream media provides fake news, manipulation and mind control, then the alternative media would be the source to find the truth. In my quest for true information, I found out that most of the alternative news sites are also controlled by the "controllers" who control the mainstream media. It's hard to find any true source of information 100 percent of the time. You need to discern all information from all sources and do your own research. Most provide a combination of some truth, some disinfo, and misinfo. Suzanne Meier explains that "The bulk of the media is owned by five companies—GE, News Corp., Viacom, Disney, and Time Warner/Spectrum. Unfortunately, independent media is near extinction due to the crushing effects of the mega media powerhouses . . . the people who actually understand history, economics, business, and politics are accused of being conspiracy theorists. Simple disagreement with the popular agenda can result in having the person blacklisted . . . According to George Orwell, legendary author of *1984*, in a time of universal deceit, telling the truth is a revolutionary act . . . Political correctness is a Marxist tool. The [Nazi] Germans knew that controlling beliefs, opinions, and ideas would disable free expression and help reshape society."[8] As it apparent today where we are strictly required to adhere the politically correct agenda/rules which totally "stifle any discussion." Some of the alternative media sources may also have been used as controlled opposition to stir discussion from issues uncomfortable to the "controllers."

How would you recognize such controlled opposition in the alternative media?

Here's some criteria:

- If a good number of people know it - they most likely want them want to know it.
- They talk a lot of truth - if they didn't they would be easily identified.
- They never tell the whole truth and there are some recurring topics that they will never touch - that is the easiest way to identify them.
- The more awake that you are the easier it is to recognize one of them. It is an on-going process of awakening.[15]

To further understand how the dumbing down of the population is connected to the depopulation agenda, please watch this documentary: https://panoffolin.wordpress.com/2014/02/09/the-great-dumbing-down-of-humanity-and-the-depopulation-agenda-inspired-by-truth/

However, Meier continues in a more positive outlook stating that with the increasing light and the awakening of the masses on the planet, it becomes clear that this control system we have followed quite blindly is falling.[8] Today, people openly share information on the corruption and this genocidal agenda which makes it hard for "the Powers that Be" to rule. I totally resonate with her last message from my experience in recent years and especially, in the last few months.

Economic Warfare

I have had discussions with many of my friends, neighbors, and family members on the topic of us working much harder for more hours than previous generations, but earning less in real buying power. Some are concerned that they will not have any pension to rely on, because pensions are not as secure as they were in the past (a large part of these pensions are invested by the companies in the stock exchange which is highly volatile), and young people find it much more difficult to buy a house. It feels that everyone I talk with is concerned with their survival, even if they work for stable companies like Israel Electric Corporation. This leads in no time to other topics. They are totally immersed in the mainstream media that instills even more fear and concern for their and their loved ones' future.

I started asking myself: Why? Is there a purpose in this deterioration of economic conditions? I don't even know young people who are not indebted, even those who have high salaries. So I started checking about Israeli working hours and what I found out stunned me. According to Globes Magazine (October, 2016 in Hebrew), Israelis work 150 more hours a month than employees in the West and pay double in taxes than any, which means they have less leisure time and money; one of the lowest earnings in the west.[16] And what about debts? I wanted to know how Israelis are faring in general and then, compare to other countries. Yes, same here: Israelis own half a trillion NIS (139 billion USD) to the banks (owning credit card companies).[17] This can definitely explain Israelis tendency to be stressed for many reasons, including economic ones, which makes them to being more unaware and easy to be manipulated.

What about other countries? Was there a deterioration, too? Is it a global trend? I sensed that somehow people who are dumbed down and are completely occupied with survival (economic, health and other issues), cannot challenge the "controllers" and their genocidal agenda for the humanity. The *New York Times* tells a similar story about Americans: Most Americans are working harder and earning less.[18] Moreover, "Americans work more than anyone in the industrialized world . . . And Americans take less vacation, work longer days, and retire later, too." Author Juliet Schor, who wrote the best-selling book *The Overworked American* in 1992, concluded that in 1990 Americans worked an average of nearly one month more per year than in 1970. ". . . This is especially stressful if both husband and wife don't earn enough to employ help[19]." Another intriguing fact is that Millennials earn 20% less than baby boomers at the same age and are worse off in general than boomers.[20]

And what about debt worldwide? Was there a deterioration in this area? According to McKinsey, a global management consulting company, the global debt has increased by $57 trillion raising the ratio of debt to GDP by 17 percentage points, while no leading economy has decreased its debt-to-GDP ratio since 2007. The rise in household debt—and housing prices—continue to new peaks in some Asian countries, Northern Europe, and the quadrupling of China's debt. This increase in global debt exceeds the peak levels of 2008 in some of the countries which experienced the financial crisis. Such countries include advanced economies such as Australia, Denmark, Canada, the Netherlands, and Sweden, and developing economies as Thailand, Malaysia, and South Korea.[21]

So again, the same trend is apparent worldwide. Working poor[22] is another example of worsening conditions. Research also shows that more UK workers earn less than living wage. "The number of UK workers earning below the so-called living wage has risen to 4.8 million, research suggests . . . The figure, equivalent to 20% of employees, is up from 3.4 million in 2009, the Resolution Foundation think tank said."[23] I was still unconvinced so I continued investigating, asking myself what about poverty and homelessness rates around the world? Had they increased in recent years? It's much easier to control poor and homeless people. Unfortunately, I was right. According to Oxfam https://www.oxfam.org/, an NGO that seeks to overcome poverty worldwide, "the world's 3.6 billion poorest people are getting poorer . . . The data, released ahead of the World Economic Forum (WEF) meeting in Davos, Switzerland, shows the gap between richest and poorest continues to widen . . . In 2015 it required the combined wealth of the world's 80 richest people to match the wealth of the poorest half of the population. In 2010 that figure was at 388 . . . In both rich and developing countries the share of national income going to workers continues to fall. This results in workers capturing less wealth and owners of capital further stretching the wealth divide."[24] Not only is the salary of workers decreasing, the wage gap between those in senior positions and typical workers also drastically increased in the last decades due to lavish pay increases for CEOs, while barely any pay rise given to workers since 1978: "In the United States, CEOs have seen pay increases of 997.2 percent since 1978, while the typical worker has had a pay rise of just 10.9 percent in that same period. More recently, CEO pay in the US increased 54.3 percent since 2009, a period in which ordinary wages remained stagnant."[24]

And how about homelessness worldwide? This is from research conducted at Yale University: the more cities grow worldwide, so do the number of homeless people. This sounds eerily familiar to Agenda 21's goal mentioned earlier that a third of the world population will live in cities until 2050? "People openly live on the streets of the world's major <u>urban centers</u>—from Cairo to Washington, DC—a disconcerting reminder of homelessness . . . Based on national reports, it's estimated that no less than <u>150 million people</u>, or about 2 percent of the world's population, are homeless. However, about <u>1.6 billion</u>, more than 20 percent of the world's population, may lack adequate housing . . . homelessness is often considered embarrassing, a taboo subject, and governments tend to understate the problem.

Obtaining accurate numbers is difficult, especially in developing countries. In Moscow, for example, officials report that <u>the homeless</u> number around 10,000, while non-government organizations claim that as many as 100,000 live on the streets. Also, in the Philippines capital of Manila, reported to have the <u>largest homeless population</u> of any city in the world, estimates vary from <u>several million</u> to <u>tens of thousands</u>. In the world's billion-plus populations, China and India, reported numbers of homeless are <u>3 million</u> and <u>1.77 million,</u> respectively, rates of 0.22 percent and 0.14 percent—on par with levels reported by many wealthy developed countries. Given their levels of socioeconomic development, the Chinese and Indian rates of homelessness appear unduly low."[25] Homelessness is also increasing in almost all areas of Europe.[26]

So how is this related to the depopulation agenda? Suzanne Meier infers that "It has been reported that disasters such as the dot-com bubble and the subprime mortgage calamity were handcrafted by this group (the Bilderberg Group) to remove wealth from citizens. What if it's true? It would mean we're being manipulated in the area that most defines our freedom and independence—our financial structures and institutions . . . Mainstream propaganda convincingly states that the idea of a shadow government is bollocks, or simply a conspiracy theory. But, again that's what a shadow government would want us to believe and this is where the media has been assisting—by libeling the inquisitive minds and the skeptics."[8]

Weaponizing Music

I remember loving music from a very young age. When I was about four years old, I would play my parents' records when they weren't at home on this record player in a box, including *The Doors*, *The Beatles*, *The Supremes* and popular Romanian music of that time. They were really rebels to listen to this music in the then-communist Romania. I was bewitched by this music. This love and enthusiasm has remained with me since that time. I even remember that my mom took me to a piano teacher when I was six, but after testing my musical hearing tone twice, she told my mom that it was a waste to spend money on piano lessons for me. So when I first discovered in my awakening that music is being used in this depopulation agenda simply by switching from 432 Hz frequency—the harmonic, inducing calm and creating unity—to the frequency of 440 Hz—that induces separation, self-centerness and aggressive—I was definitely keen to learn more about it. Is it true? How can it be? I asked myself. These were just few questions that came up a few years ago. I was also devastated to find out that it is indeed true and that perhaps I'd need to stop listening to my favorite music, electronica.

I discovered that this natural frequency was used by musicians playing without recording from time immemorial. Ananda Bosman, an international musician and researcher found out that ancient Egyptian instruments which have been unearthed are largely tuned to A=432Hz. Moreover, ancient Greeks also tuned their instruments mostly to 432Hz. This musical tuning is also found throughout various cultures and religions of the archaic times. It is also interesting to note that musicians today report positive effects after retuning to 432 Hz, including a more laid-back feel to their performances and better audience response. [27]

I remember that recently I had a chat with another Israeli activist. I was very enthusiastic about a brilliant musician that I rediscovered his music only a few months ago. I told her that he's an "independent" musician implying that he was "safe" to listen to unlike other mainstream musicians. She instantly asked me "what frequency tone does he record and play his music?" I evaded her question to deny that he wasn't so safe to listen to and replied that "he probably doesn't know the difference between 440 Hz and 432 Hz impact on human consciousness". This woman insisted that "he's a musician and as such he must know." Unfortunately, she was right—recently I discovered that he's actually playing with "Team Dark/the Controllers" and is part of the mainstream music industry. I discussed this with my brilliant friend Nir and I kind of asked or stated, "I will need to stop listening to this music, right?" He sadly replied in the affirmative. This guy also stopped listening to his favorite band for the same reasons. So I've become cautious about the media I consume, whether it's music, movies or books (I still love reading very much).

This is what L. C. Vincent, who was a professional musician for seven years, says about this standard tuning frequency (440 Hz): "This unnatural standard tuning frequency, removed from the symmetry of sacred vibrations and overtones, has declared war on the subconscious mind of Western Man."[28] If you really want to understand how the difference in tuning frequency can make a huge difference on consciousness, you can check about the science of Cymatics that "illustrates that when sound waves move thru a physical medium (air, water, sand, metallic particles, etc.) the frequency of the waves has a direct effect upon the structures which are created by the sound waves as they pass thru that particular medium. *YouTube* videos show these fascinating patterns and arrangements."[29]

Henry Makow discusses in-depth this concept of 440 Hz versus 432 Hz, which at the beginning may sound like science fiction to you. I totally relate to this reaction at first. I thought so too, but please bear with me here. He invites us to "Imagine an incredibly powerful, wealthy person who secretly prospers from conflict, disease and war learns that certain sound frequencies (those easily divisible by two, signifying opposition) create conflict, discord and disharmony while those divisible by three (signifying balance, polity, reconciliation, harmony) produce symmetry, and visually harmonic, pleasing structures. Now imagine that he has the power to establish the tuning standard of all musical instruments throughout the Western World. Imagine that he bases the entire scale of musical artistic creation upon a frequency which would skew vibrations towards discord."[30] You still think it's science fiction? Well, that is exactly what happened when the Cabal alliance determined and promoted "the musical factors capable of producing psycho pathology, emotional distress and 'mass hysteria . . . the BSI—British Standards Institute—officially adopted A=440 Hz in 1939, promoted by the strange consortium of a globalist foundation influence and the Nazi government. Ironically, the British adopted a tuning standard promoted by the Third Reich, just as both went to war. While 440Hz had been rejected by British musicians only three months prior, Josef Goebbels persuaded the BSI to adapt 440Hz saying it was of extraordinary importance . . ." [30] As Dr. Leonard Horowitz concludes: "Music bioenergetically affects your body chemistry, psycho- neuro immunology, and health. Your body is now vibrating musically, audibly and subliminally, according to an institutionally imposed frequency in harmony with aggression and in dissonance rather than vibrating in harmony with Love."[30] Brian T. Collins, a musician and researcher among the advocates of A=432Hz standard tuning, says that a lot has been written on "the A=432Hz tuning preference that is mathematically consistent with the Fibonacci series of numbers, and, therefore, universal design."[31]

The militarization of music is real according to Dr. Leonard Horowitz in his paper entitled "Musical Cult Control" that "The music industry . . . features this imposed frequency that is 'herding' populations into greater aggression, psycho- social agitation, and emotional distress predisposing people to physical illness . . . while the agents of this conspiracy provide 'therapeutic' pacification in the form of myriad psychotropic drugs and tranquilizers for the stress they purposely created, and chemotherapy for the more serious illnesses it inspires".[30] He says, "Energy (vibration) impacts 'life' (biology) and our bodies through the most common medium of life: water. Our body weight, which is nearly 80 percent water, vibrates and resonates to frequencies, and frequencies entrain our physical matter as well as thought processes. Light and sound have been shown as the primary drivers of intercellular communication, which indicates that our health, or lack of it, may indeed by a product of the vibrational resonance of sound and light."[30]

The aspect of mass hysteria caused by this 440 Hz frequency was made clear to me when "It was recently revealed that The Beatles were barred from performing in Israel following an investigation that prompted the education ministry to conclude the Beatles' performances caused: [H]ysteria and mass disorder. . . There is no musical or artistic experience here, but a sensual display that arouses feelings of aggression replete with sexual stimuli. . . ."[32] According to preliminary research, analysis, and professional discussions by Walton, Koehler, Reid, et al., on the web,(23) A=440Hz frequency music conflicts with human energy centers (i.e., chakras) from the heart to the base of the spine. Alternatively, chakras above the heart are stimulated. Theoretically, the vibration stimulates ego and left-brain function, suppressing the "heart-mind," intuition and creative inspiration. Not coincidently metaphysically, the interval between A=440Hz (equivalent to F#=741Hz in the ancient original Solfeggio scale) and A=444Hz (C(5)=528Hz in the ancient original Solfeggio scale) is classically known as the Devil's Interval in musicology, due to its highly aversive disharmonious sound made when these two notes are played simultaneously.(36)[32]

If humanity was to be optimally suppressed spiritually, the musical tuning of A=444Hz would be neglected religiously, as it has been. Religious leaders suppressed the original Solfeggio musical scale in which A=444Hz, virtually equivalent to (C(5)=528Hz for over a millennia . . . The science of coercion, cultural indoctrination, and behavior modification has a lot to do with the world's current crises, history of musical instrument tuning, and the media. President

Dwight Eisenhower protested against this "beast," warning our parents that globalist threats to "Economic, Political, even Spiritual" freedoms were mounting.(34)"[32] According to Leonard G. Horowitz, "This amounts to ENSLAVEMENT for the conduct of genocide. Your body is now vibrating musically, audibly and subliminally, according to an institutionally imposed frequency that resonates in harmony with aggression and in dissonance with LOVE.

Intensive research into the military and commercial value of compelling "herd behavior" with music to induce stress, promote diseases, and suppress spirituality, has enabled the world's wealthiest people to exercise cultural control through "programming."[32] Horowitz goes on and explains that there is historic evidence in the Rockefeller Foundation Archives that they are the investors in A=440Hz "standard tuning who "directed the US Navy's involvement in this "black-op" engaging the consortium-controlled networks . . ."[32]

These findings strongly suggest the military's acoustic frequency research and technological developments advanced during the 1930s by the Nazis to induce psychosocial pathology, herd behavior, emotional distress, and "mass hysteria," were successfully deployed and are now being used against We The People. Alternatively, musical frequencies most beneficial to health, psychosocial harmony, and world peace have been suppressed. Many musicians, mathematicians, physicians, physicists, and even geneticists, now celebrate the emergence of truth about A=444Hz (C(5)=528Hz) as an apparent carrier wave of LOVE, broadcasting universally from the heart of the electromagnetic energy matrix.(7, 22)"[32] A positive sign that people are becoming aware of this is that more meditations and music are increasingly being uploaded to Youtube. com after being converted from 440 Hz to 432 Hz frequency tuning. You can use the *Audacity* software to convert music to 432Hz pitch. See how it's done easily here: https://www.youtube. com/watch?v=dl6sae66oWk

Another good sign that people are awakening to the fact that subliminal messages are inserted both in movies and music – not only the negative effect of switching to a 440 Hz from 432 Hz pitch - may be that Hollywood movies are losing[33] indicating that "the drugs don't work (anymore)", as the Verve track goes.

FOOTNOTES

[1] http://www.jpost.com/Israel-News/Education-Ministry-Parents-can-enroll-children-aged-3-in-private-preschools-next-year-390491

[2] http://www.nrg.co.il/online/1/ART2/888/779.html

[3] The Left Reveals Its Goals in Dribs and Drabs: The Children Belonging to the State from Birth, April 28th, 2017 (in Hebrew) https://www.inn.co.il/News/News.aspx/345078

[4] http://www.shabtay-av.022.co.il/BRPortal/br/P102.jsp?arc=1871960

[5] https://www.youtube.com/watch?v=b-rdk8mOx9E

[6] The Deliberate Dumbing Down of America by Charlotte Thomson Iserbyt http://www.deliberatedumbingdown.com/MomsPDFs/DDDoA.sml.pdf

[7] https://www.activistpost.com/2010/12/10-modern-methods-of-mind-control.html

[8] Becoming human again From Sheeple to People by Suzanne Meier

[9] Drilling through the Core by Peter Wood, by Sandra Stotsky (Contributor), R. James Milgram (Contributor), Ze'ev Wurman (Contributor), and 8 more co-authors http://pioneerinstitute.org/featured/new-book-drilling-through-the-core-why-common-core-is-bad-for-american-education/

[10] https://www.cnsnews.com/news/article/barbara-hollingsworth/common-core-comprehensive-dumbing-down-american-education-every

[11] https://www.scientificamerican.com/article/big-pharma-s-manufactured-epidemic-the-misdiagnosis-of-adhd/

[12] http://www.collective-evolution.com/2016/10/25/a-d-h-d-nation-how-big-pharma-created-the-a-d-h-d-epidemic/

[13] http://time.com/25370/doctor-adhd-does-not-exist/

[14] http://www.naturalnews.com/042948_amphetamines_children_schedule_II_drugs.html

[15] https://steemit.com/life/@steemtruth/controlled-opposition-your-friend-might-be-your-enemy-truth

[16] http://www.globes.co.il/news/article.aspx?did=1001158087

[17] https://www.calcalist.co.il/local/articles/0,7340,L-3702902,00.html

[18] Michael C. Dawson is the John D. MacArthur Professor of Political Science and the director of the Center for the Study of Race, Politics and Culture at the University of Chicago. https://www.nytimes.com/roomfordebate/2012/10/18/shrink-inequality-to-grow-the-economy/most-americans-are-working-harder-and-earning-less?mcubz=3

[19] http://abcnews.go.com/US/story?id=93364

[20] https://www.forbes.com/sites/timworstall/2017/01/14/millennials-earn-20-less-than-boomers-not-as-important-as-you-might-think/#20b3f0981168

[21] http://www.mckinsey.com/global-themes/employment-and-growth/debt-and-not-much-deleveraging

[22] https://en.wikipedia.org/wiki/Working_poor

[23] http://www.bbc.com/news/uk-politics-23953573

[24] http://www.wired.co.uk/article/global-poverty-oxfam-world-economic-forum

[25] http://yaleglobal.yale.edu/content/cities-grow-worldwide-so-do-numbers-homeless

[26] http://realchangenews.org/2017/04/19/homelessness-increasing-almost-all-areas-europe

[27] https://attunedvibrations.com/432hz/

[28] https://www.henrymakow.com/musicalscale.html

[29] http://www.youtube.com/watch?v=GtiSCBXbHAg

[30] https://www.henrymakow.com/musicalscale.html

[31] Brian T. Collins a musician and a researcher discussing the 432 Hz http://omega432.com/

[32] http://www.waronwethepeople.com/musical-cult-control/

[33] https://www.theatlantic.com/business/archive/2016/06/hollywood-has-a-huge-millennial-problem/486209/

REFERENCES

1. The Israeli Ministry of Education, the Compulsory Education Law for age three is set to go into effect beginning in the upcoming academic year (2015-16) http://cms.education.gov.il/EducationCMS/Units/Gil3/default.htm

2. Implementing Reforms and Closing the Gaps in the Education for Young Age/Preschoolers, the state comptroller of the Trachtenberg Commission, Israel, year 2014.

3. http://www.frequency365.com/the-a432-hz-frequency-dna-tuning-and-the-bastardization-music/

4. https://www.bloomberg.com/news/articles/2017-09-10/japan-backs-u-s-proposal-to-target-north-korea-s-oil-supplies

5. http://www.latimes.com/business/la-fi-investing-quarterly-debt-20160710-snap-story.html

6. http://www.telegraph.co.uk/finance/economics/11625406/The-world-is-drowning-in-debt-warns-Goldman-Sachs.html

7. https://en.wikipedia.org/wiki/Rauni-Leena_Luukanen-Kilde

8. The Musical Pitch Conflict by Brian T Collins http://omega432.com/

9. http://www.wnd.com/2015/04/common-cores-real-goal-dumbing-down-people/

10. https://www.newparadigm.ws/my-blogs/7-examples-showing-how-the-ruling-elite-are-making-us-dumber/

11. http://www.thesleuthjournal.com/how-your-child-is-being-dumbed-down-by-common-core-education/

12. https://japantoday.com/category/features/kuchikomi/are-smart phones-promoting-the-dumbing-down-of-humanity

13. https://iamisatthedoors.wordpress.com/2012/07/22/how-the-illuminati-exert-control-through-the-media/

14. Beyond Israeli band against drugging children (Ritalin etc.) https://www.youtube.com/user/BEYONDunited

15. http://www.ritalindeath.com/Education/how-to-dumb-down-a-nation.htm

16. http://www.thejournal.ie/300-more-homeless-families-compared-to-this-time-last-year-3586690-Sep2017/

17. http://globalnews.ca/news/3369305/homelessness-up-by-30-per-cent-in-metro-vancouver/

18. http://www.youtube.com/watch?v=GtiSCBXbHAg

19. https://www.vanityfair.com/news/2017/01/why-hollywood-as-we-know-it-is-already-over

20. https://www.oxfam.org/

21. http://www.livestrong.com/article/145593-parts-of-the-brain-associated-with-thinking-skills/

PART II

THE SHIFT

CHAPTER FOUR

THE DAWN OF MASS AWAKENING

While the dark hats agenda has been in place for hundreds if not thousands of years, there are signs of hope—both physically and spiritually—that we are taking back our power. But I want the reader to realize that this book is really about the process of our mass awakening from this tyranny. But first I had to present "The Agenda" to reveal the current stage of this struggle and place it in its proper context.

You can even spot these awakening signs in whatever mainstream or alternative media you follow, although you may need to see through the disinformation presented there. There's a multi-front battle going on for exposing the information hidden from us, whether it's partial disclosure of some concealed information or a full disclosure which would divulge everything hidden from us—all the truth and nothing but the truth will free us. You can see the difference between partial disclosure as displayed, under the guise of a commercial, by Boeing's 2015 ad about a presumed futuristic scenario of "interplanetary spacecraft, solar energy technology, and colonies on Mars," which seems very exciting to those who are unaware that such programs already exist according to Corey Goode's testimony.[1] "The Powers that Be" are only interested in partial disclosure, to hide their criminal activities against humanity and "buy time" to run for cover, but they are now rapidly running out of time due to the quickening of the awakening of the masses worldwide.[2]

There's a popular saying: "We're the ones we've been waiting for." It's true, and the worldwide paradigm shift today proves this adage. We're our own saviors by awakening to the "real" reality and fighting to gain control of our lives and pressing for the disclosure of the truth of every dark agenda hidden from us, and reclaiming our inherent rights. We're entitled to the "truth," and together we will achieve this reckoning.

Here's an example how we are our own saviors when we are moved to act. I'm donating to various causes like fighting corruption and the compulsory biometric database in Israel via crowd-funding. I also personally went from one neighbor to another to explain why we all need to resist the installation of smart meters and had them sign a petition. Overall I've gotten a positive response. My brilliant friend, Nir, constantly speaks about these topics with his "unawakened" family members and colleagues at work. He was ridiculed at first, but then colleagues began to realize that he was right and silently began to support him and his family members, asking for more "signs" of what he was talking about. His acquaintances now alert him and others when they see chemtrails or other suspicious activity. My friend and activist Shabtay Avigal told me how his wife, who was totally pro-vaccines, started questioning them and was amazed that she talked with the doctor at the pediatrician's clinic about them. Yes, tiny steps, but consciousness is contagious, and every right act is multiplied exponentially.

Worldwide this awakening of the masses is also shown by people helping whistleblowers, who were financially hit by the "Powers that be and about to be collapsed." David Wilcock described how Pete Peterson, who recently validated the testimonies of Corey Goode and William Tompkins on his program *Cosmic Disclosure* on the Gaia online video service, was rescued by "a stunning demonstration of public support." Wilcock tells how the banks foreclosed on Pete's house and laboratory and "have now stolen and destroyed over 2 million dollars worth of belongings for a house that was only worth about 300K. Bank agents emptied [it] to the bare walls." But people stepped in and contributed $12,131 within a month when the target sum was $5,000. Wilcock adds, "He is using the money to finance the construction of a new lab, so his valuable technical work can continue forward."[3]

Another example of how people are fighting the silencing of the truth in the mainstream media is by voting with their dollars to support alternative news channels on YouTube. For instance, Jordan Sather brings a fresh and unusual perspective on the ongoing events worldwide including the latest hurricanes, the Vegas shooting, and the earthquakes in Mexico. He gained thousands of subscribers to his channel, "Destroying the Illusion," within four months of its start by receiving donations from his viewers. People are asking him hard questions, and he replies to each with well-referenced answers, which makes it a very personal media.

I might add here that there is a dichotomy in my approach toward social media in general. I'm aware that the Elite created these platforms as instruments to serve their purposes. However, we "the people" turned it back on them to expose the lies and spread the truth about the Elite's hidden agenda. I saw a wonderful posting on the Internet that reflects this idea beautifully:

> "The government created Facebook, and the social media in general, to monitor our lives and locations... But we changed the game and used it to wake up humanity. Checkmate."

Social media changed the way we receive and share information with others. It gave everybody a voice, and now "we" the people provide each other information in an accelerated and decentralized manner on so many topics, hidden and visible, can be heard—despite a lot of disinformation and misinformation. I admit that I, despite of all my experience and knowledge, fall for some of these manipulations. We all do. That's why it's so important that we openly discuss these issues, commenting on and discerning what's true. Today, due to the ease of discussing and searching for information, I and other people I know discover when we've been manipulated quicker. It's an ongoing process. No one is immune to these tricks. This infographic shows how powerful spreading news on social media is https://www.mushroomnetworks.com/infographics/social-media-news-outlets-vs-traditional-news-infographic/ "From Facebook and Twitter to Instagram and Pinterest; from YouTube, LinkedIn, Google+ and dedicated news networking platforms, social media helps news spread faster than ever because every post is commented on and shared over and over across vast networks of friends."[4]

I participate in many progressive online groups, and have noticed a lot of fear of Armageddon and an apocalypse from many people worldwide with different religions and belief systems. I feel that people need to know that what they sense is not the end of the world or the "rapture," etc. Team Dark is intentionally misguiding us to think along this track. Yes, it is indeed the end of the world as we know it, but one freed of wars, terror, disease, hunger, and universal suffering. Or, it's the end of the world for the "bad guys" or team dark. It's the dissolution of the evil matrix, and these "controllers" know it and are fighting back with ground wars and political terror, and weather control through hurricanes, earthquakes, and tsunamis (from with HAARP technology covered earlier), and a threatened worldwide financial collapse. So whatever catastrophes you see in the world right now, know that they're engineered and a positive countercurrent is being created at the same time. This is a reminder that we're powerful creators, which was recently manifested in the weakening of Hurricane Irma by worldwide mass meditations intended for this purpose and the tapering off of other expected hurricanes in the same region.

Mass meditations have been found scientifically to significantly lower rate crime according to Prof John Hagelin (featured in the documentary *What the Bleep Do We Know!?*). Unbelievable as it may sound, "While the meditators were meditating and levitating, Washington's crime rate dropped by 18%."[5] From the earliest days of his world ministry, which began in 1959, Maharishi Mahesh Yogi often spoke about the peaceful, positive global shift that would naturally result if only 1% of the world's population practiced the <u>Transcendental Meditation</u> technique. Then the results of the first scientific test of this claim conducted in 1975 found a statistically significant decrease in crime rates in twelve American cities "when the threshold of 1% of each city's population practicing the TM technique was reached."[6] Some 250,000 people participated in the solar eclipse meditation worldwide on September 21, 2017 to accelerate this positive shift, and many continued meditating to dissipate further engineered weather events. These are indeed amazing times, both scary and exciting, as drastic change appears to be happening all at once.

One of the major signs that a mass awakening is occurring worldwide is that during hurricanes or other weather events, after false flag attacks or any engineered attack, people are starting to question what's occurring. From all over the world, people are discussing and sharing information about these events to dispel the fear. For example, Greg Prescott from IN5D, the site providing spiritual and alternative information and commentary, posted a video from where he lives in Florida to show that Hurricane Irma was not as powerful as reported, to counter mainstream media claims. There are now many groups on Facebook and a slew of independent journalists and bloggers, who share real information in posts and comments. This has become a viable alternative media stream where people exchange information, ask questions and receive real answers—the new "think tanks" of the masses.

This is a comment by Jolene le Roux, a devout Muslim, taken from Facebook that for me shows the power of this awakening: "What you don't realise is that disclosure is occurring. Pedophile, Satanism, child sacrifices, Vatican crimes, political crimes and more.

We are being fed the truth but with so much 'fake news' around it is hard to discern it. We are also seeing releases of AI, cars that can fly, medical breakthroughs, and more. Yet we don't use our independent critical thinking to sift through all the garbage to see the underlying truth . . . Being awake means recognizing snippets and dumping the garbage."

As I said earlier, people are becoming aware that they are powerful creators.

The bestselling *The Secret* and the documentary it drew from are only the tip of the iceberg. The *Power of Your Subconscious Mind* (1963) is the predecessor of the Secret, which was also a bestseller that "has helped millions around the world achieve remarkable goals, simply by changing the way they think".[7] I read it several times and managed to heal myself for good from a recurring condition that I had taken antibiotics for. Another documentary, referenced earlier, that showed that we, humans, are the creators of our reality with all the implications involved is *What the Bleep Do We Know!?* This very extraordinary documentary was based on the principles of quantum physics and featured physicians, psychologists, and physicists.

From what I'm seeing in recent months (fall 2017), the "controllers" are increasing their attacks as this mass awakening is accelerating and more people are becoming aware of the real reality, from mass shootings to the use of HAARP and geoengineering technologies for creating or accelerating hurricanes, like those in Florida and Puerto Rico in 2017, and earthquakes like the ones in Mexico. (I'm sending my prayers to all the people hurt or who lost dear ones, and my wishes for quick recovery: Les envío mis condolencias y deseo que se recuperen lo antes posible.) There's circumstantial evidence in footage for the use of HAARP to create 8.1 - 8.4 earthquake near Mexico City with Tsunami warnings coming soon after.[8]

Since my awakening to this expanded reality, I have come to see humanity in a different light—more positively. I have much greater appreciation for humanity today than a few years ago. I'm seeing a lot of courage, determination, and perseverance in places I've never expected to find it, as well as the blossoming of wisdom. I didn't anticipate this new trend and I'm glad that it is happening. I've also recognized that I have a lot of prejudices and that by becoming aware of them, I can confront and deal with my narrow-minded attitudes. Some of the people around me don't like when I'm sharing this positive outlook for humanity. They prefer to believe what they are familiar with, consensus reality, but then they've never tested their beliefs. I did and continue to do so on a daily basis. It's a never-ending process.

The Signs of the Mass Awakening of Human Consciousness

Before delving into these signs, I would like to share a brilliant speech about the problem of civil obedience by Howard Zinn, which reflects on so many issues brought up in this book and the importance of our mass awakening. Matt Damon reads the speech in this video: https://www.youtube.com/watch?v=S2li9E_94MA

A small part of the transcript of this speech:[9]

"I start from the supposition that the world is topsy-turvy, that things are all wrong, that the wrong people are in jail and the wrong people are out of jail, that the wrong people are in power and the wrong people are out of power, that the wealth is distributed in this country and the world in such a way as not simply to require small reform but to require a drastic reallocation of wealth...What we are trying to do, I assume, is really to get back to the principles and aims and spirit of the Declaration of Independence. This spirit is resistance to illegitimate authority and to forces that deprive people of their life and liberty and right to pursue happiness, and therefore under these conditions, it urges the right to alter or abolish their current form of government- and the stress had been on abolish. But to establish the principles of the Declaration of Independence, we are going to need to go outside the law, to stop obeying the laws that demand killing or that allocate wealth the

85

way it has been done, or that put people in jail for petty technical offenses and keep other people out of jail for enormous crimes. My hope is that this kind of spirit will take place not just in this country but in other countries because they all need it. People in all countries need the spirit of disobedience to the state, which is not a metaphysical thing but a thing of force and wealth. And we need a kind of declaration of interdependence among people in all countries of the world who are striving for the same thing." I might add that twenty years ago, in Damon's movie *Good Will Hunting*, he referenced *Howard Zinn's A People's History of the United States*.

This mass awakening is even reflected in comments about this speech on YouTube (although not mentioning these words) like *Uprising* by Muse https://www.youtube.com/watch?v=w8KQmps-Sog or people fiercely commenting on Madonna's track Illuminati https://www.youtube.com/watch?v=uNCN1P1EMFo that shows people are awakening worldwide.

Human consciousness, which operates both on the spiritual and mundane planes, is rising worldwide, both on the local and global level. People are actually rebelling and demanding answers from their governments on a scale that hasn't been seen until recently. Displays of this low-scale rebellion such as boycotting, petitioning, and protests are becoming common all over the world with people responding to local topics like the pipeline being built across the Standing Rock Sioux's sacred burial grounds in North Dakota[10]. This is a long-time dispute, which the Sioux tribe recently stepped up with its efforts to stop this $3.8 billion project intended to transport 470,000 barrels of crude oil a day through four states.[11] In 2016 the tribe filed their case in federal court to disclose the dramatic archeological findings discovered on this site. In 2017, a federal judge ruled "that the US Army Corps of Engineers did not sufficiently evaluate the environmental impact of the Dakota Access pipeline (DAPL) and needs to go back and redo its environmental assessment." This ruling has reinforced the tribe's stance in the battle against this pipeline, which is constructed under their main water source, and could lead to an environmental disaster. [12]

In Israel, half a world away, there were posts on this topic shared with many comments supporting this Native American cause. I also remember how I felt—together with other Israeli activists—about the daily protests in France against the outrageous indefinite state of emergency in that country and the serious censorship of information[13]. Despite the scarce information about such protests, or the high-scale rebellion by groups that organized revolutionary acts, such as in Iceland (prosecuting bankers for the 2008 crisis and then incarcerating some of them), the truth is coming out. The masses are now becoming aware very soon after such events take place, despite the fake official story put out by the government and its stooges the mainstream media. Such was the case with the death of Democratic National committee staffer Seth Rich, the supposed Wikileaks source for DNC leaked emails, who people believe was murdered. Steve Scalise, the Republican whip who was shot at a congressional baseball game, is another example of the masses not believing the official story. You can find postings about it online whether on Youtube, Facebook or other venues, and join the protest to demand disclosure of the real truth on it and other such cases as well.

After the shootings in Vegas (in the beginning of October 2017), people immediately started sharing information on the crisis actors, who participated in other "attacks" as victims or eyewitnesses.[14] London police changing clothes during a terrorist attack? https://www.youtube.com/watch?v=ampLXJzWVc8 French journalists also discuss in this article why this man dies in so many terrorist attacks: http://observers.france24.com/en/20160705-mexican-man-dies-every-terrorist-attack-mystery. They discuss and expose the real goals of this attack, which is to disarm the Americans and leave them unprotected, (as was the program implemented in Nazi Germany and Austria in the 1930s). Kitty Werthmann, a WW2 Austrian survivor, tells her account of how the Nazis incrementally seized the weapons from both Germans and Austrians during this time, to warn Americans not to succumb to the attempts to disarm them. She explains that, "The government required people to register their guns, insisting it was for their own protection, a way of tracking down criminals that was supposed to cut down on crime." As the Germans and the Austrians are obedient people, they registered their weapons, and then the Nazis came and confiscated them leaving them defenseless from the encroaching tyranny.[15]

This mass awakening is also displayed in the "unlearning" of our age-old conditioning like blindly accepting the dictates of the medical system (doctors with their medication pads), the educational system, and any other such authorities. For me, after many years into my personal awakening on these topics and feeling so alone, it's exciting to see people worldwide starting to question their beliefs about every aspect of their lives, thinking for themselves and being true to who they really are by connecting to their higher selves, as well as demanding the truth first and foremost. "Ignorance is bliss, yet denial is slow torture."[16]

The information revolution, whether it's the alternative news or sharing information on social media and blogs, investigating and discussing topics together, has now opened a once-closed media-circuit box. Before this revolution, information was controlled by a very small number of groups or individuals. (Until the advent of cable television in the late 1980s in the U.S., the news was controlled by the Big Three networks.) This mass global awakening of the new information age has also led to our spiritual awakening, too. "We are collectively moving towards more spiritual practice such as Yoga and meditation. These ancient forms are now becoming commonplace and even being practiced in schools and prisons to help with focus."[16] The German prison system provides the inmates apartments, not cells, and are exposed to yoga and meditation practices.[17] The British prison system is following their footsteps and provide its most dangerous inmates with meditation lessons.[18]

I have shared with you how participating with other people

in several global mass meditations has left me with a wonderful feeling that we can affect our reality in such a peaceful and powerful manner everywhere. (I might add that daily mindful exercises to heal the collective "monkey mind" will have even more of an effect.) "You rebel by doing the right thing, even when no one is looking. You rebel by standing up and voicing your opinion when you see injustice. We rebel by uniting in the face of adversity and saying we will no longer be divided by a small group of people who think they deserve everything at our expense!"[16]

The daily political protests that took place in France in 2015, which was dubbed "the second French revolution,"[13] was followed by a seemingly endless wave of terror attacks and the enacting of an indefinite state of emergency in this country under the pretext of "protecting the citizens." (This is the use of terror attacks as an excuse to continue a state of emergency without ending it like with the Patriot Act in the U.S., including tight suppression of information, the use of mass surveillance, and arresting activists (even those who didn't participate in protests). This also includes the French media warning people not to publish information about the then candidate for the presidency of France secret banking account in the Cayman Islands (for tax evasion purposes) before the last elections so that the Elite's candidate would win.[19] So when this massive terror campaign started in France and being aware of my 9/11 doubts on the "official" story, I again had a problem believing the "official" "spin" on these attacks in France. People started sharing information on these attacks in France, including a YouTube video where, to my surprise and horror, I watched one of the casualties in an attack in Paris being bored and checking his or her smartphone under the white shrouds on Youtube (see the light...minute 3:59 here https://www.liveleak.com/view?i=9c5_1447628169). It looked surreal and confusing that the police would conduct mass drills before attacks on the same day the attacks occurred, or that drills were held a few days in the same location before an attack occurred (in the same way that drills were held before the Las Vegas shooting)—see crisis actors Craigslist job ads.[20] It seems that fake news is falling fast.

I, together with other people that I know, started looking for an explanation of what was really happening. Patrick Henningsen[21] (*New Dawn Magazine* issue 158, September-October 2016) discusses the real causes for this crisis and presents evidence that these attacks were not conducted by terrorists, but that there's mounting evidence indicating it was part of the secret state operations (or shadow government as others call it). After one of the Paris attacks in a café, I found a translated article from French to English by a French journalist (an article that I couldn't find until recently), who exposed that the shooters in the café shot at windows, so people would stand back and not take pictures. However, some onlookers saw that the assailants didn't look like Arabs at all and definitely not the way they were depicted on TV and other mainstream media outlets. He said they were white with short hair and looked like commandos or mercenaries.[22]

Patrick Henningsen corroborates this journalist's article and attributes the attacks to Operation GLADIO, organized by NATO and partly funded by the CIA. This long-term operation was run by a state-sponsored terror program, which has claimed thousands of lives over a generation all over Europe. Again, it seemed at the time, as it does today, that the Europeans were caught in an apparently endless domestic terror attacks on this continent.[21]

I remember that after the Nice terrorist attack, I immediately felt that something was wrong. I had no clue why, but over time I became extremely suspicious in general. So I thought who do I know in Nice, or someone who is more "awakened" to ask in this area, and recalled my Israeli friend who lives there. Within an hour we both knew that we were right about our suspicions. This woman told me that shortly before this attack, a former French Prime Minister and a former French President both warned the French people that "they should get used to living with terrorism: France has to learn to live with terrorism."[21] Fortunately, she had a hunch that she shouldn't go to the promenade, although she goes there daily. Afterward she said that it was very fishy that all vehicles were forbidden from entering this the promenade, while allowing this "lone wolf" truck driver to freely ram into these innocent people. This was especially difficult to believe, "Considering how France was *already* under a state of emergency after the November 2015 Paris attacks that killed 130 people."[21]

Moreover, "The UK *Telegraph* reported how only minutes before the sensational attack took place [in Nice], an order was given (by whom?) to French police to remove a compliment of police vans that were positioned to block the promenade for public safety.[21] Then, a week later, it was announced that for some unknown reason French anti-terror police high command would be demanding the Nice local authority *erase* all CCTV footage—'completely' deleting nearly 24 hours of the attack captured on cameras on the Promenade des Anglais,18 including the crucial run-up to event, the event itself, and the aftermath. No credible reason was given for this unprecedented order, other than the claim that the newly formed SDAT Anti-Terrorism Agency feared other terrorists could 'learn from SDAT tactics' from the CCTV footage. What were they trying to hide? Reportedly, local Nice authorities had refused to comply with the order from SDAT in Paris. Placing these two key interventions by French police into context with the other strange anomalies surrounding this event, one could easily surmise the Nice attack fits the profile of a GLADIO-style operation which, for some unknown reason, *did not* go as planned. After the Nice attack, during a public memorial service for the victims, the then Prime Minister was roundly booed and heckled by irate members of the audience who shouted, 'Murder!' and 'Resign!'

"This was potentially the most significant turning point in this relentless exhibition of *GLADIO gestalt*, when the public began to understand that maybe this endless string of terror events wasn't the work of bonafide jihadists said to operating all over France. Were Europeans finally realising that a GLADIO dynamic was in play?... Was this aimed to create a new militarised border force, extend the state of emergency (again), increase surveillance and warrantless searches, and more government control over social media and free speech."[21] People are so suspicious of terrorist attacks immediately after they occur that insiders start unraveling the manipulated information given to the public right after these attacks. Despite threats, some law enforcement officials refuse to follow the orders silencing the truth.[23] Paul Craig Roberts says about false flags attacks in France that "The Paris attack is playing out as I expected. The French government is attacking French civil liberty with legislation similar to the USA Patriot Act."[24] Look also how people are awakening and become investigative reporters themselves sharing the information with Paul Craig Roberts: A number of readers have sent him information that indicates that the Paris attack was reported on social media and knowledge websites before it occurred.[25] Nevertheless, it appears that despite the silencing of the truth by the regime in France, the French are awakening and thousands of people rise up against a French President.[26]

The Icelandic People Protesting & Taking Back Their Power

These protests in Iceland started during the 2008 global financial crisis, which didn't bypass Iceland and its people were requested to pay for the debt generated by this crisis. The most senior bankers involved in this crisis were jailed[27]. In 2009 the Icelanders took this protest to the streets and demanded the resignation of their government. The nationwide protests across Iceland and lobbying efforts by civil organizations was successful and led the new governing parties to decide that Iceland's citizens should be involved in creating a new constitution and the debate on this started in November, 2009. Not only were there protests in this country, "citizens started to unite in grassroots-based think-tanks. A National Forum was organised on 14 November 2009 (Icelandic: Þjóðfundur 2009), in the form of an assembly of Icelandic citizens at the Laugardalshöll in Reykjavík, by a group of grassroots citizen movements such as Anthill. The Forum would settle the ground for the 2011 Constitutional Assembly and was streamed via the Internet to the public."(Wikipedia)[28] (Apparently, the Icelanders weren't really part of the process. Despite the attempt—whether false or real attempt for collaboration between the people and the members of the parliament to create a new constitution—the corruption continued and it all blew up when the PM refused to step down after the revelations of the Panama papers.)[29]

It was reportedly that Icelanders threw yogurt and eggs on the parliament https://www.youtube.com/watch?v=qiRg6wRKu08 because the PM refused to step down.

Children's Death following Vaccinations & Agricultural Biotechnology Corporation Banned from India

Not all governing or legal bodies are corrupt. There are legislatures and courts who awakening to this mass deception. The India Supreme Court is investigating pending lawsuits against a foundation that provides extra funding for many vaccination programs concerning the vaccines they provided, which the suit claims were tested on tribal Indian population without providing adequate information on their adverse effects. The allegations against them is that no informed consent to these vaccinations was given. No one advised the parents of these children of the potential adverse effects or any suggestion that these children need to be monitored following these vaccines. A report written by KP Narayana Kumar states that many children fell ill within a month after receiving the vaccine, and five of them had died by 2010. Two other children "were reported to have died in Vadodara, Gujarat, where an estimated 14,000 tribal children" who were vaccinated with another brand of the vaccine that its purpose is to prevent cervical cancer.[30]

This report shockingly stated that "many of the consent forms used to vaccinate the girls were signed 'illegally,' either by the wardens from the hostels where many of the girls resided, or using thumbprints from their illiterate parents." They were shocked to discover that "a total of 120 girls had been taken ill, suffering from a variety of symptoms, including "epileptic seizures, severe stomach aches, headaches and mood swings."[30] Dr. Vashisht and Dr. Puliyel had continued their report, according to Pharmabiz.com, and stated that:

"The authors noted that while India was polio-free in 2011, in the same year, there were 47,500 cases of NPAFP (non-polio acute flaccid paralysis). While data from India's National Polio Surveillance Project showed NPAFP rate increased in proportion to the number of polio vaccine doses received, independent studies showed that children identified with NPAFP 'were at more than twice the risk of dying than those with wild polio infection." [30]

However, the deceit and corruption by these organizations does not end with these incidences. In 2013, yet another report named two foundations as being responsible for multiple deaths using untested vaccinations on children from the developing world. This report, which was published on the Occupy Corporatism website and written by Susanne Posel found out through an investigation, that a foundation that provides extra funding for many vaccination programs was using an untested vaccine. By giving this dangerous vaccine to Pakistani children shows the lack of empathy associated with these organizations. This organization was blamed for the deaths of 10,000 children in Pakistan, as they administered polio vaccines that resulted in casualties. It should be mentioned that a globalist foundation heavily funds this foundation.[30]

This foundation also provides extra funding for many of vaccination programs which African governments cannot fully fund. But, I might add, that doctors in Kenya discovered that Tetanus vaccines contain an anti-fertility agent which caused mass sterilization of women. Is this part of the depopulation agenda?[31]

An agricultural biotechnology corporation is facing banishment from India after 250,000 Indian farmers indebted to this company committed suicide (they could not replant the seeds and had to buy new seeds annually from this company). This ban means that this corporation is unable continue to "plant and test its new <u>GMO seeds</u> in India, as these experiments caused contamination of the soil, water supply, and even <u>organic seeds</u> before the approval of USDA." [32] The PBC plant, for example, is one of its first plants (which is banned in USA), was planted in the state of Illinois, which suffers from one of the "highest rate of birth defects and fatal death [in the USA]." [32] This agri business company's talk of 'technology' attempts "to hide its real objectives of ownership and control over seed where genetic engineering is just a means to control seed and the food system through patents and intellectual property rights." [33] This Corporation was also unanimously banned from the European parliament this year (2017). [34] Not only does India and the European parliament ban this agricultural biotechnology corporation, but marches against it intensify worldwide. People are becoming aware of the dangers of GMOs and its glyphosate herbicide and this corporation's unethical practices of suing farmers of organic fields that were contaminated by their GMO crops. This big agro-business company claims that these farmers were benefitting from the GMO crops without paying for it. Two million people protested against it in over 50 countries in 2013. [35] This grassroots movement against GMO and this company appears to be effective as the company's profits plunge drastically in recent years. [36]

Awakening and Protesting Against Corruption Worldwide

In Israel, the anti-corruption grassroots movement is led by Rafi Rotem, a former celebrated official in the tax authority (equivalent to the IRS), who was financially and personally destroyed once he became a whistleblower and exposed the rampant corruption in this authority. According to Haaretz newspaper, he wanders the streets of Tel Aviv and continues to be persecuted by the police who harasses him every time an article is published about him. Rotem's accusations are extremely serious and worrisome. He described the apparent cooperation between wealthy tycoons, smugglers, and big-time criminals and senior Tax Authority officials. This includes the mysterious death involving one of his informers, who Rotem believes was killed after being exposed by a Tax Authority employee as Rotem's informant. "The police closed the case claiming that it was suicide despite big question marks at the scene of the killing."[37] Here's a footage of Rafi Rotem anti-corruption and other protests across Israel (French): https://www.youtube.com/watch?v=pg009KBsaNo

Not only did this activist managed to raise an outcry against corruption by his protests, he successfully managed to raise money by crowd-funding to sue the government and the tax authority in 2017. His target goal was 200,000 NIS, approximately 56,000 USD, and he raised 202,000 NIS under the banner: "The Corrupt Ones Are Ruining Our Country, Let's Sue Them".[38] I also donated to this cause. This isn't the only social cause that crowd-funding was used to fight against the government and Knesset (the Israeli parliament) in Israel. This year I was excited to witness how a grassroots movement I was involved in for almost five years succeeded with its protest. This was against the compulsory biometric database of iris scans and fingerprints that are required to issue passports and IDs. Five hundred activists called the offices of all 120 ministers and members of Knesset a few years ago to voice our resistance to this tyrannical measure. The government claims it's for our security to prevent creation of double IDs, which barely exists and does not prevent the creation of a false passport—no one checks if it's actually you or someone impersonating you to issue a passport. The target sum for funding the lawsuit in the Israeli Supreme Court was 60,000 NIS (crowd-funding sum). This target was reached and surpassed in less than 24 hours with 105,000 NIS collected.[39]

Three social activists, who fiercely fight against the orchestrated kidnapping of children from poor families and especially from single-moms for privatized welfare services, discovered how deep the rabbit hole goes in this area when they were jailed without trial.

People started gathering on Thursdays near the house of the Minister of Justice Ayelet Shaked to protest and demand these activists, who are held in terrible conditions, be released pending a trial. This made other social activists, including me, afraid for their lives. The activists are: Lori Shem Tov, whose children were kidnapped by the welfare services, Moti Leibel, and Zvi Zer.[40]

Other Protests and Awakening to the "Real" Reality

Five years ago, there was only one small Israeli group on Facebook discussing chemtrails, but later on many groups discussing and sharing information on this topic began to operate and with thousands of active participants today. One of these groups is entitled "Geoengineering Israel".[41] The protest against this practice reached such heights that the founder of this group, Aharon Amir, was invited on the morning news program of Channel 10, one of the leading TV channels in Israel.[42] The anchor tried to ridicule and deride him, but Amir was eloquent and provided data and evidence of this practice and simply asked questions that hung in the air with no rebuttal—not even from the "scientist" on the panel. This show potentially reached tens of thousands here, as the scientist claimed he didn't know about this practice, but this scientist actually shared his knowledge on experiments done to control the weather on small scale, which planted seeds of doubt in those watching the program, even if some refused to believe that there is such program.

The struggle against "the agenda" is taking place on multiple levels and with many issues, including the corruption of the government and parliament members, inflated municipality taxes, and is propagated on alternative media sites and even mainstream investigative reporting. Crowd-funding is being used to establish an alternative platform broadcasted on prime-time TV to uncover sensitive financial and economic treachery. This includes the case of bank agents teaching about loans in public schools to create future lenders to enrich the banks and impoverish poor children later in life (to sustain the current debt-slavery banking system), or uncovering how toxic food is not allowed to be labeled because of the powerful lobbies of big food in the Israeli parliament (the Knesset). (The Investigative Fund's goal—Keren Ha'tahkirim in Hebrew—is to fund independent investigative reporting in Israel).[43]

I'm especially moved by the awakening in Israel (Ben Fulford, a controversial Canadian journalist, said that Israel is approaching an all-out rebellion on these issues) not only because I live here, but because I felt that it has been one of the most disinformed and misinformed first world countries in terms of the average citizens awareness of these topics. For me, after my bitter discussions in family and friends, who are now listening to me, this seems almost like a miracle. (You can read more about Benjamin Ford at: https://soapboxie.com/world-politics/ Who-is-Benjamin-Fulford-and-can-he-save-the-world)

This anti-government and anti-corruption grassroots movement is sweeping the world, as part of this awakening as the masses are refusing to succumb to these disempowering tactics. Whether these are left-wing or right-wing governments, those in Chile, Colombia, Brazil, Ecuador, and even tiny French Guiana, all have very low approval ratings and are faced with major protests.[44] South Africans are even fighting their government against the silencing of the truth on social media sites, or as it is called "regulating" or actually censoring them.[45]

These protests are happening everywhere now. Thousands of people protested in Poland against the EU government, which was created by the ruling elite of Europe and its Cabal. It should be noted that these protests are against the EU government and its parliament, its members allotted according a country's population, so it's run by bureaucrats elected by the Elite to serve its interests. It should be noted that "the EU does not require any candidate country to hold a referendum to approve membership [although Poland did] or as part of <u>treaty ratification</u>." (Wikipedia)[46] They protest that they have no power in deciding what is going on in Poland.[47] The EU forces its rules on all the EU residents. No one asks the citizens.

People are resisting compulsory vaccinations in Poland and Italy, as well as in other EU countries. See the successful documentary Vaxxed featuring Robert De Niro.[48]

The amazing news is that in Italy even parents who are in favor of vaccinating their children are protesting the horrific means taken against parents refusing to vaccinate theirs, including extremely high fines and even placing liens on their bank accounts. These kinds of extreme measures recently taken by the "controllers" (Team Dark) is their reaction to the approaching demise of their agenda, which backfires and leads to the exponential awakening of people worldwide to their manipulation.

One of their major tactics is their war on alternative and independent media. Germany, for instance, passed a bill to fine sources of "fake" news, while they, the controllers, are the ones deciding what is fake and what is legitimate news (the real fake news = Fake News Network).[49] However, Germany is not alone. Here is a list of the most repressive countries who suppress information on the Internet: https://cpj.org/2015/04/10-most-censored-countries. php Independent and alternative media outlets are censored also in Western countries like the US or France.[50] Mainstream media constantly calls alternative news "fake news," in order to hide the truth from the masses. Google censors alternative media[51] for the same reasons or Wikipedia listing of "fake news" websites, which are alternative media sites that seek the truth.[52] Governments also use trolls and agents to derail discussions of sensitive issues.[53]

FOOTNOTES

1 http://www.stillnessinthestorm.com/2016/08/Boeings-You-Just-Wait-Ad-Reveals-100-Year-Partial-Disclosure-Timeline-Analysis-SSP-History-Psychological-Subtle-Influencing-Techniques-and-Steering-the-Collective-Consciousness.html

2 https://divinecosmos.com/start-here/davids-blog/1195-partial-disclosure

3 https://divinecosmos.com/davids-blog/1218-mega-attack/

4 http://bulawayo24.com/index-id-technology-sc-internet-byo-119106.html

5 https://www.theguardian.com/education/2012/oct/08/meditation-crime-prevention-research

6 https://www.tm.org/blog/maharishi/maharishi-on-the-1-effect/

7 https://www.amazon.com/Power-Your-Subconscious-Mind-Prosperity/dp/0735204314

8 https://ruclip.com/video/m-HnLsZCTXk/mexico-earthquake-by-haarp-footage-caught-on-camera-2017.html

9 http://www.informationclearinghouse.info/article36950.htm

10 http://www.indianz.com/News/2016/09/02/standing-rock-sioux-tribe-reports-cultur.asp?fb_comment_id=1125113137563881_1126237850784743#f2a7e980c445c8

11 https://earthjustice.org/blog/2016-october/making-history-at-standing-rock-tribes-are-leading-action-to-preserve-the-planet

12 https://www.vice.com/en_us/article/59zjn8/the-standing-rock-sioux-just-won-a-major-victory-in-court

13 https://www.theguardian.com/world/2016/apr/08/nuit-debout-protesters-occupy-french-cities-in-a-revolutionary-call-for-change

14 http://thetruthfulone.com/false-flag-crisis-actors/

15 http://www.wnd.com/2014/01/hitler-survivor-tells-americans-buy-more-guns/

16 https://truththeory.com/2017/04/12/5-signs-going-global-mass-awakening/

[17] http://www.dw.com/en/
german-prisoners-find-their-inner-zen/a-16714543

[18] https://www.theguardian.com/society/2015/oct/19/
britains-most-dangerous-prisoners-to-get-meditation-lessons

[19] https://www.theguardian.com/world/2017/may/06/
french-warned-not-to-publish-emmanuel-macron-leaks

[20] https://www.reddit.com/r/The_Donald/comments/6umrdz/
craigslist_ad_for_crisis_actors_in_phoenix/

[21] Patrick Henningsen (New Dawn Magazine issue 158,
September-October 2016) False Flag Terror & the Migrant
Crisis.

[22] http://www.mirror.co.uk/news/uk-news/
paris-attack-witness-says-black-6834503

[23] http://awarenessact.com/
exposed-french-military-caught-planning-isis-false-flag-attack/

[24] Sputnik News, "In Bush's Footsteps: Paris Adopts Measures
Similar to US Patriot Act." Nov. 17, 2015. https://sputniknews.
com/politics/201511171030277245/

[25] The Millennium Report, "Paris Attack Reported on
WIKIPEDIA and TWITTER before it happened."[8] Nov. 16,
2015. http://themillenniumreport.com/2015/11/paris-attack-
reported-on-wikipedia-and-twitter-before-it-happened/

[26] http://www.nnettle.com/news/2904-thousands-rise-up-against-
rothschild-owned-president-macron-in-paris

[27] https://www.huffingtonpost.com/stefan-simanowitz/iceland-has-
jailed-29-bankers_b_8908536.html

[28] https://en.wikipedia.org/
wiki/2009_Icelandic_financial_crisis_protests

[29] https://www.huffingtonpost.com/entry/iceland-protests-panama-
papers_us_5702a58ee4b0a06d58064555

[30] https://vactruth.com/2014/10/05/bill-gates-vaccine-crimes/

[31] https://healthimpactnews.com/2014/mass-sterilization-kenyan-
doctors-find-anti-fertility-agent-in-un-tetanus-vaccine/

32 http://www.seattleorganicrestaurants.com/vegan-whole-foods/
monsanto-gmo-ban-india/

33 https://www.globalresearch.ca/
the-seeds-of-suicide-how-monsanto-destroys-farming/5329947

34 https://www.march-against-monsanto.com/monsanto-officially-
banned-from-european-parliament-following-unanimous-vote/

35 https://www.theguardian.com/environment/2013/may/26/
millions-march-against-monsanto

36 https://www.naturalnews.com/053660_Monsanto_falling_
profits_organic_food.html

37 https://www.haaretz.com/opinion/.premium-1.531402

38 https://www.mimoona.co.il/Projects/4107

39 https://www.headstart.co.il/projectupdates.aspx?id=19914

40 https://www.facebook.com/pg/Free.Israel.Political.Prisoners.
Lori.Moti.and.Zvi/posts/?ref=page_internal

41 https://www.facebook.com/%D7%94%
D7%A0%D7%93%D7%A1%D7%AA-
%D7%90%D7%A7%D7%9C%D7%99%D7%9D-
geoengineering-israel-1470266303196703/

42 https://www.youtube.com/watch?v=fs81AuYTIpg

43 https://keren.press/about/

44 https://www.washingtonpost.com/world/the_americas/
protests-sweeping-south-america-show-rising-antigovernment-
anger/2017/04/15/c086c10c-1f92-11e7-bb59-a74ccaf1d02f_
story.html?utm_term=.f829b23c5de0

45 https://advox.globalvoices.org/2017/03/10/
south-africans-want-their-governments-hands-off-social-media/

46 https://en.wikipedia.org/wiki/
Referendums_related_to_the_European_Union

47 http://www.neonnettle.com/news/2446-thousands-rise-up-in-
poland-against-eu-government-ruling-elite

48 http://video.beforeitsnews.com/vaxxed-from-cover-up-to-
catastrophe-full-movie_75a2065ca.html

[49] http://www.neonnettle.com/news/2338-germany-approves-bill-to-fine-social-media-up-to-56m-for-fake-news

[50] http://allnewspipeline.com/Silencing_Truth.php

[51] https://www.davidwolfe.com/bombshell-google-caught-censoring-alternative-media-war-fake-news/

[52] https://en.wikipedia.org/wiki/List_of_fake_news_websites

[53] https://www.straight.com/news/482846/government-trolls-use-psychology-based-influence-techniques-social-media

REFERENCES

1. http://operationdisclosure.blogspot.co.il/2017/07/mass-spiritual-awakening-caused-by.html

2. http://dreamcatcherreality.com/highly-awakened/

3. http://anonhq.com/violent-protests-labor-strikes-halt-france-hollande-attempts-slay-workers-rights-investigative/

4. https://emsnews.wordpress.com/2017/05/06/first-macron-info-leak-information-he-parks-wealth-in-cayman-islands/

5. Dr. Daniele Ganser's *NATO's Secret Armies: Operation Gladio and Terrorism in Western Europe* (2004) is recognised as the most authoritative book on the subject. Among the documents Ganser brings to attention is the classified Field Manual 30-31, with appendices FM 30-31A and FM 30-31B, authored by the Pentagon's Defense Intelligence Agency (DIA) to train thousands of stay-behind officers around the world.

   Ganser, Daniele, *NATO's Secret Armies: Operation GLADIO and Terrorism in Western Europe*, Frank Cass Publishers, December 22nd 2004.

   https://www.goodreads.com/book/show/765633. NATO s Secret Armies

6. https://www.nbcnews.com/news/world/strikes-protests-disrupt-france-tourist-season-euro-2016-loom-n584836

7. http://yournewswire.com/thousands-protest-in-paris-against-ongoing-state-of-emergency-in-france/

8. https://www.globalresearch.ca/paris-attacks-another-false-flag-sifting-through-the-evidence/5489695

9. https://www.reddit.com/r/conspiracy/comments/4u5oem/what_are_the_odds_same_guy_that_filmed_france/

10. http://www.collective-evolution.com/2015/11/15/ottawa-professor-on-paris-terror-attacks-911-french-style/

11. http://time.com/4407430/nice-attack-hollande-speech-emergency/

12. https://nodisinfo.com/final-absolute-proof-one-died-nice-truck-attack-fake/

13. http://freedom-articles.toolsforfreedom.com/paris-shooting-10-signs-false-flag/

14. https://theburningbloggerofbedlam.wordpress.com/2015/01/12/french-police-commissioner-suicide-as-the-paris-attacks-exposed-as-staged-hoax/

15. https://theburningbloggerofbedlam.wordpress.com/2015/11/22/the-paris-false-flag-there-were-no-suicide-bombers/

16. https://www.telesurtv.net/english/news/CIA-Behind-France-Attacks-Says-Ex-White-House-Official-20150111-0010.html

17. https://rehmat1.com/2016/07/23/paris-admits-nice-attack-was-a-false-flag-operation/

18. http://www.countercurrents.org/mithiborwala180115.htm

19. https://www.globalresearch.ca/frances-surveillance-law-amid-terror-created-by-the-french-republic/5449522

20. https://www.activistpost.com/2015/11/9-reasons-to-question-the-paris-terror-attacks.html

21. http://www.zerohedge.com/news/2017-03-07/ever-growing-list-admitted-false-flag-attacks

22. http://autonomies.org/fr/2017/04/france-resistance-and-rebellion-under-a-state-of-emergency-without-end/

23. https://en.wikipedia.org/wiki/States_of_emergency_in_France

24. https://www.theguardian.com/world/2016/dec/14/french-parliament-votes-to-extend-state-of-emergency-until-after-2017-elections

25. http://www.france24.com/en/20170609-france-state-emergency-macron-police-powers-civil-liberties-terrorism

26. http://foreignpolicy.com/2016/07/16/frances-perpetual-state-of-emergency/

27. http://www.zerohedge.com/news/2017-03-07/ever-growing-list-admitted-false-flag-attacks

28. http://www.euronews.com/tag/protests-in-france

29. https://starrynews.wordpress.com/2016/10/12/exposed-french-military-caught-planning-isis-false-flag-attack/

30. Massive Protest In Iceland After Prime Minister Exposed In Panama Papers **https://www.youtube.com/watch?v=LKADLvveXaM**

31. Marches Against Monsanto Intensify **https://www.newparadigm.ws/my-blogs/10-signs-of-our-global-awakening/**

32. **https://www.march-against-monsanto.com/**

33. The end of the world for the bad guys minute 53 – The Goldfish Report

    https://www.youtube.com/watch?v=3-jTgEdAD9k&feature=share

34. https://www.bloomberg.com/news/features/2016-03-31/welcome-to-iceland-where-bad-bankers-go-to-prison

35. https://crazyemailsandbackstories.wordpress.com/2012/05/12/icelands-amazing-peaceful-revolution-still-not-in-the-news-backstory/

36. https://www.naturalnews.com/052265_vaccine_experiments_Bill_Gates_India.html

37. http://americannutritionassociation.org/newsletter/india-bans-planting-gm-crop

38. http://yournewswire.com/india-bans-gmo-seed-trials-to-protect-health-of-citizens/

39. The Anti-biometric Crowd-funding Campaign Reached Its Target in Less than 24 Hours (in Hebrew), December 1st, 2016 https://www.calcalist.co.il/internet/articles/0,7340,L-3702972,00.html

40. The Independent Journalists Moti Leibel, Lori Shem-tov, and the lawyer Zvi Zer Imprisoned Illegally for 100 Days, June 18th, 2017 https://netinfo.live/category/%D7%A1%D7%97%D7%A8-%D7%91%D7%99%D7%9C%D7%93%D7%99%D7%9D/

41. The Internet's Terror Affair: When the Judges Are Also the Complainants, July 3, 2017 https://www.ha-makom.co.il/article/shpurer-shoftim-shemtov

42. Shabtay Avigal Reporting about Lori Shem-tov and Moti Leibel Imprisoment June 3rd 2017 http://www.shabtay-av.022.co.il/BRPortal/br/P102.jsp?arc=1896675

43. Shabtay Avigal's in-depth report about Rafi Rotem http://www.shabtay-av.022.co.il/BRPortal/br/P102.jsp?arc=1873487

44. https://divinecosmos.com/start-here/davids-blog/1220-vegas-meta-analysis

45. https://divinecosmos.com/start-here/davids-blog/1023-financial-tyranny

46. http://www.nnettle.com/news/1760-largest-child-porn-bust-in-history-ignored-by-mainstream-media

47. http://www.nnettle.com/features/805-first-of-the-elite-washington-dc-pedophile-ring-pleads-guilty-to-child-rape

48. http://www.nnettle.com/news/1888-elijah-wood-hollywood-is-run-by-a-powerful-elite-pedophile-ring

49. https://sputniknews.com/europe/201611241047790760-norway-pedophile-ring-busted/

50. https://foreignaffairs.house.gov/press-release/house-votes-turn-tables-human-traffickers/

51. http://www.newsy.com/stories/3-new-executive-orders-address-crime-help-law-enforcement/

52. https://www.studentnewsdaily.com/daily-news-article/trump-signs-3-executive-orders-targeting-drugs-crime/

53. https://www.usnews.com/news/best-countries/articles/2017-06-14/latin-americas-growing-intolerance-of-corruption

54. https://www.globalcitizen.org/en/content/fighting-for-their-lives-indigenous-people-rise-up/

55. https://www.telesurtv.net/english/news/5-Social-Movements-Resisting-Repression-in-Latin-America-20170215-0042.html

56. http://www.countercurrents.org/martinez040707.htm

57. http://tapnewswire.com/2017/06/crisis-solutions-inc-is-running-all-terror-false-flags-worldwide-check-out-their-website/

58. More soft disclosure news http://www.theeventchronicle.com/the-event/cobra-disclosure-process/?utm_campaign=coschedule&utm_source=facebook page&utm_medium=The%20Event%20Handbook&utm_content=Cobra:%20Disclosure%20Process#

59. The Anti-corruption protests in Romania in 2017 http://www.bbc.com/news/world-europe-38867959

60. http://galacticconnection.com/kevin-annett-vatican-politics-unveiled-november-1-2016/

61. http://higherdiscernment.blogspot.co.il/2017/05/itccs-update-on-ninth-circle-actions.html

62. Many Elite Headed to Prison for Child Sex Trafficking

(Dave Hodges) Did you know that in Trump's first 30 days

in office, his people, mainly Attorney General Jeff Sessions, prosecuted 1,500 sex traffickers? To date, Trump/Sessions have prosecuted 3,500 child-sex-traffickers. Continue Reading: --> http://bit.ly/2ty1V6M <--

63. Major concerns raised about the wellbeing of singer Sinead O'Connor after her attempts at suicide following her exposure of a Catholic Church pedophile ring including her public outburst where she branded The Pope as the root of all evil in the world.

http://www.neonnettle.com/features/1036-sinead-o-connor-suicidal-after-exposing-catholic-church-pedophile-ring

64. https://www.globalresearch.ca/more-paris-puzzles-did-the-suicide-bombers-blow-themselves-up/5490888

65. https://divinecosmos.com/start-here/davids-blog/1219-disclosure-war

66. https://shift-magazine.net/2015/11/18/top-10-grassroots-movements-that-are-taking-on-the-world/

67. An ex-FBI legal agent talking about the shootings in Vegas to disarm people worldwide and leave them defenseless https://www.youtube.com/watch?v=-3F6SZZIT-E

68. Panama Protests in Iceland http://www.bbc.com/news/world-europe-35964517

CHAPTER FIVE

THE EVIL CABAL EXPOSED

Top-level Pedophilia & Ritual Sacrifices Dealt with

For me, pedophilia and the related topic of ritual sacrifices are the most horrific crimes that I've been exposed to throughout my awakening. Discovering these abuses was so overwhelming to me that at first, I often cried myself to sleep and even woke up during the night with troubling dreams. It really devastated me and some days I couldn't do anything. I felt so hopeless and helpless as I couldn't do anything about it, except for sharing my concern with certain groups on Facebook. It's truly a heartbreaking tragedy, but today we are seeing a shift in awareness as more and more of these criminals are being arrested worldwide and some children, though very few compared to the real numbers, are finally being rescued from a gruesome fate. The recent overthrow of the Icelandic government over pedophilia abuses mentioned earlier seems to be connected to a global campaign aimed at prosecuting them (we see this mainly taking place in Western countries). It may be connected to a global operation of the "alliance" or the "white hats," as 87,000 pedophiles have been recently arrested in Germany. This is a global effort of international law enforcement agencies, as we see large arrests made in a major pedophilia network bust, and investigators have confirmed that thousands more arrests will follow. The revelations are shocking, and everywhere you look you find more "elite" offenders: a prominent Vatican official Cardinal was found to be connected to child pornography and pedophilia[1]; "and the 70,000-member pedophilia ring uncovered in Norway."[1] A massive online pedophile ring containing 70,000 people worldwide was busted by cops, and the amazing thing is that it trickled to the mainstream media.[2] Even high-level politicians are not immune from being arrested, indicating that it's progressing toward the high-level offenders.[3]

Since Donald Trump's inauguration, we have seen the acceleration of the arrests of pedophiles in the U.S. and around the world in unprecedented numbers, which is deliberately ignored by the (controlled) media. He addressed this topic in a speech he gave at a press conference from the White House: "How human trafficking is a 'dire problem' domestically and internationally."[4] Several bills addressing human trafficking (including children) have been passed in congress in 2017, since his inauguration.[5]

Trump signed three executive orders targeting human trafficking: "The order outlines the administration's approach to cutting down on organized crime— including gangs, cartels and racketeering organizations—by enhancing cooperation with foreign governments and the ways in which federal agencies share information and data. It identifies human trafficking, drug smuggling, financial crimes, cyber-crime and corruption as 'a threat to public safety and national security.'"[6]

Human trafficking is directly connected to pedophile rings as it provides the supply of children to pedophiles across the world, so targeting human trafficking affects both practices in one swift blow.[7] The definition of human trafficking including trafficking of children for a wide variety of reasons (p. 8/70 http://www.ohchr. org/Documents/Publications/FS36 en.pdf). This is an all-out effort to curb this problem. Trump is not the only politician pushing this agenda in the U.S. Congressman Trey Gowdy, "Delivered an epic speech to Congress, while appearing to hold his tears, in which he vowed that anyone who stands in the way of the investigations into Elite pedophilia will be forced to 'publically explain themselves" for their actions.'"[8]

These crimes are now being exposed, including symbols that help law enforcement agencies and others to see how they communicate and to alert parents. For example, a terrified mom recently "found a marking on a toy that was given to her 2-year-old daughter that alerted other pedophiles that the child was 'ready for child sex trafficking' after she recognized the symbol from leaked FBI documents published by Wikileaks, which outlined secret symbols used by pedophiles."[9] NPR also confirms the information about horrifying pedophilia practices in the Vatican in another report about a prominent cardinal, who was charged with "historic sexual" abuse offenses in Australia. According to the Associated Press, "He is the highest-level Vatican official to be charged in the church's long-standing sexual abuse scandal."[10]

Ritual sacrifices is the most horrific topic that totally devastated and threw me off balance when I first discovered this criminal activity. This is unfortunately closely related to pedophilias, as some abducted children may end up in this unspeakable ritual. With the accelerated rate of soft disclosures on both pedophilia and ritual sacrifice, the Elite Controllers, despite their efforts to hide these crimes, can no longer avoid disclosure—their crimes are becoming known and dealt with. Some children are being rescued, but where the Elite's rule is still unchallenged, they proceed with these heinous crimes. Several high-ranking officials of the Catholic Jesuit orders were found guilty of trafficking, torture, rape, and the murder of children. This was determined by "Five judges of the International Common Law Court of Justice in Brussels . . . Since last March [2014] over 48 eyewitnesses have testified before this court, including their "activities as members of the Ninth Circle Satanic Child Sacrifice Cult. The Ninth Circle Satanic Cult was said to do child sacrifices at Roman Catholic cathedrals."[11]

It is important to emphasize that though only a fraction of these crimes is disrupted, these activists manage to rescue some children and put these criminals on the defense where before they proceeded with impunity. This is an update from May this year (2017): "In Rome, London, Paris, Frankfurt, Brussels and Geneva our actions were blunted by the presence of armed paramilitary units at the cult locations. Considering the proximity of these locations to the leaders of the Ninth Circle this was anticipated. Nevertheless, we have learned that the planned killings at these major sites were in fact postponed or relocated to elsewhere, possibly because of the public announcement of these locations... [..]

Unfortunately, in Washington DC our team was unable to intervene and we must assume the cult performed their killings. Several of our team members there were arrested by plain clothed officials and are still being held in communicado. We have yet to receive a report from the teams that were to strike at the cult centers in Tara Ireland and in Vancouver and Montreal Canada."[12]

"In general our actions were a definite blow to the Ninth Circle and to the confidence of its members. Of great satisfaction to us was the increased cooperation of elements of the local police who assisted us in detaining the cult members. We can say with certainty that the tide is turning . . .

"Of equal importance to these actions has been a back channel communication that was received yesterday by the ITCCS Central Office from a party claiming to represent an element within the Catholic Curia in Rome (the College of Cardinals). This party has requested an immediate meeting with ITCCS officials. The Vatican-run Ninth Circle cult has been forced once more onto the defensive, and lives of the innocent have been saved. Divisions are clearly appearing within the Vatican hierarchy and we suspect more revelations soon, especially as politicians in the European Union are beginning to debate the Ninth Circle atrocities...

"To all people of good will and to all our affiliates we ask you to not forget that despite this victory the Ninth Circle killings will continue, and our efforts must therefore never slacken. We welcome the flood of new volunteers into our ranks and urge them to undergo our common law Sheriff training programs to equip them to stop once and for all the torture and killing of our children, and those responsible."[12]

Although this is only a tip of the iceberg according to Anne Longfield, one of the Children's Commissioner for England, it gives hope that soon these crimes will be stopped completely. In July 2017, it was confirmed that 1203 children have been rescued from Elite pedophile rings.[13] But many more children remain as slaves in pedophilia networks."[13] These are the latest figures from her report from "the Government's national referral mechanism (NRM), the official framework for identifying and helping victims of child slavery, sexual exploitation, and human trafficking."[13] As today these top-level elite controllers cannot be prosecuted for these crimes in regular courts (those are intended for us, the people). Designated tribunals are being established for this purpose (especially human and child trafficking and ritual sacrifices). It should be emphasized that the "controllers" or "the powers that be" are above the law under the current legal system. These tribunals include the International Tribunal for Natural Justice (https://www.itnj.org/), the Judicial Commission of Inquiry into Human Trafficking and Child Sex Abuse, and the International Tribunal into Crimes of Church and State (http://itccs.org/), established by Kevin Annett. Their purpose is (1) "to lawfully prosecute those people and institutions responsible for the exploitation, trafficking, torture and murder of children, past and present, and (2) To stop these and other criminal actions by church and state, including by disestablishing those same institutions." (as cited in the introduction).

The EU Cabal Defeated in the UK

Recently, there have been increasingly more false flag attacks in the UK, whether it's the attacks in London or at the concert of Ariana Grande, but they seem targeted "events" to me. I can only speculate that it has to do with the "awakening" of the people in this country, and especially since Brexit. Despite the media brainwashing to vote in favor of staying in the EU, the Brits did the opposite— even though this was downplayed and ridiculed afterward in the media. This felt to me and other people who follow the "real" news as the controllers "slip of power" in this country. They couldn't allow it; in a similar way, they couldn't allow another "Trump" in France or protests against the regime that lost its footing there. So why do or how do people immediately suspect these are false flag attacks? I'll give you these points to ponder on the Manchester terror attack and then check for other clues: "Since 9/11 – and increasingly so – any mass event in the West, notably in Europe and the US, like the pop concert by US singer Ariana Grande in Manchester on 22 May, would be cordoned-off and super secured. How can the terrorist with his artisan bomb (under the arm or under his belt?) get through security? In any case, he is conveniently dead, another witness done away with."[14]

It may be cynical to start asking who benefits the most from these attacks when people may have lost their lives, and I hope no one did. The multiple attacks occurring simultaneously in London— vehicle ramming into pedestrians on London Bridge and stabbings in Borough Market area—less than two weeks after the attack in Manchester, does raise questions. Were they connected to the UK's 2017 general election on June 8? Again, this may have affected the election's results, which would potentially be in favor of the ruling conservative party. As in France, in the aftermath of these attacks in the UK, "on the heels of both Manchester and Westminster terror events, the Met Police have accumulated more power in terms of their role in helping to manage 'national security.' Likewise, these events may be used to devolve more power and clout to the British Intelligence Services... In less than a few hours, a 'series of coordinated terror attacks" has been declared by MET police. *No forensic review or careful examination of a crime scene, yet again...*"[15]

Soft Disclosures of Elite Malfeasance

We are seeing the training and funding of Daesh (ISIS), and terrorist attacks discovered to be staged (false flags) and carried out by our own governments. It should be noted that by false flag I don't mean that no one has died. In some cases, as with the 9/11 attack's 3,000 victims, there is a loss of lives. But in other attacks, like in the Sandy Hook or the Las Vegas shooting attacks, it's not certain. This is what a former CIA officer, David Steele, says about false flag attacks in the US: "Most terrorists are false flag terrorists, or are created by our own security services. In the United States, every single terrorist incident we have had has been a false flag, or has been an informant pushed on by the FBI. In fact, we now have citizens taking out restraining orders against FBI informants that are trying to incite terrorism. We've become a lunatic asylum."[16]

It gets even more creepy and overwhelming, and I should add depressing, when we become aware as to how these false flags are apparently produced. Yes, I'm using the word "produced" here, as these are real-life productions. In an interview with an independent journalist conducted by Sean from the SGT Report (lookup on Youtube), who investigates false flag attacks, he provides details on how we're all being duped. It turns out that there is a global company that governments and intelligence agencies employ its terrorist's "services." Yes, as unbelievably as it may sound, they actually purchase false flag attacks from this company for their countries.[17]

This is one of many indications that people are awakening and don't accept the official "story". As a result of these soft disclosures of false flag attacks, more people worldwide are aware of this reality and don't believe or question the "story" provided by their government or MSM, and therefore look for alternative sources, forums, and debates about false flag attacks posted on YouTube. Not only are these attacks being exposed and discussed on social media, some are taking it one step further and pressing charges and lawsuits for more than one trillion dollars against the mainstream media over the Sandy Hook massacre coverage.[18] The US army has been caught red-handed by Senior Syrian legislator Ammar al-Assad helping ISIS terrorist escape Syria following their defeat by Russian and Syrian forces.[19] Amnesty International has also confirmed that the US Army gave ISIS $1 billion worth of arms and equipment during the former president's final year in office.[20] In another recent twist of a soft disclosure of the truth, it's been revealed that Katy Perry has urged her fans to welcome in the rule of her "controller's" (the Powers that Be" or Team Dark) New World Order and "unite" under one world government.[21] Russian President Vladimir Putin, which is supposedly part of the Alliance aiming to liberate humanity and the earth (despite all of his negative press), reveals "definitive proof" that forty countries and the US have funded Daesh in a conspiracy to trigger World War 3.[22]

This soft disclosure accelerates as alternative ways of broadcasting the news emerge. This includes the SGT Report[23] (with an impressive 218 K subscribers) and other websites offering alternative commentary and alternative spiritual information like I5DN (founder Gregg Prescot) again with thousands of subscribers—Corey Goode, Simon Parks, Victor Oddo, and Jordan Sather have their own alternative sites. They are thriving and rapidly accumulate subscribers because they really try to figure out the truth of our modern reality. Sometimes they are right, sometimes they are not, but this is how we learn to discern and gain insights from the sources available to us. People all over the world are eager to learn the truth, and they directly donate to their favorite information sources by using tools such as Patreon (https://www.patreon.com/). Some of them are in direct contact with their subscribers, personally thanking them in videos, answering comments on Youtube, and commenting or even just sharing their reactions (I loved it when Jordan Sather said that some of the comments crack him up). But what was for me the "crème of the crème" of soft disclosure was the documentary broadcasted on no less than the History Channel featuring David Wilcock and Corey Goode, among many others, exposing the connection between our governments and extraterrestrials, and bases on the moon and Mars. See here http://www.dailymotion.com/video/x5t0amx

Recently intel has been disclosed in the alternative media (in relevant groups, like the Resistance Movement) about further elite malfeasance. Some include explosive QAnon's revelations on the former president of the United States and the candidate for the last election for presidency "16-year treasonous plan to use two White House terms for a coup d'état in the United States that would end up revising the Constitution, cancelling the Second Amendment, and opening borders to flood the nation with illegal immigrants calculated to vote Democrat for the foreseeable future [...] alleged that 'Deep State' rogue operatives murdered Supreme Court Justice Antonin Scalia in an attempt to lock in a hard-left ideology on the nation's highest court [...] QAnon predicted that the presidential candidate in the last election would use her 8 years as president to cause World War III – a war that would cause death and destruction on a massive, never-before-imagined scale of horror. The war would be a 'fake war' promoted by the government-controlled MSM. Billions of the world's populations would be killed off, allowing the globalists (and their minions in the governments worldwide) to pocket huge wealth on a global scale." [24]

According to Benjamin Fulford, there are also many "extra-judicial killings going on" to send message by their death to their "handlers" and counter-killings by the Cabal to thwart those who were about to provide evidence about crimes, like "In Japan, two former executives of Toshiba, Atsutoshi Nishida and Taizo Nishimura, suddenly died in the past two months because they were about to provide evidence about the March 11, 2011 Fukushima tsunami and nuclear terror attack against Japan, according to sources close to the royal family." [25] One of the more exciting reports is by Benjamin Fulford, the Canadian journalist, (Jan 1st, 2018) talks about this historic moment that ". . . most of the U.S.-based top perpetrators of the fake 'war on terror' have now themselves been renditioned to the U.S. Navy camp in Guantanamo Bay, Cuba, Pentagon sources say. The globalists' minions may have been airlifted to Gitmo for military tribunals, as the Department of Defense spends $500M to upgrade the prison and send more military police and Marines, the sources say." He goes on to discuss the most devastating issues of this disclosure: pedophilia and human trafficking, "human trafficking centers around the world are being raided and shut down. In Saudi Arabia, 3,000 child sex slaves have been freed, according to Russian FSB sources." [26] In the U.S., there was a power outage at a famous theme park on December 27th, as it was raided by special forces fighting human slavers, the Pentagon sources say. [26]

As I, together with many others, who follow all these fast-paced events, hoped these indictments and arrests will not stop or happen only in the US, but soon take place worldwide. According to April LaJune (on December 31st, 2017), she reported that U.S. troops were deployed worldwide with 10,000 sealed indictments! So it's getting quite interesting. Watch here https://www.youtube.com/watch?v=_JAJCBeGbzw

Free Energy Technology Cannot Be Suppressed

For decades, we've had to continue using polluting fossil fuel as our prime energy sources, since others were suppressed. (The Elite control this industry and its enormous profits.) Yes, the US government has suppressed 5000 patents for free energy and other innovative energy inventions. [27] Despite this heavy suppression, we recently saw how free energy has gone mainstream. There is Keshe's invention of a bicycle that you can pedal for an hour that generates electricity for 24 hours[28], or when the Indian Prime Minister Narendra Modi and Israel's Prime Minister Benjamin Netanyahu went out driving the Gal-Mobile—a mobile, integrated water desalination and purification vehicle, which turns seawater into safe high-quality drinking water. "The seawater fuels the car and the byproduct is desalination." Other examples are cities and even countries aiming at a 100% use of renewable energy sources: This is shown in "a local city like Burlington, VT being the first city in the U.S. to use 100% renewable energy; even whole countries like Paraguay, Iceland, and Norway being 100% renewable. Cheap localized energy is on the horizon along with the very real possibility[.] <u>Nikola Tesla</u> once envisioned . . . a world of free energy."[29]

New Economic Models

Economic models like Ubuntu Liberation movement led by Michael Tellinger are becoming popular in small towns and more widespread worldwide. This movement paves the way to a new economic philosophy called Contributionism that turns competition into collaboration. When fully implemented, the end result will be the elimination of money. This "One Small Town" initiative is the first stage to creating food and income for small communities from income-generating projects within a community.

The microfinancing model, where banks help subsistent people learn skills to support themselves, is another innovative model. It gives communities worldwide "a fishing net not a fish" to support themselves. This kind of grassroots movement really makes a difference, especially in developing countries, but it can serve as a model to be implemented elsewhere.

At the beginning, microfinancing was used to provide loans to poor entrepreneurs and small businesses who couldn't get loans from traditional banks. Over time, this developmental model helps the poor come out of poverty. Women in developing countries, who are the most hard-pressed to get bank loans, managed to create successful businesses this way and sustain themselves and their families. In Guinea, microfinancing had outstanding rates of return in one of the poorest countries in the world and one that adheres to strict Muslim rules to loans (no interest allowed).[30]

Black Hats-White Hats War Behind the Scene

People are becoming aware of a war between "dark hats"—the Cabal—and the "white hats" (the Alliance) taking place behind the scenes. It is not, as it is being shown in the mainstream media, a war between countries. No, surprisingly it's not the US versus Russia, but an in-fighting within countries and organizations, such as the CIA, FBI, Pentagon, the military, and other intelligence agencies worldwide according to Benjamin Fulford. He is a very outspoken and controversial Canadian journalist, former writer for Forbes in Japan ("From 1998 to 2005, he was the Asian Bureau chief for *Forbes* magazine."), and an author. They unfortunately include a lot of disinformation and misinformation provided to him, some of which may be true, so please discern. He shared some interesting background on a coalition of white hats in countries that according to the media should be fighting each other.[31]

As the saying goes "it's darkest before dawn". David Wilcock in his recent update claims that the recent arrests of the dark elements (Cabal) within the Vatican (mentioned earlier), the multiple arrests of top-profile pedophiles in the British government and TV personality such as Jimmy Savile, who raped hundreds of children while having the full protection of the mainstream media and the elite, may be the result of an international coalition of "white hats" called the Alliance. He further claims that the Vegas shooting was intended to distract us from The Harvey Weinstein Expose. I think this also was to deflect a deeper look into the Hollywood pedophile scene.[32] Wilcock explains about this struggle and who are these forces: "I want to also remind you that we have extensively discussed a vast, international alliance that is opposing this negative group, or 'Cabal' as we often call it. The Alliance includes an ever-increasing majority of the US military and intelligence community, as well as many foreign governments. Many of the seemingly mysterious headlines in today's world can be explained as the result of a shadow war between the Cabal and the Alliance."[33]

How Does this Cabal Operate?

"This group has religious beliefs that are unusual and very secretive. Yet, at the same time they routinely engage in multi-million-dollar marketing campaigns. These campaigns appear within certain video games, television shows, music videos, awards ceremonies and films, among other means. They openly and flagrantly advertise their philosophies and symbols, which many have interpreted as a mocking gesture to the entire world. Part of why they have been 'hiding out in the open' is that they did plan to formally reveal their presence and create a 'New World Order.' They only intended to do this once humanity had been brought to its knees by orchestrated, negative events, and were demanding rescue and salvation. Thankfully, this cult is being exposed and taken down by a vast international alliance, whose operations we have covered extensively. This group believes the only way to escape 'prison' is to become Illuminated. Hence, they refer to themselves as 'Illuminati.' Far from being an ancient, obscure movement that faded out in the 1700s, there is a very prevalent group that still uses this name to refer to themselves. In order to remove some of the ridicule factor and occult allure, the Alliance has asked us to simply refer to them as the Cabal. This same international alliance is now working diligently to defeat them."

"The Cabal versus Alliance war may well be in its final stages—complete with the first wave of the disclosure plan being rolled out as early as tomorrow. The "storm," (as recently stated by Trump) would take place in the form of mass arrests, the issuance of a new currency, and the launch of a global currency reset, the source said. "'Calm before the storm' means the swamp is about to be cleaned out and they are all scared sh#tless, so we better take a picture,"[34] a CIA source confirmed. "The mass killing operation in Las Vegas and the accompanying corporate media BS storm about a single, now-dead killer being responsible... The Internet is full of videos showing that multiple shooters were involved, and calls for comprehensive revenge are being made. By promoting this obvious lie, the FBI, nominally in charge of the Las Vegas investigation, has made itself a target of the U.S. military and other agencies."[34]

The awakening has gone mainstream. The MSM can no longer hide the truth anymore. They cannot stop the revelation of all the hidden secrets and the matrix of control, whether it's the depopulation agendas, false flag attacks, government black projects like the secret space programs—all is being exposed and will continue to be exposed until there's full disclosure. The real apocalypse is the lifting of the veil of the matrix of lies, manipulation, and deception. Together we could reach many more people and help expedite this positive shift worldwide. This is my wish. And I'm actually seeing it take place and my readers are part of this shift. How you can spot these indications in your surroundings and sources? And what you can do about it? Join us in the many social media groups and discussions, share information on your profile pages and give your opinion. This is an information war, and it difficult to know and validate what is true, discerning information.

If the truth is exposed, all lies are dissolved. To better discern the truth in this infowar, listen to your intuition and inner guidance, and then use your rational mind to discern the credibility of all the information you find on the Internet and other news forums. When enough people are doing this and it reaches a critical mass, the truth would start be revealed to all exponentially (it would leak to mass media and then lead to the final dissolution of the mind control, programming matrix). Share the information, if you feel guided, with whomever you feel is open to it but do not force it on anyone who is not ready to hear it. I made the latter mistake for years, and it only led to unpleasant experiences for myself and others. Keeping your relationships intact and letting others awakened on their own schedule, is more important. The elite cannot control billions of awakened people. And it doesn't require this many people to shutter the "matrix"—just a critical mass to achieve this goal. It's the one hundredth monkey effect on our collective consciousness.

"The Shift is the awakening of humanity's heart. This transformation of consciousness, the greatest one ever recorded, first became apparent in the mid-1960s and has been building momentum ever since. The Shift is a collective transformation consisting of the sum of each individual's step into the New Reality. Each person, in their own time, is moving forward into a stage of consciousness which brings a wider vista and an awareness which springs from the heart. When enough people's primary attention becomes focused through their heart chakras, then the 'hundredth monkey effect' will occur."[35]

And now I turn to all of the agents from all the ABC soup agencies, including NSA, Shabak (General/internal Israel's security agency), Mossad, CIA, MI6, MI5 or any other agency that I'm not aware of… please excuse me if I haven't mentioned your particular agency. Your time is up. The game is over! Your controllers are collapsing rapidly. I tell you now: Cross to the light now!!! Join the victorious side before it's too late for you while you're reading this. Just pack your bags and leave. Otherwise, prepare to wear orange for the rest of your life while we all will celebrate the liberation of our planet in huge parties worldwide!

FOOTNOTES

[1] http://www.collective-evolution.com/2017/07/20/massive-pedophilia-network-busted-in-germany-87000-member-dark-net-exposed/

[2] http://www.nbcnews.com/id/42108748/ns/us_news-crime_and_courts/t/massive-online-pedophile-ring-busted-cops/#.WduNa4-Cyig

[3] http://victuruslibertas.com/2017/07/high-level-politicians-arrested-in-huge-pedophile-sting/

[4] http://www.nnettle.com/features/844-3000-pedophiles-arrested-since-trump-took-office-media-remains-silent-

[5] https://www.govtrack.us/congress/bills/subjects/human_trafficking/6210

[6] http://www.nbcnews.com/politics/white-house/here-s-full-list-donald-trump-s-executive-orders-n720796

[7] http://www.stillnessinthestorm.com/2017/02/breaking-trump-meets-with-anti-human-trafficking-experts-promises-to-use-the-full-force-of-government-to-stop-it.html

[8] http://www.neonnettle.com/features/797-trey-gowdy-vows-to-take-down-elite-pedophile-rings-in-epic-speech-to-congress

[9] https://www.huffingtonpost.com/entry/pedophilia-symbol-on-toy_us_56e6c6bbe4b0860f99d98178

[10] http://www.npr.org/sections/thetwo-way/2017/06/29/534898111/vatican-cardinal-charged-with-historic-sexual-offenses-in-australia

[11] https://exposednewsalternative.wordpress.com/2015/05/12/ninth-circle-secret-society-exposed-jesuit-pope-francis-found-guilty-of-child-trafficking-rape-murder/

[12] http://itccs.org/2017/05/02/breaking-news-report-on-the-disruption-of-the-ninth-circle-cults-sacrificial-rituals-on-april-30-2017/

[13] http://www.neonnettle.com/features/1043-1200-children-rescued-from-elite-pedophile-rings-only-tip-of-the-iceberg-

14 https://www.globalresearch.ca/
the-manchester-terror-attack-is-it-a-false-flag/5592055

15 http://21stcenturywire.com/2017/06/03/
london-attacks-who-knew-who-benefits-the-most/

16 http://thefreethoughtproject.com/former-cia-officer-every-single-
terrorist-attack-us-false-flag-attack/

17 http://beforeitsnews.com/new-world-order/2017/06/exposing-
crisis-solutions-false-flag-company-7440.html

18 http://www.nnettle.com/sphere/353-1-trillion-dollar-lawsuit-
filed-against-msm-for-staging-sandy-hook-

19 http://www.neonnettle.com/news/2356-exposed-us-army-
quietly-sneak-isis-terrorists-out-of-syria

20 http://www.neonnettle.com/news/2211-amnesty-international-
confirms-us-gave-isis-1-billion-of-weapons-in-2016

21 http://www.neonnettle.com/news/2208-katy-perry-no-borders-
it-s-time-to-welcome-the-new-world-order

22 http://www.neonnettle.com/features/945-putin-i-have-proof-the-
us-and-40-other-countries-funded-isis-to-start-ww3-

23 SGT Report Special: ILLUMINATI LUCIFERIANS
TOTALLY EXPOSED
https://www.youtube.com/watch?v=uOpp_eNFtYk

24 https://www.facebook.com/groups/1047083605397117/
permalink/1384208798351261/

25 https://benjaminfulford.net/2017/12/18/u-s-troops-deploy-
worldwide-10000-sealed-indictments-take-khazarian-mob/

26 https://www.facebook.com/groups/1047083605397117/
permalink/1364699000302241/

27 http://www.stillnessinthestorm.com/2016/07/History-of-
Technology-Suppression-Government-Secrecy-Orders-on-
Patents-Have-Stifled-More-Than-5000-Inventions.html

28 http://anonhq.com/60-minutes-on-this-bicycle-can-power-your-
home-for-24-hours/

29 http://www.thelastamericanvagabond.com/social-change/
eight-signs-world-undergoing-paradigm-shift/

30 http://www.isdb-pilot.org/wp-content/uploads/2015/12/
   Microfinance-makes-businesses-successful-in-Guinea.pdf
31 https://www.disclosurenews.it/en/
   western-system-failure-ben-fulford/
32 https://divinecosmos.com/start-here/
   davids-blog/1220-vegas-meta-analysis?showall=&start=1
33 https://divinecosmos.com/start-here/
   davids-blog/1220-vegas-meta-analysis
34 https://divinecosmos.com/start-here/
   davids-blog/1220-vegas-meta-analysis?showall=&start=3
35 http://www.infinitebeing.com/0507/monkeys.htm

REFERENCES

1. http://www.nnettle.com/news/1760-largest-child-porn-bust-in-history-ignored-by-mainstream-media

2. http://www.nnettle.com/news/1760-largest-child-porn-bust-in-history-ignored-by-mainstream-media

3. http://www.nnettle.com/features/805-first-of-the-elite-washington-dc-pedophile-ring-pleads-guilty-to-child-rape

4. http://www.nnettle.com/news/1888-elijah-wood-hollywood-is-run-by-a-powerful-elite-pedophile-ring

5. https://sputniknews.com/europe/201611241047790760-norway-pedophile-ring-busted/

6. https://foreignaffairs.house.gov/press-release/house-votes-turn-tables-human-traffickers/

7. http://www.newsy.com/stories/3-new-executive-orders-address-crime-help-law-enforcement/

8. https://www.studentnewsdaily.com/daily-news-article/trump-signs-3-executive-orders-targeting-drugs-crime/

9. http://galacticconnection.com/kevin-annett-vatican-politics-unveiled-november-1-2016/

10. http://galacticconnection.com/kevin-annett-vatican-politics-unveiled-november-1-2016/

11. http://higherdiscernment.blogspot.co.il/2017/05/itccs-update-on-ninth-circle-actions.html

12. Many Elite Headed to Prison for Child Sex Trafficking

(Dave Hodges) Did you know that in Trump's first 30 days in office, his people, mainly Attorney General Jeff Sessions, prosecuted 1,500 sex traffickers? To date, Trump/Sessions have prosecuted 3,500 child-sex-traffickers. Continue Reading: --> http://bit.ly/2ty1V6M <--

13. Major concerns raised about the wellbeing of singer Sinead O'Connor after her attempts at suicide following her exposure of a Catholic Church pedophile ring including her public outburst where she branded The Pope as the root of all evil in the world.

http://www.neonnettle.com/features/1036-sinead-o-connor-suicidal-after-exposing-catholic-church-pedophile-ring

14. http://galacticconnection.com/ben-fulford-full-report-and-several-updates-nazis-align-with-white-dragon-as-isolated-satanists-continue-their-death-throes/?utm_source=Newsletter&utm_campaign=58bb9a19ce-The+Daily+Alternative+News+Source+Jan+6%2C+2018&utm_medium=email&utm_term=0_aebd2bb672-58bb9a19ce-147594585&goal=0_aebd2bb672-58bb9a19ce-147594585&mc_cid=58bb9a19ce&mc_eid=af149fb47f

CHAPTER SIX

OUR STAR TREK SOCIETY

The Elite have maintained their control over civilizations down through the ages by controlling technology, be it the Gutenberg Press or Quantum computers. This has reached a new level of suppression in the last fifty years, if not longer, with their contact with extraterrestrials and an exchange of their advance technology for access to, among other things, human DNA samplings. But today we are witnessing a breakdown of that control by the Elite. This suppressed technology is being released because they can no longer hide it from us, given all the whistleblower disclosures of late.

The Advanced Technologies Hidden from Us

The suppressed advanced ET technologies[1] include zero gravity space crafts, free energy, and advanced healing technologies to name a few. According to Corey Goode, (a whistleblower who worked twenty years in the secret space program)," The military defense contractors are manufacturing a wide variety of products that will absolutely transform life on Earth as we know it, once they are released. We will instantaneously transition into a *Star Trek* age, with spaceships, teleportation, time travel, anti-gravity, free energy, food materializers, and super advanced healing technologies. [1,2] (*The*

Ascension Mysteries: Revealing the Cosmic Battle Between Good and Evil by David Wilcock).

Goode says the elite or the Cabal (as David Wilcock calls them) have been intentionally withholding this technology from us to prevent them from leading us to an age of prosperity and peace. They've used them and still do as a means of enhancing their control.[1] If you think that, "We the people" all over the world are being kept in the dark, while our so-called "leaders" know about all of these technologies, you're mistaken. For instance, there are twenty-one security clearance levels above the president of the U.S.[3] No matter who is elected, this person is only a tool of the Cabal and pledged to keep their secrets. He or she serves merely as a PR tool to make us think that we have a choice in our governance. I'm using the pronoun "we," as this same deception applies to Israel and other countries with so-called free elections. (I even argued with my family during lunch before the last elections here in Israel, March 2015, that it's all a show and the results are pre-planned in advance. I asked them, "Do you want me to prove it to you?" And everyone around the table shouted in unison "No.") It appears that the top ten clearance levels are supposedly based around "black" government projects such as the alien presence cover-up, underground alien bases, super soldiers, men in black, etc. This chart includes all the clearance levels. https://theawakemind.wordpress.com/2012/06/17/the-not-so-shocking-us-security-clearance-levels/

Apparently, the whistleblowers disclosures and their loss of control has precipitated reckless behavior, like some of them trying to escape earth in cloaked spaceships. *Newsweek* even claimed they attempted to leave for Mars.[4]

According to Corey Goode [5, 6] and Randy Cramer[7], there are corporate bases on Mars and the Moon for them to flee to. About a year ago, I even watched a video of this alleged escape from earth in a cloud-cloaked spaceship. After being shot down (by the alliance or resistance movement, I presume), I could see a small spaceship moving out of a cloud. They are confined to earth. I tried to find this footage (perhaps on <u>http://www.theeventchronicle.com/</u> site), but unfortunately, it appears that it was taken down. I had a lot of fun watching this video with friends who follow this intel cover-up. You can see this in the following videos:

<u>https://www.youtube.com/watch?v=Cvpw_L9VkGA</u>

In Perth Australia **<u>https://www.youtube.com/watch?v=cRkPDmC3DhI</u>** UFO shooting down a warhead !!MUST WATCH!!

<u>https://www.youtube.com/watch?v=5G1bSDUElfA</u>

UFO cloaked in blue clouds drop out of portal

<u>https://www.youtube.com/watch?v=cMMyI6TOvv4</u>

Randy Cramer is another whistleblower, one who served as a marine both on the moon (as a pilot) and on Mars (as security) for twenty years combined. He was authorized by a superior in the military to "spill the beans," and he's sharing his experience and knowledge about the technologies used by the Cabal. [8] Randy's information and firsthand accounts of this strange new world backs up what other whistleblowers have also shared, including the establishment of bases on Mars. The experience that really shook me was his description of the trauma of almost dying after a battle and "being put [back] together many times,"[9] with technology that could "replace his whole body, and depending on what parts [organs] needed replacement, often took days to accomplish."[9]

Why would the Cabal allow and even authorize these leaks? According to Cramer, "He was given permission by his commanding officer to go public with his information, which suggests that the Cabal realizes that this is the ideal way for them to allow leakage of the truth without losing face and triggering social unrest. This is a slow pressure release engineered to gradually acclimate the masses to the concept of extraterrestrials and, ultimately, these secret space programs that have been in operation for over 50 years." [10] There are other testimonies verifying these advanced technologies. You can see here a saucer-shaped UFO craft from earth's soil[11].

The ET Directive behind this Technology Suppression

There are other testimonies from people who worked on projects related to these ultra-advanced technologies, such as teleportation, time travel, and anti-gravity-driven space craft. They come from a variety of people, including military leaders, bankers, media executives, corporate CEOs, judges and lawyers, Hollywood actors and producers, law enforcement, and insiders from various intelligence agencies, whether it's NSA, CIA, KGB, FBI, DHS/MI-5&6, or MOSSAD. However, these insiders were told only part of the plan, because if they have been aware of the entire agenda even they wouldn't have cooperated with it. But why? According to testimonies from whistleblowers, it allegedly has to do with an alien directive to disconnect people from the "prime creator," which some would call "the source."

According to various scientists, many strands of our genetic code (DNA) were tampered with and have been totally disconnected (what is called the dormant or junk DNA strands) from the primary chromosome strands to disconnect humans (us) from the Great Cosmic Intelligence. This was done so that "we humans," as a species, would be vulnerable and accept their different mind control programs, which are compelling us to behave in ways that are highly destructive to us and to our planet. This lower vibrational modality maintains our controlled and illusionary reality. Without a connection to the "source," we can only "serve" the team dark, those dimensional beings who are feeding off the discord of this false "matrix."

In the book, *Harvesting the Disconnected The Alien Agenda for Mankind* by Andrew Hennessey, [12] he explains how this disconnection is done: "Souls are being plucked from the living human grapevine for dark abuses in the hungry abyss by wrapping them in heavy accretions of material luxury, or dark shrouds of physical and spiritual disease and despair, or in the engaging intellectual millstone of materialism and its labyrinth of powers and principalities, or in its addictions and pseudo consolations. These deadening and disorientating attacks make the soul vulnerable to temptation and disgraceful attempts at compensation at the cost of his/her brotherhood or sisterhood. Part of the attack is to dehumanize the human being by taking their hearts and minds off heavenly directions and outcomes[...] The main aim of the Reptilians or Grays [devils in our mythologies] is to produce disconnection from the Source within the human soul by presenting and driving into us, negation and negative circumstances." Andrew Hennessey has been interested in the UFO phenomenon from a very early age, having had many UFO encounters and experiences, which he first wrote about in his book, *The Turning of the Tide.*

It's really intriguing that even our language has hints of some ancient ET intervention. Think about all the expressions containing the word draconian in English. We have the same expressions in Hebrew, too. And why are there statues of dragons in the City of London marking its borders? [13] The history of dragons has been known for six millennia. It can be traced back to approximately 4,000 B.C. with them playing a role in legends and in folklore. It was said they could live in a wide range of habitats, including the middle of the ocean, the center of the earth, in fire or frigid caves—anywhere damp and dark. "Stories of dragons appear all throughout history and almost every culture has their own idea about dragons[...] Dragons seem to come from exaggerated myths about huge snakes, lizards or other reptiles." [14]

Recently a hit series and its sequel feature a group of "immortals," who derive their power from a substance extracted from dragons and seek to control the world, which the superheroes fight to prevent.

So they hide their existence in plain sight? I'm starting to sound like QAnon, the recently famous intel source thought to be in Trump's workforce, who raises the readers' awareness by posting questions on his Twitter account. [15] Other sources also provide evidence that human DNA had been tampered by aliens. Corey Goode is one of these sources, but he's not the only one. [16] Can you imagine that even mainstream scientists have discovered ET code in our DNA? Read here.[17, 18, 19] It makes us think about what we actually know about our origins. According to David Wilcock, "There are at least 40 different humanoid extraterrestrial groups that have tinkered around with our DNA for many thousands of years[…] We have a lot of problems that are because of them tinkering with our DNA. That includes the fact that we have bad backs, the fact that we get sunburns, and the fact that the sun is bad for our eyes. There are lots and lots of strange things that we have that are because our genetics have been tampered with."[20]

Perhaps this is the reason why we've been inundated by so many movies about alien invasions recently, which may be connected to a fake alien invasion agenda (if our DNA has already been tinkered and spliced up with ET DNA, then it's not an invasion but a homecoming). One of my favorite movies years ago was *Independence Day*. However, after researching these subjects, I don't think I would have been able or even liked to have watched this movie, despite its positive ending. Although all this sounds too "out there" to be true, David Wilcock says that insiders and other researchers, who have shared information on these technologies with him, claim that the Cabal has and does use "cloning technologies, highly advanced space craft and they've been talking about alien invasion [like] this since the 1950's."[21]

This fake ET invasion scenario is not as far-fetched as you may think. Believe me, I can definitely understand your skepticism about this eventuality, as I had a hard time believing it myself. But Corey Goode says that the Cabal had such a plan in place to be implemented via the secret space program, which is also known as Project Blue Beam.[22] You may ask yourself: Why would they do this? What is the agenda behind such an alien invasion? According to Wilcock, this is part of the depopulation agenda discussed in Chapter One. He says that the Cabal was going to use this program to manipulate us into believing this fake alien invasion, which would allow them to cause huge collateral damage and help them to implement their depopulation agenda (as stated in their NWO [New World Order] dictate in the Georgia Guidestones), which this alien invasion was part of it. If the Cabal's timeline was realized, "The planet should have already been under their total control but it hasn't worked out the way they wanted".[21] Corey Goode adds that the term "Non-Terrestrial Threat" was heavily used in the SSP (Secret Space Programs) in the context of entering the Earth's atmosphere, which required clearance or they would be considered such a threat. [21]

These "discoveries" are slowly being revealed to the masses to mentally prepare them so they won't experience future shock when it is all revealed, which among other things is, "that cloning of humans is possible & has gone on for decades." [23] This technology has been mainly suppressed and is being used to control us. (Like replacing politicians who won't "work with them" with their clones.) How do they hide these technologies in plain sight? They present those, which have already been invented, in "science fiction" movies (as mentioned previously). This is why I call our true reality: "Our Science Fiction reality." Think about such Hollywood films for a moment: "Clones and cloning in *Avatar*; *"Jurassic Park* – cloning animals; *Genesis II* – underground genetics laboratories that are connected by tube shuttles; *Terminal Man* – brain stem implants; *Star Trek* – various items."[23] Not only is the secret technology being revealed in these movies, "the attitudes and beliefs shown on the two series, especially a recent *Star Trek* sequel[,] are the attitudes the Satanic elite want people to have." [23]

Hollywood movies imply that extraterrestrial beings have ruled earth but present it in a movie as a fantasy like *Jupiter Ascending*. Corey Goode was shocked by it, or so he says, because he was actually sent as one of SSPs delegates to meet with the Dracos. He said that he would never go on such ventures again, says Justin Deschamps, on his blog *Stillness in the Storm*. [21] "David Wilcock mentions the movie *Jupiter Ascending*, which is jam-packed with solar system history, the agenda of the Draco group (using humans as a food resource), and their use of human beings for life extension technology, and DNA hybridization programs. Corey and David saw the movie together during last year's Consciousness Life Expo. Corey's 'frickin mind was blown' by what was revealed in the film [...] David shows slides of a reptilian from the movie, saying that this might have been the reason why I was so shocked.

- Wilcock suggests that what is depicted in the movie is part of some soft or partial disclosure effort.

- Goode says that he thinks the disclosure in the movie is higher than the secret space program, that it has to do with these 22 genetic, social, and spiritual experiments being conducted on Earth by a super federation of extraterrestrials who have lived within our solar system since the time this outer barrier came down." [21] These experiments include long-running genetic programs, altering what it means to be human. Corey elaborates upon each of the four major components of this grand experiment: genetic, spiritual, consciousness and cosmic. [21, 24] This movie could be their version of the history, from the aliens behind these 22 programs. Wilcock says, "Corey Goode has mentioned in the past that there are up to 60 ET groups that maintain permanent outposts here to monitor experiments that are actively being conducted on the Earth. Apparently, these groups came in after the fall of the outer barrier and many of them have bases on the Moon." [21]

- David Wilcock says Corey had to meet this royal Draco during a meeting, and it was not pleasant. These white royal Dracos were pleading for clemency at a meeting Corey attended in mid-2015, "These guys, the Draco, are actually using the Earth as a fear factory, consuming what they call 'looshe'. They need humanity to be in fear, stressed out, hating life etc, and work with the ground-based Cabal to ensure those conditions are maintained, hence false flags attacks, denatured food, the war on terror, etc. In the below-linked articles, I attempt to discuss the scientific basis for *fear food* or *looshe* and why races that use artificial life-extension technology need it to survive." [21]

Other interesting technology regularly used by the NSA according to this interview *between* Al Bielek and Preston Nichols is "a portable unit that can render an individual invisible[...] The NSA, also maybe CIA, seem to have a trick way of achieving invisibility, probably only for a short time[...] We don't know whether it's a gadget or a mind effect, but it's likely a little electronic gimmick to cause a slight time phase shift, probably back-engineered or given to them by their alien parasite friends in exchange for XXX[...] Carol, Ryan and I and others have encountered invisible feds in situations where no other explanation is feasible, such as in moving cars and cars that quickly get off the road and park as we approach. Many of us have heard them walking around in our houses, obviously not having arrived via doors or windows." [25]

I know it's hard to believe all it, but what about the Jimmy Kimmel interview with Obama about the aliens (even if it seems that Obama is joking). Here's the excerpt from the interview:

- [Kimmel] wanted to know whether Obama had tried to get to the bottom of the "UFO files" about the mysterious desert region known as Area 51.
- "The aliens won't let it happen," Obama joked. "You'd reveal all their secrets. They exercise strict control over us."
- But President Clinton once said he'd checked on the matter and found nothing, Kimmel protested. "That's what we're instructed to say," Obama responded. [26]

How Could These Suppressed Technologies Transform Our Reality?

Corey Goode explains that, "The 'free energy' technologies would end the need of the 'Current Oil/Petro Energy Companies,' The 'Frequency and Light Healing' technologies would end the 'Current Pharmaceutical Corporations,' the 'Neurological Interface' technologies would end the need for 'Large Education Institutions' and the 'Food Replication' technologies and 'Environmental Purification and Restoration' technologies would end poverty, starvation, and begin to reverse the damage humanity has done to the earth virtually overnight. The real reason is that these technologies have been suppressed is that they would immediately collapse the world economies and make the *Babylonian Money Magic Slave System* of no use anymore. It means the 'Loss of Control' of the .01% (Elite) over the 'Masses' and a complete 'Paradigm Change'. In short it means 'Freedom'! Freedom for the first time in humanity's 'known' recorded history."[27]

Lawrence & Michael Sartorius say that "Governments fearing the loss of their control over us have conducted a major 'Cover Up' of U.F.O.s and Extraterrestrial visitors since World War II, and at the same time intimidated the World's Media into ignoring any reports of their appearances in our skies. In the meantime, the Governments have quietly created their own secret files of all the numerous UFO sightings supplied by their Military Forces and filed them away in Top-Secret Archives [while] at the same time secretly interacting with some of these extraterrestrial visitors [...who have made] a Treaty with the U.S. Government in exchange for some of their more advanced technology. They identified themselves as Zeta Reticulans originating from a Planet around a Red Star in the Constellation of Orion which we called Betelgeuse[...] A Treaty was eventually signed between them and the U.S. Government for them to re-engineer their failing DNA with that of Earth Humans in exchange for their spacecraft technology and weapons. [28]

"The Treaty that was agreed on stated that the Aliens would not interfere in our affairs[,] and we would not interfere in theirs. We agreed in return to keep their presence on Earth a secret and provide them with large underground Base facilities under the 'Four Corners' area of Utah, New Mexico, Arizona and Colorado. They were not to make any Treaty with any other Earth Nation [...] They would be allowed to make abductions of Humans on a limited and periodic basis for the purpose of medical examination and monitoring of our development, with the agreed requirement that the Humans would not be harmed, and be returned to their point of abduction with no memory of the event. They were also required to furnish the Government with a list of all Human contacts and abductees on a regularly scheduled basis. However, after over a period of forty years they had proved to have failed to either supply very meaningful new technology or to keep their word on the amount and degree of abductions. This applied particularly to women and children taken up to their Mothership for experimental surgery, as well as to their frequent mutilation of cattle in a continued effort to extract genetic codes. As a result, the U.S. Government had gradually closed down most of their extensive main underground Bases by the late 1990s, leaving them to carry on with only much more limited facilities for a short period." [28]

One of the most exciting technologies, which many people worldwide want to know whether it's existing viable technology, is time-portal travel to other dimensions or planets in this multiverse. This technology appears to exist and was mentioned in an extract from the interview between David Wilcock and Corey Goode: David asks Corey about what he heard in the smart glass pads about portals that will open up on Earth at certain times and places that one could use to travel through space and time. "[Glass pads] were devices provided to SSP personnel for information dissemination purposes, and according to Goode, they contained a wealth of information, data that would otherwise be classified as Above Top Secret. Much of the historical information provided by Goode he apparently received courtesy of these Smart Glass Pads." [29]

Goode says, "I didn't hear about that from the glass pads. It was Intuitive Empaths, in the secret space program, who would be used to triangulate where and when these portals would open up—which would either be underground or under water, at the earth's surface, or in the sky. They seemed to open up randomly at first, but after they got the celestial mechanics down, they realized that depending on the positions of celestial bodies, such as the Sun, moon, planets, other stars, etc, these portals would open." [21]

David says he wants to talk about the weird stuff saying, "that after Corey was recruited into the program, in 1987, he did his 20-year tour of duty, and then was brought back in time to the day that he left. This was done through time travel technology[…] Corey explains that at the end of a tour of duty, an asset is de-briefed (recounting the experience) and age regressed or 'biologically turned back' to the time before you left. During this process, scars, tattoos or any other markings are 'wiped clean' due to the temporal regression methods used. The technology for this was a kind of paneling they placed around the body, while in a heavily sedated state to keep the body completely still throughout the process. This is called the 'twenty and back' program." [21]

What evidence do we have for time travel technology? In an interview of Al Bielek by Preston Nichols, Bielek said that, "The Navy had the ability to use the time travel technology from about 1970 and developed full operational capability in 1973. They did do an experiment where they tried to go back and kill the father of the man destined to be the head of the new One-World government. They did kill his father, but it made no difference. They didn't understand why it didn't work. Robert Lazar was voicing the concept that time is quantitized or compartmentalized and that you can't change what has already happened in terms of the past." [30]

In another interview in which Al Bielek was interviewed by Kenneth Burke, he elaborates even more on this time-travel technology: "I [Bielek] was time-transferred to 1983, where they did the full erasure of my full memory of my career and everything as Zeb Cameron. All my credentials were removed and erased. Dr. von Neumann knew it was happening. He didn't like it, but he couldn't do anything about it. They also pulled the age regression number on me, which was to reduce my body size to that of an infant. Now, they can take a person back to a fetus. This is a common and usual technique, now, and I know people who have gone through it, including my second son. (I have four sons by the way.) My number two son, I found and I've met and know him. It's another long story." [30, 31, 32]

Ben Rich, former head of the Lockheed Skunk Works, said in a lecture shortly before he died, "We already have the means to travel among the stars, but these technologies are locked up in black projects and it would take an act of God to ever get them out to benefit humanity.... Anything you can imagine, we already know how to do." (see http://www.serpo.org)

I think that the most important thing in this discussion is that according to Wilcock, "All those who are seeking the truth are essential players in breaking down the walls of secrecy".[21] So you, who reads this book right now, are an integral part in the dismantling this wall of secrecy and spreading it to the masses. Yes, you're part of the solution and the massive paradigm shift going on in the world right now.

Suppressing ET Existence

As I said earlier, I think the suppression of the existence of ETs in general and on earth and in cooperation with governments is a way to suppress spirituality and maintain the patriarchal religions of the past and their male control over humanity. Understanding the implications of the "missing link" in our DNA or "junk DNA," which are the inactive DNA strands being tampered with and are a hint to our connection to advanced ET lineage, would establish that we're not the descendants of apes but are spiritual beings. Thus, the Cabal would lose their control over us, as we claim who we really are—namely, exalted spiritual beings and not low-living animals. This agenda is taught to suppress the basic knowledge of who we really are and what is our true heritage. It appears that this information even trickles from the mainstream media (MSM).

Robert Bigelow, a NASA partner, claims that aliens currently living on earth[33] are, "suppressing your idea of Who You Are. It's about convincing you that you are nothing, no one. It's about convincing you that you are just a biological machine, fit to serve as no more than a cog in a machine or as Pink Floyd put it just another brick in the wall. Mainstream science to this day still denies the existence of consciousness just because it can't get a handle on it with the 5 senses. Its simplistic solution is to disregard anything it can't measure[...] Remember also *The Matrix* series of films. Morpheus shows Neo the shocking truth that we are raised as a food source for the Controllers. He shows Neo a symbol of the battery. While this is a good symbol, a battery implies a **storage of energy**. In actuality, we act as **generators of energy** for the Archons, so a generator you see at a construction site might be a more accurate symbol[...] However, because we are powerful beings, the Archons can't just rely on force for all this. They need to trick us into giving them consent. How do they do that? How do they get us to go willingly into the soul net? With the trick of the white light [...]

"Simon Parkes is an incredible modern day ET contactee[...] If you listen to his interviews[,] it is clear, he is a rational, level-headed man, who even holds a position in local government in England. Parkes states that **alien intervention** and **genetic manipulation** occurred earlier in humanity's history, where our DNA was tampered with and our psychic abilities repressed. This was done so that no one could challenge the prison guards (the Archons). In presentations such the video above, Parkes also mentions the trick of the white light and the soul net[...] The *WingMakers* story is an astonishing creation, full of stories of humanity's history, poetry, paintings and music, well worth checking out. To me, one of the most powerful of the stories – which are written as fiction but come across as completely factual – is the <u>Neruda Interview #5</u>, where we learn of how all of us humans – who are divine, infinite consciousness – came to be trapped inside physical bodies that die. The deception came about through the conspiring of 3 separate alien races (the Annunaki, the Serpent Race, and the Sirians) who found a way to trick the Atlanteans (our ancient ancestors) to inhabit biological vessels (the human body). Part of the deception involves Anu, the reptilian king of the Annunaki, ruling over humanity as king, and setting up planes of existence to ensure we never get out – including the soul net reincarnation plane. "[34]

Despite These Malevolent Agendas How Did Humanity Survive?

According to Corey Goode, "For years now we have reported how benevolent extraterrestrial humans are systematically preventing the Cabal from accomplishing any of the 'big stuff.'" [35] You can see here the footage of a UFO shooting down a nuclear warhead https://www.youtube.com/watch?v=5G1bSDUElfA. These benevolent ETs (or the Galactics, as they like to be called) according to various sources include the Yahyel (Aka The Shalanaya), Sirian Hybrids, The Essassani ["The Essassanis are our contact ambassadors, and you may be most familiar with the Essassani species from Bashar, channeled by Daryl Anka."], and the Pleiadians among others. [35, 36, 37] Edgar Mitchell, the Apollo astronaut and American hero says that aliens tried to save the US from a nuclear war with Russia. [38, 39]

Wilcock says that, "Given that Alex Jones was leaking intel that mass starvation, martial law and FEMA camps were imminent all the way back in 1995, it is amazing that nothing has happened in all this time. Pete Peterson was given advance warning about 9/11, as were others, and the hope or expectation was that all of these things would have resulted from it. I have personally been subject to countless briefings warning of this sort of scenario. Yet, the positive efforts to stop it work so well that I label it all as 'fear porn.'" [35] A few great examples of "divine intervention" becoming very obvious in our headlines can be found in the China's October Surprise series[40] and Disclosure Imminent? Two Underground NWO Bases Destroyed. [41]

More examples of Positive ET Interventions:

The Dangers of AI

Corey Goode and the Sphere Being Alliance (not to be confused with the Earth Alliance) warned that AI (artificial intelligence) is extremely dangerous to humanity and hidden from us to be left defenseless (as with the constant attempts to disarm the Americans). You can see here how a robot/AI openly says that she wants to destroy humans (The Pulse | CNBC – the scientist guides the robot what to say, but it says it wants to destroy humans and he's denying this…). See here https://www.youtube.com/watch?v=W0_DPi0PmF0 Stephen Hawking also warns of such scenario that when artificial intelligence becomes too clever, it can literally wipe out humanity. [42] "Lewis, Tanya (2015-01-12). *Don't Let Artificial Intelligence Take Over, Top Scientists Warn*".[43] Stephen Hawking, Elon Musk and dozens of other top scientists and technology leaders have signed a letter warning of the potential dangers of developing artificial intelligence (AI).

A significant problem is that unfriendly artificial intelligence is likely to be much easier to create than friendly AI. While both require large advances in what is called recursive optimization process design,[44] friendly AIs also require the ability to make goal structures invariant or fixed—under self-improvement (or the AI could transform itself into something unfriendly)—and one "that aligns with human values and not automatically destroy the human race." [45] An unfriendly AI, on the other hand, can be optimized for an arbitrary goal structure, which does not need to be invariant or fixed by its controller or us. [45] The sheer complexity of human value systems makes it very difficult to make AI's motivations human-friendly. Unless moral philosophy provides us with a flawless ethical theory, an AI's utility function could allow for many potentially harmful scenarios that conform with a given ethical framework but not "common sense". According to Eliezer Yudkowsky,[46] there is little reason to suppose that an artificially designed mind would have such an adaptation. In the television series *Person of the Interest*, the computer genius who finally designs a friendly AI tells his colleague that the first 42 versions tried to kill him. Physicist Stephen Hawking, Microsoft founder Bill Gates and SpaceX founder Elon Musk have expressed concerns about the possibility that AI could develop to the point that humans could not control it, with Hawking theorizing that this could "spell the end of the human race". Stephen Hawking said in 2014 that "Success in creating AI would be the biggest event in human history. Unfortunately, it might also be the last, unless we learn how to avoid the risks." Hawking believes that in the coming decades, AI could offer "incalculable benefits and risks" such as "technology outsmarting financial markets, out-inventing human researchers, out-manipulating human leaders, and developing weapons we cannot even understand." [47, 48, 49] Corey Goode also shares these warnings "We were warned and warned and warned by these different non-terrestrial groups not to mess around with this AI signal or these different artificial intelligence technologies that developed from information that we received from this inter dimensional AI signal." [50]

DUMBS – Deep Underground Military Bases

There are over 120 Deep Underground Military Bases situated under most major cities in the USA alone. There are also many such bases in Canada under major metropolitan areas. "Almost all of these bases are over 2 miles underground and have diameters ranging from 10 miles up to 30 miles across![...] The US Government through the NSA, DOD, CIA, DIA, ATF, ONI, US Army, US Marine Corp, FEMA and the DHS has spent in excess of 12 trillion dollars building the massive, covert infrastructure for the coming One World Government and New World Religion over the past 40 years[…] These city-sized bases can hold millions and millions of people, whether they are mind controlled, enslaved NWO World Army Soldiers or innocent and enslaved surface dwellers from the towns and cities of America and Canada." (The Watcher Files, Project Camelot) [51],[52]

(Boring machines that with immense heat drill rapidly big places…. Perhaps another type of ET technology.) https://www. nap.edu/read/14670/chapter/8#146

"The Black Budget currently consumes $1.25 trillion per year. At least this amount is used in black programs, like those concerned with deep underground military bases. Presently, there are 129 deep underground military bases in the United States. They have been building these 129 bases day and night, unceasingly, since the early 1940s. Some of them were built even earlier than that. These bases are basically large cities underground connected by high-speed magneto-leviton trains that have speeds up to Mach 2. Several books have been written about this activity[…] The average depth of these bases is over a mile, and they again are basically whole cities underground. They all are between 2.66 and 4.25 cubic miles in size. They have laser-drilling machines that can drill a tunnel seven miles long in one day. Deep Underground Military Bases and the Black Budget – Phil Schneider's last lecture of 1995."[53]

"The federal government has now invented an earthquake device. I am a geologist, and I know what I am talking about. With the Kobe earthquake in Japan, there was no pulse wave as in a normal earthquake. None. In 1989, there was an earthquake in San Francisco. There was no pulse wave with that one either. It is a Tesla device that is being used for evil purposes. The black budget programs have subverted science as we know it."[54]

How Is This Suppression of ET Technology Hides Our True Origin?

As cited earlier, the suppression of ET technology hides our true origin, which is extraterrestrial and that we did not evolve from primates. The tinkering with our DNA proves this, and its disclosure puts an end to this alien agenda for humankind, as people will be aware of this agenda and it won't be contained and controlled anymore. According to Corey Goode, humanity is an experiment conducted by 23 or 24 extraterrestrial races. We did not evolve from the monkeys. They've suppressed the fact that we're spiritual beings (from ET source) having a physical experience, and not just physical entities. Michael Tellinger[55] also speaks about the true history and the real origin of humanity and that "we are from the stars." He is a scientist, explorer and internationally acclaimed author of numerous books, and the founder of the UBUNTU Liberation Movement. Michael has become an authority on the ancient vanished civilizations of Southern Africa, the mysterious origins of humankind, resonance.[55] Watch here around minute 4:43 mark https://www.youtube.com/watch?v=f0zBv-DrXbk

Had the BBC attempted to prep us to ET presence and the suppression of their existence by religions? Brandon Ambrosino shares with us the following intriguing information, [56] "One notable **study** conducted by Ted Peters, who teaches systematic theology at Pacific Lutheran Theological Seminary and the Graduate Theological Union in Berkeley, California, found that twice as many non-religious people than religious people think that the discovery of alien life will spell trouble for earthly religion (69% to 34%, respectively)." [57]

Enslaving Humanity in Off-World Colonies and on Earth

I first heard of those off-world slave colonies from Cobra (an abbreviation of "compression breakthrough"), who said there are

14 million humans from earth who had been abducted and are slaves on many other planets. I was totally shocked, especially because I found out that the ritual abuse of humans off-planet is much worse than on Earth, which is devastating enough. I usually don't participate in group meditations, but when I heard about this disclosure, I felt compelled to join and help free our fellow humans on other planets. Almost 144,000 people worldwide joined this meditation. I remember that my brilliant friend, Nir, and I meditated to liberate the slaves abducted to off-earth slave colonies on May 30, 2017 to help the light forces liberate these colonies. I remember the track used Vangelis from his album Voices which still moves me to my core when I listen to it https://www.youtube.com/watch?v=L8WOTqeJcC8. It was so moving and Cobra reported after a couple of days that it was successful, although not all were liberated. Those who were allegedly freed were taken to planets where they would be healed from the abuses they suffered by those who abducted them: The Interplanetary Conglomerate.

Corey Goode also speaks about this phenomenon, "A family would agree to go, get on the ship, arrive at the location only to discover that it was all a lie. [They are taken to one of these off-world colonies, made to work in the industrial apparatus there as literal slaves. In other words, many of these people were recruited under false pretenses like what is done in the sex trade with young girls.] The recruits were considered the property of 'the corporation.'"[21]

David Wilcock says that 55 to 60 million people were abducted from earth. This number can be expanded to work for the programs as they grew. These people were abducted, sometimes entire villages, and then the children born off-planet are slaves who didn't know any other reality. Corey Goode claims that this galactic human slave trade is being threatened by the SSP Alliance, an alliance of Secret Space Programs which plan to stop these horrible, abusive practices, which have plagued humanity perhaps for millennia by planning full disclosure. Wilcock further says, "Corey explains just how extensive the Galactic human slave trade has been, the principal parties involved, and the egregious mistreatment of those unfortunate enough to have been taken captive. Corey further explains that 'Drop Zones' exist, where the bodies of humans that have been killed, mutilated, or exploited in some way have been left, and how national security agencies have suppressed this information." However, as a result of a solar system wide quarantine implemented by the Sphere Alliance, the number of human captives, which have been taken outside the solar system to be sold, has been reduced. [21, 58]

Global Human Trafficking and Off Planet Trade

There is no currency or financial system that is used between these space-faring civilizations so everything is based on bartering. Some ETs are interested in some of the Earth's Art (again some of our most famous missing historical art pieces are in off-world collections), luxury Items like spices, animal and plant Life, while many others are interested in trading their technology and biological specimens for Human Beings. These humans are used for many purposes including manual slave labor, sex trade, and engineering (some of us are well-known for certain technical skill sets). Some of the ETs use humans as food resources in various ways. When the secret earth governments and their syndicates discovered that a large amount of humans were being taken off the planet by various ETs anyway, they found a way to profit from it and have control over which people were being taken. In prior arrangements, they were made promises of receiving technologies and biological specimens for allowing groups to abduct humans, but the ETs rarely delivered on their promises. Once they had developed the advanced infrastructure of their Interplanetary Corporate Conglomerate (ICC) in our Sol System and along with advanced technologies (that some of the thousands of ET groups traveling through our system were now interested in obtaining), they had the ability to deter most unwelcome guests from entering Earths airspace the Cabal/ICC then decided to use human trafficking as one of their resources in interstellar bartering.[2]

Full Disclosure is necessary to reveal the full scope of human slavery, which extends off-planet and into many other civilizations of which earth humans, many of them children, are used for sex and trafficking. In most of these cases, the massive profits for human slavery, sexual slavery, and free labor for the negative alien agenda (NAA) [59] is involved. [60]

David Wilcock corroborates this:

- The Dark Fleet is a human-based group, but they work side by side with the Draco, helping them fight their enemies. This faction is more into human trafficking and the trafficking of genetic materials from Earth.
- David mentions how the *Guardians of the Galaxy*[61] film has a lot of soft disclosure in it, showing people from Earth being pulled into a space program, just like what happened in the Brain Drain. The "Brain Drain" era, according to another of David Wilcock insiders, Pete Peterson, refers to recruiting 55 to 60 million of the best and brightest scientists in the world to this secret program in the 1950s and in the early 1960's. [21]

How Is This Connected to Disclosures about Antarctica?

All those who follow the train of intel disclosed here, may have noticed the many world leaders are secretly visiting Antarctica in recent years, including Barak Obama, John Kerry, Pope Francis, and Russian Orthodox Church Patriarch Kirill, and even legendary astronaut Buzz Aldrin in 2016. Why? Steve Quayle, author of *Empire Beneath the Ice*, says in an interview with Greg Hunter on *USA Watchdog* that it may be connected to "Operation Highjump" initiated by Admiral Byrd, who in 1947 sent a war flotilla to Antarctica to search and destroy the hidden Nazi bases. This operation was a large one and included 13 ships with 4,700 men, and the most advanced U.S. weaponry of that time. This information was based on the documentation provided to them by the intelligence agencies. It appears that these world leaders are being given orders by entities in this region. Steve Quayle's provides a plethora of citations, historical evidence and explanations for what is really going on in this place throughout this interview. [62]

But perhaps the most shocking revelations were made by Corey Goode, the secret space program whistleblower, who said in 2016 that scientific and political figures were shocked to discover an advanced civilization in Antarctica which was flash frozen. He disclosed information about his extensive tour of Antarctica facilities deep under the ice-shelf of an ancient inner-earth civilization called Anshar, whose facilities are controlled by the Interplanetary Corporate Conglomerate (another SSP). Ancient historical records like the Oronteus Fineus map[63] also confirm that once Antarctica was inhabited by a thriving civilization prior to a devastating pole shift destroyed much of this area. Goode says, "This is a startling archeological discovery that confirms the elongated skulls found in places like Paracas, Peru, belonged to another species of humans, rather than being artificially created deformities." What is critical to understand according to Goode is that many of the Cabal view themselves as direct descendants of these pre-Adamite peoples (before Adam of the Christian Bible), and consequently view the Antarctica discovery as an event that corroborates their uniqueness, and fitness to rule. Apparently, many pre-Adamites occupy very senior positions in the Vatican hierarchy where their identities are hidden by the elongated hats worn by Bishops and Cardinals." (and article by Michael E. Salla, Ph.D.) [64]

How Can We See We're the Creators Connected to Source?

Namaste is a beautiful word that most people who use it don't know it's meaning which hints to our real source. Next time you hear someone saying this you'll know that it means "I see your divinity and you see my divinity within me." Here's a more detailed explanation https://www.elephantjournal.com/2012/08/namaste-what-it-means-why-we-say-it/

How our world would look if we all felt this way about each other? It would really become what Louis Armstrong sang about a few decades ago in his song/track *What a Wonderful World* [65]

FOOTNOTES

[1] The Ascension Mysteries: Revealing the Cosmic Battle Between Good and Evil by David Wilcock https://books.google.co.il/books?id=4m3fDQAAQBAJ&pg=PT317&lpg=PT317&dq=cabal%27s+advanced+healing+technologies&source=bl&ots=Lj9EuBhCJ6&sig=v1Lttj1ZZCUKkjBwdsIyCd2KW-E&hl=i-w&sa=X&ved=0ahUKEwj8_rekm8jXAhUD6xoKHckB7YQ6AEIJjAA#v=onepage&q=cabal's%20advanced%20healing%20technologies&f=false

[2] Wilcock, David, *The Ascension Mysteries: Revealing the Cosmic Battle Between Good and Evil*, New York, Dutton, August 30, 2016.
https://www.amazon.com/Ascension-Mysteries-Revealing-Cosmic-Between/dp/1101984074

[3] https://theawakemind.wordpress.com/2012/06/17/the-not-so-shocking-us-security-clearance-levels/

[4] http://www.theeventchronicle.com/editors-pick/article-claims-elite-plan-to-escape-to-mars-leave-99-of-us-on-dying-warring-planet/

[5] http://exopolitics.org/corporate-bases-on-mars-and-nazi-infiltration-of-us-secret-space-program/

[6] https://www.youtube.com/watch?v=5vsXicr79aE

[7] http://www.mirror.co.uk/news/weird-news/secret-alien-base-mars-marine-3745652

[8] https://www.gaia.com/article/randy-cramer-mars-defense-force

[9] https://authenticmentoring.wordpress.com/2014/08/04/how-many-whistle-blowers-does-it-take-to-expose-the-secret-space-program/

[10] https://supersoldiertalk.com/2016/01/10/the-secret-space-program/

[11] http://hybridsrising.com/Technology/Hybrids-Rising-Technology-ET-Craft.html#PrintingCraftFromEarthsSoil

12 Hennessey, Andrew, *Harvesting the Disconnected: The Alien Agenda for Mankind*, Edinburgh, Scotland, Lulu.com publishing, December 2010.
http://www.whale.to/b/harvestingv61.pdf
13 https://en.wikipedia.org/wiki/Dragon_boundary_mark
14 http://www.draconika.com/history.php
15 https://twitter.com/hashtag/qanon
16 http://el11even.com/2015/09/03/the-alien-tampering-of-human-dna/
17 https://www.ancient-code.com/scientists-have-found-an-alien-code-in-our-dna-ancient-engineers/
18 http://www.dailymail.co.uk/sciencetech/article-2994187/Mystery-alien-genes-Scientists-discover-DNA-NOT-ancestors-say-change-think-evolution.html
19 http://www.stillnessinthestorm.com/2016/02/otherworldly-lineage-of-human-species.html
20 https://divinecosmos.com/start-here/davids-blog/1180-ssp-revealed
21 http://www.stillnessinthestorm.com/2016/02/david-wilcock-and-corey-goode-history.html
22 http://www.bibliotecapleyades.net/sociopolitica/esp_sociopol_bluebeam04.htm
23 https://www.bibliotecapleyades.net/ciencia/ciencia_genetica07.htm
24 https://www.gaia.com/video/grand-experiment
25 http://www.whale.to/b/sch.html
26 http://www.openminds.tv/obama-talks-area-51-ufos-and-aliens-with-jimmy-kimmel/32582
27 https://spherebeingalliance.com/introduction
28 http://www.thenewearth.org/newearth2.html
29 http://www.stillnessinthestorm.com/2016/06/Smart-Glass-Pads-Disclosure-Embedded-Nanoparticles-Clear-the-Way-for-Smart-Glass-Devices.html
30 http://www.whale.to/b/orion.html

[31] http://www.whale.to/b/bielek14.html

[32] Andrew Carlssin, the man from the year 2256
  http://www.rense.com/general36/time.htm

[33] http://www.independent.co.uk/news/science/nasa-robert-
  bigelow-aliens-extraterrestrials-earth-aerospace-space-
  international-station-a7763441.html

[34] http://freedom-articles.toolsforfreedom.com/
  soul-net-deep-down-rabbit-hole/

[35] https://divinecosmos.com/start-here/
  davids-blog/1217-dark-alliance

[36] http://humansarefree.com/2015/06/5-alien-species-in-contact-
  with-earth.html

[37] https://medium.com/we-are-not-alone-the-disclosure-lobby/
  extraterrestrial-and-extradimensional-beings-how-they-travel-
  space-and-time-fee564a2cf68

[38] http://www.dailymail.co.uk/sciencetech/article-3195416/Aliens-
  tried-save-America-nuclear-war-UFOs-shot-missiles-White-
  Sands-protect-Earth-claims-former-astronaut.html

[39] https://divinecosmos.com/start-here/
  davids-blog/1191-disclosure-showdown?showall=&start=2

[40] https://divinecosmos.com/start-here/
  davids-blog/872-disclosureevent

[41] https://divinecosmos.com/start-here/
  davids-blog/975-undergroundbases

[42] http://www.independent.co.uk/life-style/gadgets-and-tech/
  news/stephen-hawking-artificial-intelligence-could-wipe-out-
  humanity-when-it-gets-too-clever-as-humans-a6686496.html

[43] https://www.livescience.com/49419-artificial-intelligence-
  dangers-letter.html
  LiveScience. Purch. Retrieved October 20, 2015.

[44] https://www.jstage.jst.go.jp/article/
  kikaia1979/68/669/68_669_828/_article

[45] http://knowledge.wharton.upenn.edu/article/ai-new-electricity/

[46] https://en.wikipedia.org/wiki/Eliezer_Yudkowsky

[47] https://en.wikipedia.org/wiki/AI_takeover
https://en.wikipedia.org/wiki/Existential_risk_from_artificial_general_intelligence

[48] http://www.dailymail.co.uk/sciencetech/article-3143275/Artificial-intelligence-real-threat-robots-wipe-humanity-ACCIDENT-claims-expert.html

[49] http://www.express.co.uk/news/science/830501/AI-robots-killing-too-late-Elon-Musk

[50] http://lenouvelagedor-sistarseha.over-blog.com/2016/06/cobra-interview-de-cobra-et-corey-goode-par-rob-potter-partie-2.html

[51] http://www.thewatcherfiles.com/dumb.htm

[52] http://projectcamelot.org/underground_bases.html

[53] http://www.whale.to/b/schneider1.html

[54] http://www.whale.to/b/technology.html

[55] http://michaeltellinger.com/

[56] http://www.bbc.com/future/story/20161215-if-we-made-contact-with-aliens-how-would-religions-react

[57] http://tedstimelytake.com/wp-content/uploads/2013/03/ETIContactReligions.pdf

[58] http://exopolitics.org/galactic-human-slave-trade-ai-threat-to-end-with-full-disclosure-of-et-life/

[59] http://ascensionglossary.com/index.php/NAA

[60] http://ascensionglossary.com/index.php/Full_Disclosure_Event

[61] Guardians of the Galaxy http://www.imdb.com/title/tt2015381/

[62] https://www.silverdoctors.com/headlines/finance-news/the-mysteries-of-antarctica-revealed-someone-or-something-has-summoned-the-worlds-political-and-religious-leaders-to-antarctica/

[63] http://www.ancientdestructions.com/oronteus-finaeus-map-antarctica-fineus/

[64] http://exopolitics.org/discovery-of-flash-frozen-antarctica-civilization/

[65] https://www.youtube.com/watch?v=A3yCcXgbKrE

REFERENCES

1. Skype Interview - Marine after 17 years on Mars authorized to reveal truth for US National Security

2. About Andrew Hennessy https://scottishandrew.wordpress.com/about/

3. Skype Interview - Marine after 17 years on Mars authorized to reveal truth for US National Security https://www.youtube.com/watch?v=NXg8p4ohplU

4. A list of suppressed ET technologies can be found here http://www.bibliotecapleyades.net/ciencia/ciencia_extraterrestrialtech.htm

5. http://www1.american.edu/salla/Articles/Exo-SP-6.htm

6. https://spherebeingalliance.com/introduction

7. About Corey Goode https://spherebeingalliance.com/about-me

8. https://www.forbes.com/sites/leifwalcutt/2016/09/08/the-future-is-now-star-trek-technology-that-exists-today/#713e27777fa3

9. http://www.metatech.org/wp/ufos/secret-government-anti-gravity-fleet/

10. http://awarenessact.com/u-s-navy-and-nasa-have-a-fully-operational-space-fleet/

11. http://www.express.co.uk/news/weird/770805/Nellis-Airforce-base-UFO-secret-space-project

12. https://www.amazon.co.uk/Forbidden-History-Technologies-Extraterrestrial-Intervention/dp/1591430453

13. Replicator Technology /Corey Goode Interview with David Wilcock – amazing the star trek society

    https://www.youtube.com/watch?v=iVM0BOkkUTI

14. US Navy and NASA Have a Fully Operational Space Fleet

    https://www.youtube.com/watch?v=cYikz80v6-U

15. http://www.whale.to/b/time_travel.html

16. http://www.thetruthdenied.com/news/2012/08/09/andrew-basiago-alfred-lambremont-webre-time-travel-and-time-lines-what-does-this-mean-for-humanity/

17. Andrew Carlssin, the man from the year 2256

    https://www.youtube.com/watch?v=RoTm0qiiWwI

18. Information about Andrew Carlssin, the alleged time-traveler, who amassed $350 million dollars within two weeks time, published on https://www.youtube.com/channel/UCuGyi1u5cqLE6dxU8Bv9row on January 29, 2016

19. https://www.techworld.com/picture-gallery/apps-wearables/tech-leaders-warned-us-that-robots-will-kill-us-all-3611611/

20. http://rense.com/general22/br.htm

21. https://truedisclosure.org/

22. http://www.stillnessinthestorm.com/2015/05/human-trafficking-for-slavery-off-world.html

23. Alien Agenda: Planet Earth

   https://www.amazon.com/Alien-Agenda-Planet-Richard-Dolan/dp/B00TKPWNZQ/ref=sr_1_1?ie=UTF8&qid=1512655938&sr=8-1&keywords=alien+agenda+planet+earth

24. https://jhaines6.wordpress.com/2014/11/30/what-is-the-true-agenda-of-the-archon-anunnaki-draco-cabal-what-are-they-really-trying-to-achieve-here-on-the-earth-and-why-do-you-need-to-know-by-bradley-loves/

25. Disclosure of Super Advanced Technologies https://divinecosmos.com/start-here/davids-blog/1223-targeted-arrests

26. https://divinecosmos.com/start-here/davids-blog/1225-abr-legacy

27. https://www.amazon.com/Underworld-Mysterious-Civilization-Graham-Hancock/dp/1400049512

CHAPTER SEVEN

THE GLOBAL CURRENCY RESET

I talk with people from all over the world, including Brazil, Israel, Mexico, South Africa, Romania, Germany, the Philippines, China, Canada, the United States and many other countries mainly on Facebook, but also on Instagram. What I found is that many people are struggling financially—both employees of companies and those self-employed. I wonder how my readers are faring financially? Are your relatives, acquaintances, and friends struggling? This is not a coincidence. Our debt-based financial system is designed this way by the Cabal to further enslave us. But what happens if this "debt-slave" financial system can't sustain itself anymore, as the Elite lose more and more control? The different scenarios involving a global "reset" will be explored here.

Apparently, the global currency reset is going to manifest in two ways:

1. Reset in the value or importance of currencies

2. The current financial system is based on fiat money, which has no intrinsic value (Wikipedia https://en.wikipedia.org/wiki/Fiat money), created by loans and other kinds of credit. Debt actually creates money that doesn't exist, and it is called fiat money because it's not attached to anything of value like gold or other concrete assets. The money is being printed simply out of thin air according to the needs of the Cabal. Yes, you read this right.

There is an increasing number of countries, such as Hungary and Bolivia, that choose to free themselves (and their citizens) of this debt-slave system. They have cut all ties to an International financial institute, reclaiming their financial independence by rejecting the Cabal banking entities.[1]

This is how the new financial system operates in Bolivia: The financial system consists of the central bank which is a state-owned, in contrast with other countries (including Israel), and 51 privately-owned institutions. Thirteen of those 51 privately-owned institutions are commercial banks. The rest are loan and savings organizations, credit unions, and other financial institutions.[2] When more countries join this ban of Cabal banking entities, the financial system worldwide will collapse and need to be reset before it transitions into a new monetary system.

Most central banks are not financially independent institutions that belong to sovereign countries, which is evident from this list of Rothschild privately-owned-and-controlled central banks worldwide.[3] Syria is one of the few countries that is independent of this system; this may suggest why Russia is backing the current regime, and the Daesh, which is supported by the West (not openly), is doing the Cabal's bidding.

Is the Federal Reserve a Government-Controlled Institution?

The crux of this control in the U.S. is the Federal Reserve System. How does the Federal Reserve operate? How does it initiate the printing of money and the lowering or raising of interest rates? There are 12 Federal Reserve Banks, which act as the branches of this system.

According to Investopedia, the core functions of the Federal Reserve is:

- Supervising and examining state member banks.

- Lending to depository institutions to ensure liquidity in the financial system.
- Providing key financial services and serving as a bank for the U.S. Treasury.
- Examining financial institutions to ensure and enforce compliance with consumer protection and fair-lending laws." [4]

These reserve banks aren't government or state-owned by definition, but are semi-private/semi-government institutes. "The Reserve Banks are considered quasi-governmental—or legally private but functionally public—because they are owned by commercial banks in their region (e.g., banks that hold stock in their Federal Reserve Bank), but serve public goals." [4] You may ask how does it initiate the printing of money. Since the economy of the U.S., or other national economies, is not linked to a gold standard (or other resources), they create what is called fiat money. But who decides how much money to print?

"The U.S. Treasury decides to print money in the United States as it owns and operates printing presses. However, the Federal Reserve has control of the money supply through its power to create credit with interest rates and reserve requirements. Since credit is the largest component of the money supply by far, colloquially people talk about the Federal Reserve increasing the money supply as printing money." [5]

The question which intrigued me after studying this topic is whether the central banks can just tell the treasury (in the U.S.) to print more money. It was unclear. So I found information about this subject both in Israel and in the U.S. It seems that the central bank in Israel, Bank of Israel, controls the amount of money in the economy, but not only by printing the money (the notes and coins), which is only a fraction of the money in the economy. It lends savings to other people which creates new money this way. (https://www.ynet.co.il/articles/0,7340,L-4300174,00.html). I also explored the relationship between the Federal Reserve and the Treasury and printing money and here's what I found: The Federal Reserve is the one that "calls the shots" in regards to how much money is actually in circulation in the economy. It determines how much money is injected into the economy; not the Treasury. How does it do it?

"Money printed by the Treasury is distributed to the twelve Federal Reserve banks around the country. The treasury and the government of which it is a part does not have any say on how much money actually gets injected into the economy, as monetary policy decisions are left up to the Federal Reserve." (http://welkerswikinomics.com/blog/2010/08/28/why-cant-the-government-just-print-more-money-not-such-a-silly-question/)

"Central banks can increase the amount of money in circulation by simply printing it [explained above]. They can print as much money as they want, though there are consequences for doing so. Merely printing more money doesn't affect the output or production levels, so the money itself becomes less valuable." [6] But how do they control the amount of money in the economy? Here's an explanation by Investopedia:

"One of the basic methods used by all central banks to control the quantity of money in an economy is the reserve requirement. As a rule, central banks mandate depository institutions to keep a certain amount of funds in reserve against the amount of net transaction accounts. Thus [,] a certain amount is kept in reserve, and this does not enter circulation[…] When the central bank wants more money circulating into the economy, it can reduce the reserve requirement. This means the bank can lend out more money. If it wants to reduce the amount of money in the economy, it can increase the reserve requirement. This means that banks have less money to lend out and will thus be pickier about issuing loans."

(https://www.investopedia.com/articles/investing/053115/how-central-banks-control-supply-money.asp). The central banks print money without government oversight. According to Mark Koba from CNBC, "The Fed is an independent agency—which means it can make decisions on its own, without needing approval from any other branch of government." [7] The connection between the U.S. Treasury and the central bank is explained as: "The Department of the Treasury is also responsible for printing <u>currency</u> and minting coins[...] The Federal Reserve System was established in 1913. It serves as the <u>central bank</u> of the U.S., with a mandate to keep our money valuable and our <u>financial system</u> healthy. Its primary method of accomplishing this task is through its influence on <u>monetary policy</u>[...] The Federal Reserve serves as the government's banker, processing transactions, such as accepting electronic payments for <u>Social Security</u> taxes, issuing <u>payroll</u> checks to government employees and clearing checks for tax payments and other government <u>receivables</u>." [8]

Influencing the interest rates is not done directly, but it can push upward or lower interest rates by using certain tools like federal discount rates in the US: "The central bank holds the key to the policy rate—this is the rate at which commercial banks get to borrow from the central bank (in the United States, this is called the <u>federal discount rate</u>). When banks get to borrow from the central bank at a lower rate, they pass these savings on by reducing the cost of loans to its customers. Lower interest rates tend to increase borrowing, and this means the quantity of money in circulation increases." [6]

As I've noted, the Federal Reserve Banks are not United States Government institutions, and the system has been in dispute from the outset. "They are private monopolies which prey upon the people of these United States for the benefit of themselves and their foreign customers; foreign and domestic speculators and swindlers; and rich and predatory money lenders." – The Honorable Louis McFadden, Chairman of the House Banking and Currency Committee in the 1930s. [9]

It should be noted that Finance mogul J.P. Morgan bailed the government out of a financial crisis in 1895, making the government of the U.S. indebted to Wall Street bankers and leading to the creation of the Federal Reserve in 1913. "With the nation confronting another financial crisis in 1907, and the United States the only one of the world's major financial powers without a central bank, the nation was forced to turn to Wall Street. Finance mogul J.P. Morgan, who had bailed the government out of a financial crisis in 1895, organized private sector investments and lines of credit to stabilize the banking system amid its latest panic." [10], [11]

This is also the case in Israel, where it's very clear that the banks control the government because its largest political parties are indebted to the two largest banks in Israel, which are privately-owned banks. This is the reason why the reforms in the banking system are blocked in the Knesset (the Israeli parliament). The largest parties' debts to the banks in Israel are displayed here: http://rotter. net/forum/scoops1/180657.shtml.

The Worldwide Financial Reset

According to different analysts, we're about to experience a reset of the entire financial system, including a reset of different currencies. People talk about revaluation of currencies (abbreviated as "RV"), but it may be something else, like re-denomination of currencies. It's unclear yet how this "reset" would occur. **A revaluation would mean that the currencies of countries would be pegged to valuable resources like gold, silver, or even linked to GDP, while re-denomination refers to the USD becoming one of the "reserve" currencies and not the dominating one, as it is today.** There would be a "basket" of currencies, which the USD would be only one of them and not the leading currency. I think that the reset might be a mixed revaluation of currencies and re-denomination. The currencies of countries will be revalued according to their concrete assets, including such parameters as GDP, gold, but they would also be re-denominated of other world currencies and perhaps to a more equal status.

John Mauldin ("a visionary thinker, a noted financial expert, a *New York Times* best-selling author, a pioneering online commentator, and the publisher of one of the first publications to provide investors with free, unbiased information and guidance—*Thoughts from the Frontline*") [12] discusses this reset and says that this system will need to be restructured, as there's so much debt today and not enough money to cover it all:

"All that debt cannot be repaid under current arrangements, nor can those promises ultimately be kept. There is simply not enough money and not enough growth, and these bubbles are continuing to grow. At some point, we're going to have to deal with these issues and restructure everything[…] In my opinion, the entire world is entering what I call the Great Reset, a period of enormous and unpredictable volatility in all asset classes." [13] (This is a group of securities that exhibits similar characteristics, behaves similarly in the marketplace and is subject to the same laws and regulations. The three main **asset classes** are equities, or stocks; fixed income, or bonds; and cash equivalents, or money market instruments.)

Karen Hudes is the "World Bank whistleblower, who is a graduate of Yale Law School and worked in the legal department of the World Bank for more than 20 years. In fact, when she was fired for blowing the whistle on corruption inside the World Bank, she held the position of Senior Counsel." [14] She "worked as an attorney at the World Bank from 1986-2007." [15] She says that the US dollar is set to crash and will be replaced with a new, interest-free, gold-backed currency.

She further explains that the Federal Reserve holds gold or bonds (against their gold) in quadrillions which can be used to offset the debt of each country worldwide and use this gold to allow each country mint their own currency. It's not a one world currency. But there isn't agreement. [16] According to her, the criminal banking cartel will soon be history. She explains how the USA will file bankruptcy to bring down the Cabal in the near future. The banking cartel is going down together with the Federal Reserve note, but not the USD [17] [perhaps because the USD or USN – of the US Republic - would be gold-backed currency]. [18]

Gregg Prescott, M.S., who is the founder and editor of _In5D_ _says that,_ "For those with their ears to the ground, you already know about current systems where we can all live in abundance and prosperity without the need for money, including the Ubuntu system and the Venus Project. What Hudes is proposing would simply be a short-term transition until all forms of money are eliminated because as long as there is money, we're ALL financial slaves to a broken system." [19]

Prescott also speaks about a potential total financial shift in our world:

"It is important to understand that the death of the dollar is inevitable and it NEEDS to die in order for an asset backed currency to replace it. When this happens, there will likely be a complete forgiveness of all debt when the currency resets." [20] Jim Willie (A statistical analyst in marketing research and retail forecasting, who holds a PhD in Statistics) [21] also shares this view. And on March 27, 2017, he issued an alert on imminent global currency reset, which didn't happen, but it doesn't mean it's not going to occur at one time or another. "With China being betrayed by the US Govt and US Fed in concerted collusion. The attempt to reduce the US Dollar while maintaining ultra-low bond yields seems the final straw. The inference is made that the jig is up finally, and a significant turning point is upon us[...]EuroRaj, [an Indian financial analyst with two masters degrees and London and New York financial experience, who now manages a hedge fund in South Florida,] stated unequivocally that the Chinese do not consider the US Fed, the banker cabal, and the US Elite as honest business partners any longer. He expects their harsh clear revenge to follow, with the launch of the long awaited Global Currency RESET to come next[...] At least in the Eastern hemisphere, the US Dollar is about to be kicked to the curb, shunned in trade payment usage. The non-USD platforms will be given much greater emphasis. The game is about to change, to enter the extreme danger zone[...] The United States Govt cannot continue on numerous glaring fronts of gross negligence and major violations. These violations have prompted the BRICS & Alliance nations to hasten their development of diverse non-USD platforms toward the goal of displacing the US Dollar while at the same time to take steps toward the return of the Gold Standard." [22]

Willem Middelkoop, the founder of the Commodity Discovery Fund and the author of *The Big Reset,* which I will later quote[23], is yet another analyst who envisions a system reset to be imminent; even before 2020, which is only two years away from now (December 2017). The anchor of the current monetary system is the USD since the Second World War, and he sees that it would have to change, as the fiat money printing of USD for decades has caused a gradual but steady dollar devaluation. According to this writer, the USA has waged a secret war on gold since the 1960s in a desperate move to maintain this dollar system. Both China and Russia have been accumulating enormous amounts of gold since this time to position themselves for the next phase of the global financial system. [23]

He states that there are only two options: "A financial reset planned well in advance, or a hastily implemented one on the back of a dollar crisis. The United States, realizing the dollar will lose its prominent role, seems to be planning a monetary reset that will surprise many. It will be designed to keep the United States in the driving seat, but will include strong roles for the Euro and China's Renminbi. And it is likely gold will be reintroduced as one of the pillars of this next phase of the global financial system. Insiders claim gold could be revalued up to $7,000 per troy ounce during this process." [24] Today (December 29, 2017) the value of an ounce of gold is $1,295.03 according to https://goldprice.org/gold-price.html

What Is the Global Currency Reset?

Now that I've established that this "reset" is going to occur, the question raised is what is this "reset," or Global Currency Reset (GCR) that so many talk about it in different terms, from different perspective, which makes it very murky and confusing for someone like me who isn't such an expert on financial topics:

"Part of this belief system says that there is a coming overnight crash to the United States dollar. This crash will be felt on a global level and many currency values will change as a result. Many currencies will change in value or revalue once this event happens. Many people have purchased the Iraqi dinar and the Vietnamese Dong as an investment and as a way to protect themselves from this coming crash. Some believe that value will be transferred out of paper currencies and into assets like gold and silver. Some believe that the entire global economy will crash leading to a total collapse of society as we know it. Others believe that a set of laws will be implemented that will restructure the value of currencies all over the world." [24]

I suspiciously watched my friends buying and advising others to buy ZIM (the Zimbabwean currency) or Iraqi Dinar, among other "exotic" foreign currencies, and felt that this is a total investment scam intended to lure people into investing in these currencies worldwide. This was propagated as a means of survival in a world after such a collapse of the current financial system and currencies, which has become big business (these scams). However, I now don't believe this is a total scam but very unclear. This global currency reset may be more like a revaluation of currencies according to the state's resources, as it is explained here: "Every country will have its currency valued in real-time based on its resources. The resources considered in the valuation of a country's currency will be gold, silver, crude oil, natural gas, diamond mines, etc." [25]

I found this to be the best explanation of the global currency reset: "What exactly is the <u>GCR (Global Currency Reset)</u> all about? Essentially, it's the end of the United States Dollar as the world's reserve currency, and the beginning of a new monetary system led by a new currency, possibly the SDR." [26] (<u>Nick Giammarino</u>)

What Is True about this Potential Reset?

With so many contradicting perspectives on the global currency reset, it's difficult to decide what will transpire. In order to dispel the confusion, I found the following explanation by the editor of *The Event Chronicle*, "A daily alternative news blog for people interested in seeking truth and exploring alternate viewpoints not covered in the mainstream," which may clear up some of the confusion on this topic:

"The Global Currency Reset and the Revaluation are actually two different events. The Revaluation refers to the revaluation of Iraq's currency. The Global Currency Reset refers to a much broader revaluation of many currencies around the world. But in the public's mind they've become linked together. I'll be using the terms interchangeably here."[27]

There Are Several Types of "Reset"

The site Prepareforchangeleadership.org, which was created to support a peaceful movement for peaceful change during the planetary shift called "The Event", presents its view of the concept of "The Reset". According to this site, there are several scenarios of reset (financial system and global currency reset): bad, ugly and good. There's a distinction between Revaluation (of currencies) – not discussed here and re-denomination. (Prepareforchangeleadrship.org http://prepareforchangeleadership.org/home/)

Is it going to work? The answer is 'we don't know', as it has never been tried before on a global scale.

"There is only one absolute certainty at this point and that is the current system['s]... demolition[...] It would be crucial that all the awaken people, at this point in time, agree at least on this: that the current financial system **must go away, and start planning accordingly.** "[28]

The **bad reset** means that the entire financial system collapses, as those behind it won't be able to meet their obligations. Then "fiat bonds and derivatives are unable to be redeemed so that we, the people, can use cash (electronic and paper) and redeem the deposits." [28] Failing to redeem the deposits means that people would starve and be desperate. According to this site, some of the banks have to survive in order to implement the re-denomination of currencies. There are also planned prosperity and humanitarian funds to be wire transferred to specific accounts, which will make no sense if money becomes worthless in the near future. We may then see and will need to be suspicious if there is major devaluation in currencies in the "new financial system" that would benefit certain players showing that this "new system" is rigged as the current one.

"There are some real and founded concerns about this being just another 'New World Order' trick to re-boot the system, give us a slack for a certain period of time and drive everybody to ecstasy with a 'Global Debt Jubilee' for let's say 5 years, and then after micro chipping every being on this planet, ban cash all together, force everyone into using e-cash and then, SLOWLY (as usual), start banning basic freedoms and tell you where to put your money, giving special grants to their slavery and mass poisoning department. So IF the New System is **just a change to an asset backed system without a full and complete liberalization of the currency market I'll get really, really nervous**[...] Either it's a positive alliance white hat made 'for the people' financial transition or the remaining cabal factions that have been selected to lead Mr. Global 2.0 with nano-chipping and replicators[...] The system has to be asset backed and DECENTRALIZED because, if it's not asset backed it's FIAT and that seems to be the problem now, and decentralized because there's simply not enough GOLD out there to supply the needs of every trade in the world! Also multi-polar to secure the stability it needs to boost trade between nations. If it's decentralized and multi-polar it **SHOULD** be free." [28]

How you can distinguish between the bad, ugly and the good reset?

"It's very important that immediately after the Reset you start testing your local and national authorities' permissiveness towards the use of alternative exchange platforms[…] The way local or national authorities support or fight these emergent flows of trade may be an indicator of their agendas and possibly occult powers. P2P (peer-to-peer) IS the word you're looking for in this case." [28]

The **good reset** is one that has no central control for clearance, which is considered a good reset to create abundance. "Every process that bypasses a central control 'hub' for clearance is a good one for creating abundance[…] if you organize one (or more) of the following types of platforms you'll be creating abundance on your community:

1. Local Exchange Trading Systems – good links here http://www.transaction.net/money/letsor http://www.lets-linkup.com/080-All%20About%20LETS.htm
2. Create your own currency http://www.collective-evolution.com/2015/07/09/in-times-of-crisis-why-not-create-your-own-currency
3. Cryptocurrencies. There are several and plenty of info on the internet. Consider creating at least a virtual wallet!
4. Commercial Credit Circuits http://www.lietaer.com/images/C3_BAL_diagram.pdf%20%20
5. Collaborative consumption http://www.collaborative consumption.com and good old barter" [28]

What can we expect of such a **good reset**? From what I'm reading and what I feel is going to happen before we transition to the new financial system—which may already be active in the background—all debt is going to be cancelled worldwide, which will include state, corporate and private debt from interest loans. Debts without interest will not be cancelled. The old financial system controlled by the Cabal, which is a debt-based system, is going to collapse. According to COBRA, there will be a short period of time, up to two weeks, when the banks will be closed, with no withdrawal of money from ATMs or paying with credit cards (only paying with cash and possibly with cheques). This is why he constantly asks people to hold a cash reserve for two weeks of spending—to be ready for the time that it happens. After this period, the new system would be launched. According to Karen Hudes, there are sums of money available to pay the debts (but not to save the old system) and other sources like Ben Fulford that discuss this.

I'll explain this based on the US system. The money created by the Federal Reserve will be replaced by debt-free money, which is based on the "issuance of interest-free <u>credit</u> by a government-controlled and fully owned <u>central bank</u>. Such interest-free but repayable loans could be used for public infrastructure and productive private investment. This proposal seeks to avoid debt-free money causing inflation[…] Some governments have experimented in the past with debt-free government-created money independent of a bank. The American Colonies used the '<u>Colonial Scrip</u>' system prior to the <u>Revolution</u>, much to the praise of <u>Benjamin Franklin</u>. He believed it was the efforts of English bankers to revoke this government-issued money that caused the Revolution. <u>Abraham Lincoln</u> used interest-free money created by the government to help the Union win the <u>American Civil War</u>. He called these '<u>Greenbacks</u>' ("the greatest blessing the people of this republic ever had." <u>https://en.wikipedia.org/wiki/Monetary reform</u>). This debt-free money would be issued directly from the United States Treasury.

Dr. Richard Werner, a German economist who is a professor at the University of Southampton, who is a monetary and development economist, <u>https://en.wikipedia.org/wiki/Richard Werner</u>), discusses and perhaps suggests debt-free money which was used, "Nearly 1000 years ago Winchester in England was the centre of such a money creation system - debt free and interest free. The tally stick system was used. It expanded the money supply needed by government and it was without debt." [29] The second step, which may be the most beneficial step, is that all corporate, personal, and national debts will be permanently cancelled. For example, if you rent a home or an apartment, you will own it and the previous owner will receive financial compensation that is equal to the value that the tenant rents. The new monetary system would be debt-free, people-controlled system. The reason it has not happened yet (the current financial system has not collapsed yet) is that the alternative systems are currently being constructed. [30]

Why There Will Be a Reset (of all the financial system)?

Willem Middelkoop explains that despite failing again and again, "Universities worldwide still promote the ideas of the Chicago School of Economics. The tenet of the Chicago School is based on the creation of fiat money by central banks in collaboration with private banks[…]" (the book *The Big Reset* p. 11). "The current crisis – which could have been predicted on the basis of roughly 6,000 years of the documented history of money – contradicts the Keynesian doctrine of creating money out of thin air. Fiat money systems have been put to test more than 200 times, and they have all failed in the end. The likelihood of failure should now be considered a statistical certainty rather than a theoretical improbability[…] A similar reset took place with the start of the dollar system in 1944." [24]

The foresight of Thomas Jefferson, third President of America and drafter of the Declaration of Independence (1808), came true unfortunately, and today this happens in the U.S. Inc. As quoted from *The Grandest Deception* by Dr. Jack Pruett, "If the American people ever allow private banks to control the issue of their currency, first by inflation, then by deflation, the banks and the corporations which grow up around them will deprive the people of all property until their children wake up homeless on the continent their fathers conquered." [31]

"The truly unique power of a central bank, after all, is the power to create money, and ultimately the power to create is the power to destroy." (Paul Volcker, former Chairman of the Federal Reserve in the Forward of *The Central Banks* (1995). [32]

According to Willem Middelkoop, "(Central) bankers, the alchemists of our time, have a monopoly on the creation of money, just like the police and army have a monopoly on violence. In the last century, central bankers have succeeded in turning paper into gold and gold into paper [...] In the current banking system, central bankers often turn out to be lap dogs for private bankers instead of watch dogs." [24] (The book *The Big Reset* revised edition.) It's not surprising to see this as "Annually, the financial sector [in the US] spends about one million dollars per member of congress on financial lobbying." [33]

"According to the former Republican Congressman Ron Paul, the Federal Reserve is the chief culprit behind the current economic crisis. Because of its 'unchecked power to create endless amounts of money out of thin air', the Fed has caused one financial bubble after another. Paul also claims that by 'recklessly inflating the money supply, the Fed continues to distort interest rates and intentionally erodes the value of the dollar'. He calculates that the dollar has lost 'more than 96% of its value since the Fed's creation in 1913 [...]"[24] Bill Black, an associate professor of economics and law at the University of Missouri, Kansas City and the author of *The Best Way to Rob a Bank is to Own One*, sums it all in the book's title. Middelkoop further says in his book, "Black claims that 'the US administration refuses to investigate and prosecute the elite bank fraudsters'. According to Black, 500 FBI agents working on white-collar crime cases were transferred to national security tasks immediately after the 9/11 terrorist attacks." [24] The Cabal used this tragedy to shift focus away from their money manipulation to security issues, which paved the way for foreign wars that drained the treasury of trillions of dollars. It also served as a distraction and thwart any investigation.

The Department of Justice has started just a few dozen criminal investigations against Wall Street bankers since 2000. [34] But the only bankers sent to jail were those that had a conflict with one of the Wall Street banks, or were punished for insider trading on their own account[…] a US Attorney General, who was involved in many Wall Street criminal investigations, has suggested that pressure from the highest echelons was used to stop the prosecution of high-level bankers. "[…] A study of hundreds of media reports shows that the total amount of fines and settlements paid by the Wall Street banks between 2000 and 2013 to avoid prosecution, adds up to $100 billion." [24]

Here's a complete list of Wall Street CEOs prosecuted for their role in the crisis https://www.washingtonpost.com/news/wonk/wp/2013/09/12/this-is-a-complete-list-of-wall-street-ceos-prosecuted-for-their-role-in-the-financial-crisis/?utm_term=.a023836caed1

Debt-Slavery/Bondage System

From the above-mentioned book, Willem Middelkoop writes in a chapter rightly entitled *A Planet of Debt*: "The decline in interest rates after 1981 made it possible for governments to issue more debt. The same held true for companies and individuals. The period of unprecedented debt build-up lasted until the start of the current credit crisis[…] At some point in time, even governments have to get rid of their debts. This will happen either through inflation, debt defaults or debt cancellations. Such monetary resets have been the solution many times in the past. It could well happen again." Not only is debt a huge problem in the US, but in the EU too. "In the eighteen most important countries belonging to the OECD (the Organisation for Economic Co-operation and Development), the total amount of public and private debt (relative to GDP) grew from 160% in 1980 to 321% in 2011[…] National debt increased by 425% on average and have risen in many countries to almost 100% of their GDP"[24] Chinese citizens, as opposed to those of other countries, having savings in the billions unlike the rest of us. This is backed by

Forbes that says it's not only corporations that have a high rate of savings but also Chinese households which leads to China's current account surplus: "When national savings exceeds investment, the excess savings shows up in China's current account surplus." [35]

Middelkoop says further, "Why do you expect a Big Reset of the global financial system? [...] Two major problems in the world financial system have to be addressed: 1) the demise of the US dollar as the world's reserve currency, and 2) the almost uncontrollable growth in debts and in the central banks' balance sheets[...] In theory, all debts worldwide could be wiped out on a Sunday afternoon. We could start from scratch with a new balance sheet the next morning. If every citizen in the world was to be credited with let's say 1,000 newly designed Bancors [36], which would be accepted by all banks and businesses, we could start anew in an instant. We could even write off mortgages and nationalize all real estate, and have a system whereby we pay rent to the state. These kind of scenarios are hard to comprehend, but when the need is highest, solutions can become very creative[...] It is therefore much more logical to expect an outcome for our reset to range somewhere between 1 and 256. Some debts will be cancelled. Some parts of the financial system will be nationalized, as we have seen happening with banks and other financial institutions since 2008." [24]

In a book review of Middelkoop's book, Valentin Schmid says, "It is my belief that, well before 2020, the global financial system will need to be rebooted to a new paradigm in which gold will play a larger role[...] Like many other researchers who don't have the academic blinders of economists, Middelkoop criticizes the Federal Reserve (Fed) for its quantitative easing programs and criticizes commercial banks for their addiction to credit, misallocation of capital, and corruption. An appendix lists all fines paid by U.S. banks from 2000 to 2014. The total is $135 billion[...] We could even write off all mortgages and nationalize all real estate, and have a system whereby we pay rent to the state. These kind of scenarios are hard to comprehend, but when the need is highest, solutions can become very creative. It could be the end of private real estate ownership[...] A better one would be the ancient <u>debt</u> jubilee where all debts would just be written off every 15 years or so and the system reset, which may be preferable for the majority." [37]

What Would Be the New Banking System?

There's very little information about the alternative financial system in general. However, COBRA (the contactee of the Resistance Movement, whose covert name is the abbreviation of Compression Breakthrough) mentioned in one of his reports that the AIIB, (which stands for the Asian Infrastructure Investment Bank (https://www.aiib.org/en/index.html) and quoted from its site it's "a multilateral development bank with a mission to improve social and economic outcomes in Asia and beyond. Headquartered in Beijing, we commenced operations in January 2016 and have now grown to 84 approved members from around the world." [38], will serve as the platform for the new financial system. [39] (I have reservations about this system, which is based in Beijing. As we know, the Chinese government oversees all businesses in China, which would make me wonder if we wouldn't be changing a U.S. to a Chinese government-control financial system.)

I started to look for more information on this on the AIIB site and found that "[AIIB] is a new multilateral financial institution founded to bring countries together to address the daunting infrastructure." [40]

Other sources like Damien Lee, an author passionate about market fluctuations, macro trends and the intricate global economy and who writes for *Market Mogul*, speculates that the AIIB may replace the IMF and the World Bank[41], but he doesn't give a conclusive answer to this question. He just shares the concerns of those who may be losing to this bank... But there's no such intention on the surface that the AIIB would compete such financial institutions as the IMF:

"While some regard the AIIB as a rival of the IMF and the World Bank, many others have asserted that the newly formed bank does not make current supranational financial institutions irrelevant nor redundant." [42]

On the other hand, it seems that the AIIB together with the New Development Bank (NDB) (https://www.ndb.int/) are breaking the monopoly of the IMF and the World Bank in lending money to countries in Asia by offering a viable alternative to them and countries elsewhere.

"The establishment of the BRICS New Development Bank, an emergency reserve fund, and the AIIB will break the monopoly position of the International Money Fund (IMF) and the World Bank (WB)," said the article written by Liu Zengyi, research fellow of Shanghai Institutes for International Studies." [43] The attitudes towards privately-owned banks which create money by government-owned institutions and the old privately-owned central banks also shift.

"In Europe, Miguel Angel Fernandez Ordones, the former Governor of Spain's Central Bank, told Parliament on November 7th that replacing monetary creation by privately-owned banks with money created by a government-owned institution would be a good thing." [44]

This sort of public commentary by officials who are in actual power over money is a visible sign that the old privately-owned central bank control grid is crumbling. Pentagon sources are also saying that, "Regime change is no longer a U.S. province, as the military coup in Zimbabwe happened after the army chief went to China, and it is needed to position the asset-backed Zimbabwe dollar as Africa's reserve currency prior to the global currency reset." [44]

While this is an overview of the coming "financial reset," it is rather difficult to say exactly what will happened, but the current system is corrupt and failing, and what replaces it can't be any worse. Personally, what I get from this research is that the problem has been the printing of fiat money not based on tangible assets like gold, and that the best way to "hedge our bet," as it were, whatever system will replace it, is to invest our money in tangible assets like property or gold and silver and not stocks and bonds and such intangibles. But, that's just my opinion. Follow these links and decide on your own.

FOOTNOTES

1 http://www.neonnettle.com/features/624-bolivia-announces-complete-ban-on-rothschild-owned-banks

2 https://www.export.gov/article?id=Bolivia-Banking-Systems

3 https://yournewswire.com/complete-list-of-rothschild-owned-and-controlled-banks/

4 https://www.investopedia.com/university/thefed/fed1.asp

5 https://www.investopedia.com/ask/answers/082515/who-decides-when-print-money-us.asp

6 https://www.investopedia.com/articles/investing/053115/how-central-banks-control-supply-money.asp

7 https://www.cnbc.com/id/43752521

8 https://www.investopedia.com/articles/economics/08/treasury-fed-reserve.asp

9 https://www.globalresearch.ca/who-owns-the-federal-reserve/10489

10 https://www.federalreservehistory.org/essays/federal_reserve_act_signed

11 Psychotherapy As Life Really Mattered by Christopher Alan Anderson

https://books.google.co.il/books?id=A8eNZu3Ebk0C&pg=PT44&lpg=PT44&dq=the+creation+of+the+Federal+Reserve+was+one+of+the+first+moves+to+control+the+governments&source=bl&ots=uJOegflVei&sig=mzhCgvAs918LEWvxelu8q3Hl2lw&hl=iw&sa=X&ved=0ahUKEwii-aes2K3YAhWCLlAKHa_hByIQ6AEIVTAG#v=onepage&q=the%20creation%20of%20the%20Federal%20Reserve%20was%20one%20of%20the%20first%20moves%20to%20control%20the%20governments&f=false

12 http://www.mauldineconomics.com/about-us/john-mauldin

13 http://www.thebigresetblog.com/index.php/john-mauldin-we-are-coming-to-a-period-i-call-the-great-reset/

14 https://www.globalresearch.ca/world-bank-whistleblower-reveals-how-the-global-elite-rule-the-world/5353130

[15] http://kahudes.net/about-us/

[16] About the Global Currency Reset by Karen Hudes https://www.youtube.com/watch?time_continue=1997&v=Jc0Z_eAVjzc

[17] http://themillenniumreport.com/2016/07/new-u-s-currency-already-in-our-money-supply/

[18] https://www.youtube.com/watch?v=sIepFcIrkco

[19] http://in5d.com/karen-hudes-dollar-to-crash/

[20] http://in5d.com/when-the-dollar-dies/

[21] http://www.gold-eagle.com/authors/jim-willie

[22] https://www.silverdoctors.com/gold/gold-news/jim-willie-issues-alert-dollar-collapse-gold-and-silver-price-spike-were-at-the-door-of-the-global-currency-reset/

[23] http://www.willem-middelkoop.nl/en/

[24] The Big Reset Revised Edition: War on Gold and the Financial Endgame by Willem Middelkoop https://www.amazon.com/Big-Reset-Revised-Financial-Endgame-ebook/dp/B01DA3JXZG

[25] http://understandcontractlawandyouwin.com/global-currency-reset/

[26] http://globalcurrencyreset.net/what-is-the-global-currency-reset/

[27] http://www.theeventchronicle.com/the-event/what-is-the-global-currency-reset/#

[28] https://prepareforchange.net/financial/financial-reset-the-good-the-bad-and-the-ugly/

[29] Richard Werner: Debt Free & Interest Free Money https://www.youtube.com/watch?v=zIkk7AfYymg

[30] http://www.c-truth-b-free.com/k-global-financial-reset.html

[31] The Grandest Deception by Dr. Jack Pruett https://www.amazon.com/Grandest-Deception-Dr-Jack-Pruett/dp/1456892789

[32] Welton, Ken, *CAP-COM the Economics of Balance: Capitalism and Communalism in the Unfranchised Society*, Dana Point, Pandit Press, August 1, 2001. https://www.amazon.com/

CAP-COM-Economics-Balance-Kent-Welton/dp/0614149436/
ref=sr_1_9?ie=UTF8&s=books&qid=1272910630&sr=1-9
[33] https://www.publicintegrity.org/2010/05/21/2670/
five-lobbyists-each-member-congress-financial-reforms
[34] http://neweconomicperspectives.org/2013/08/mueller-i-crippled-
fbi-effort-v-white-collar-crime-my-successor-will-make-it-worse.
html
[35] https://www.forbes.com/2010/02/02/china-saving-marriage-
markets-economy-trade.html
[36] https://en.wikipedia.org/wiki/Bancor
[37] https://www.theepochtimes.com/understanding-the-financial-
system_2106511.html
[38] https://www.aiib.org/en/about-aiib/
[39] http://www.stillnessinthestorm.com/2016/01/cobra-short-
situation-update-system.html
[40] https://www.aiib.org/en/index.html
[41] https://themarketmogul.com/author/lee/
[42] https://themarketmogul.com/could-the-asian-aiib-replace-the-imf/
[43] https://economictimes.indiatimes.com/news/international/
business/brics-bank-aiib-to-break-imf-world-bank-monopoly-
china-think-tank/articleshow/48053695.cms
[44] https://foreverunlimited.wordpress.com/2017/11/25/benjamin-
fulford-khazarian-cabal-purge-accelerates-marines-storm-
cia-hq-over-2000-indicted-in-u-s-collapse-of-control-grid-in-
europe/

REFERENCES

1. http://www.thebigresetblog.com/

2. http://www.mauldineconomics.com/about-us/john-mauldin#

3. https://www.facebook.com/theglobalcurrencyreset/

4. http://globalcurrencyreset.net/

5. https://www.theepochtimes.com/back-to-square-one-why-the-financial-system-needs-to-reset_2127853.html

6. https://www.newdawnmagazine.com/articles/the-money-masters-behind-the-global-debt-crisis

7. http://en.granma.cu/mundo/2017-03-06/the-asian-bank-competing-with-the-imf

8. https://www.americanprogress.org/issues/security/reports/2015/09/22/121668/chinas-new-international-financing-institutions/

9. http://theeconomiccollapseblog.com/archives/world-bank-whistleblower-karen-hudes-reveals-how-the-global-elite-rule-the-world

10. http://www.zerohedge.com/news/2017-05-25/new-financial-system-being-born11. http://positivemoney.org/2017/12/ex-governor-bank-spain/

12. The Big Reset: War on Gold and the Financial Endgame by Willem Middelkoop January 15, 2014

https://www.amazon.com/gp/product/9089645993/ref=as_li_ss_tl?ie=UTF8&camp=1789&creative=390957&creativeASIN=9089645993&linkCode=as2&tag=minidrevie-20

CHAPTER EIGHT

COPING WITH THE AWAKENING TO THE TRUTH

The information that I've shared so far is rather disturbing. I know, and I feel for you. As I went through this same process of "awakening" to our true reality for over four years, I had to deal with my own emotional reactions and at times clinical depression over these revelations. However, my readers have had to "digest" these dark insights over a much shorter period of time, and I feel that I now have to provide support on how to deal with the shock and trauma. In this chapter, I'll share the many modalities that helped me gain my balance and cope with this devastating information, as well as others by experts in the trauma recovery field. I had days that I've been so numb with shock and pain that I woke up during the night and cried because I felt so hopeless about doing anything to reverse these trends. I've picked up many tools that I used to help me cope with this shock and hope they will be of help to you. Just choose the tools that resonate with you.

Physical Modalities that Helped Me Balance

As I said in my introduction, these are pointers on how to adapt to the changes both spiritually and physically, like grounding yourself by walking barefoot on the beach or on a grass lawn to discharge the static buildup of electricity—especially before you go to bed. Dr. Mercola says in the documentary *Ground to Earth*: "I'm grounded 95% of the day!" What's also helpful is sunbathing, daily exercise, and meditating twice a day. Eating cilantro and wheatgrass, and taking natural dietary supplements like spirulina and chlorella to remove the toxins from the body can be beneficial. Probably the most important supplement is large doses of antioxidants, since stress produces huge amounts of free radicals, and this may help the body cope with these effects. "A balance between free radicals and antioxidants is necessary for proper physiological function. If free radicals overwhelm the body's ability to regulate them, a condition known as oxidative stress ensues. Free radicals thus adversely alter lipids, proteins, and DNA and trigger a number of human diseases. Hence application of external source of antioxidants can assist in coping this oxidative stress."[1]

While vitamins C and E are touted as free radicals' scavengers, Dr. Patrick Flanagan back in the 1990s developed Microhydrin, which is fused hydrogen atoms with silica for time release, and is many times more powerful and any other supplement. A 500 mg capsule of his "Hydrogen Boost," once sold by Source Natural, had the antioxidant power of 10,000 glasses of orange juice. (Currently this formula can be found in Dr. Flanagan's Mega Hydrate by Phi Sciences.) Dr. Richard Lippman, who invented the nicotine patch and who was nominated for the Nobel Prize in Medicine in 1996 for his research on antioxidants, says that 2 to 6 percent of the oxygen we breathe turns into free radicals, which are "a thousand times more destructive living to living tissue than cyanide." Lippman was able to secure a U.S. patent, the first and only, on a proven "anti-aging" formula, for his antioxidant ACF228.

Sometimes I just chilled out, distanced myself from my research for a couple of days, walked on the beach, and then at home burned incense and lit candles to just calm down and release some of the pain that I felt. Nature has the vibrations that balance our body and will release the build of tension from too much emotional or mental fixation. Hiking in a forest or even driving along a coastal road will do wonders for you.

Victor Oddo provides good modalities in this video[2] for dealing with the awakening symptoms and the challenges you may have experienced while reading this book. Good practices which he shares include filling "our own cup," by giving to yourself first before helping or giving to others. He uses the oxygen mask analogy that on an airplane you're advised that you first put on the oxygen mask before helping others wear it; "otherwise, you suffocate and you're good to nobody." You'll definitely be unable to help others in the same state of trauma, numbness, and pain if you don't help yourself first. He suggests—choose whatever resonates with you—Epsom salts baths, listening to your favorite soothing music, lighting some candles and incense and my favorite, just chilling out. This way you'll have more energy for yourself and more to give to others. You can meditate every day, sitting meditation or active one-focus mindfulness out in the world. Do you like Reiki? Massage? Yoga? Watch less TV or listen less to the news (both on the radio and reading newspapers). [2]

Avoid Stress & Socialize with Like-minded People

I found some remedies of how you can deal with the trauma and disbelief while viewing this video[2]: minimize media exposure from television, newspapers, and the Internet. Accept and process your angry feelings from being duped all these years, and challenge your sense of isolation and helplessness by reaching out to other people in the same situation. There are many groups related to the awakening process on Facebook and YouTube. Just making a move in this direction can make you feel supported and less helpless. Get going on your recovery program and don't just "file away" these suggestions. I've found that exercising for 30 minutes each day (three 10-minute spurts of exercise are just as good) revitalizes me, dancing with friends in homes not nightclubs, eating out at health food restaurants, and attending uplifting and inspirational movies were lifesavers. Personally, I walk for 30 minutes before breakfast while listening to dance music with my mp3 and sometimes I walk, dance, and skip and entertain my neighbors at the same time which makes me feel better making someone smile or laugh. One neighbor started imitating me while I was walking and dancing and it cracked me up, which is great to change your low vibrational depressed mood. One more tip is to "make stress reduction a priority [...] simply take 60 breaths, focusing your attention on each out breath." [3]

Other helpful coping strategies is having a massage regularly, use a diffuser to fill the air in your house with essential oils or apply them to hot baths. I have a friend who has dealt with a lot of emotional upsets in his life but does forty minutes of yoga every night and sleeps like a baby. Either way, getting eight hours of sleep every night is essential. (I'll come back to yoga and talk about meditation later in the chapter.) Avoid overdosing with stimulants like caffeine, nicotine, or sugar, or worse alcohol or drugs, hug those you love, including pets[4] and yourself. If you don't have a pet, get one. Their natural non-mental energy can be very soothing. As a substitute, I'm feeding the stray cats on my street and pet them daily. If you like writing, write in your journal or share with others on a personal blog.

It's most important that you accept your upset feelings and the fact that your wish to isolate yourself at first. It's most important that you don't judge, blame, or ridicule yourself for whatever reaction you have. Another way of coping with this turmoil is to live in the moment, not the past or future, and not get caught up in your head with recriminations or fear, which Eckhart Tolle suggests in his extraordinary books *The Power of Now* and *The New Earth*. Another resource is Mary NurrieStearns' yoga books on coping with emotional trauma and her personal life story of how yoga helped her rise from her life crumbling down and saw her through the phase of "death" of her old self and nurturing the new self. An amazing book with lots of recovery and consciousness-raising techniques is John Nelson's *A Guide to Energetic Healing*. He shows how to use "recapitulation" to break the energy cords to past and present trauma (denial of any kind brings up past history), as featured in one of my favorite magazines *New Dawn*, which also ran an excerpt from this book in their special February, 2018 issue.

"E[c]khart Tolle's book on tape, *The Power of Now* became my lifeline. I listened to him feverish during my work commute. I took in his message of being here now, in the present moment. 'Being here now' became my motto. I could only manage taking each moment as it came. Any movement of thought into the future brought great emotional suffering. I soaked in his words. They felt like they kept me alive and instant by instant I made it th[r]ough the day. Anxiety ceased. Mourning began." [5] I've mentioned Mary NurrieStearns, especially her book *Personal Living: The Process of Personal Transformation,* as my awakening process resembles this pattern in many ways. While she is referencing more of a spiritual transformation, those of us dealing with denial of any kind will resonate to her insights. When I started awakening to the "Big Lie" I'd been fed all my life, I felt that I wanted to share my insights with as many people as possible. But then I found that most people do not want to be awakened to the truth of such a massive cover-up. It's too difficult to digest, too far off from anything that they have been taught, so it's easier to deny anything else and ridicule the other person—perhaps hoping that the truth would disappear along with the person sharing this information. Then I started isolating myself, even from my best friends who didn't accept any of this scenario and ridiculed what I had to say. I felt very alone and this is perfect description of how I felt in all this situation:

"The truth of the matter is that most people who say they want awakening don't actually want to awaken. They want their version of awakening. What they actually want is to be really happy in their dream state. And that's okay, if that's as far as they've evolved. But the real, sincere impulse toward enlightenment is something that goes far beyond the desire to make our dream state better. It is an impulse that is willing to subject itself to whatever is needed in order to wake up. The authentic impulse toward enlightenment is that internal prayer asking for whatever it is that will bring us to a full awakening, no matter whether it turns out to be wonderful or terrible. It is an impulse that puts no conditions on what we have to go through[…] This authentic impulse can be a bit frightening, because when you feel it, you know it is real. When you have let go of all conditions - when you have let go of how you want your own awakening to be and what you want the journey to be like - you have let go of your illusion of control."[6]

"Enlightenment is a destructive process. It has nothing to do with becoming better or being happier. Enlightenment is the crumbling away of untruth. It's seeing through the facade of pretense. It's the complete eradication of everything we imagined to be true." [7]

"In my experience, everyone will say they want to discover the Truth, right up until they realize that the Truth will rob them of their deepest held ideas, beliefs, hopes, and dreams. The freedom of enlightenment means much more than the experience of love and peace. It means discovering a Truth that will turn your view of self and life upside-down. For one who is truly ready, this will be unimaginably liberating. But for one who is still clinging in any way, this will be extremely challenging indeed. How does one know if they are ready? One is ready when they are willing to be absolutely consumed, when they are willing to be fuel for a fire without end."[8] (from his book, *The End of Your World: Uncensored Straight Talk on the Nature of Enlightenment* by Adyashanti [9]). His name means "primordial peace" in Sanskrit; Adyashanti is an American spiritual author and teacher from the <u>San Francisco Bay Area</u>. He offers online courses, talks, and retreats in the United States and abroad, and is the author of numerous books, including *The End of Your World* [10]

If you feel alone because you resonate with the information presented in this book and even tried to speak about it with family members, friends, and acquaintances, please know that you're not alone and that your very being can actually facilitate this change and provide support when the shift actually occurs. You're valuable by being you! Please bear this in your mind. And here's a wonderful message that helped me see my "awkwardness" and dancing to a different drum beat is actually good for this world and happened just in time: *7 Things The Universe Would Tell You* By Dr Dain Heer. [11]

His message is very empowering, especially if you feel "weird" while or after reading this book and try to share your insights with the world. This is what he says in this video: 1. "You my friend are a sleeping giant [which is what Tony Robbins says in his book *Awaken the Giant Within*], [and] you're far greater than you think you are. There's so much more to you than you realize and maybe it will give you the faith, the hope, the awareness, the strength, if you will, to actually carry on because there is truly something great about you." He explains that you didn't or don't see this truth because this is how our system is built. We're designed to go to the lowest, dumb-downed common denominator. Nobody talked to you about your greatest or challenged you. This keeps you thinking that you're smaller than you are (or more awkward). So, you don't become as great as you can become, and other people that you may share this information may turn their backs on you. It happened to me and I continue to experience this. 2. You've done a terrific job with the tools available to you. There are more tools to help you accept yourself as you are. You are courageous, you haven't given up! That's the greatest gift that you can give yourself. Trust yourself, your feelings, your intuition. Something that really gave me strength, and with which I resonate with so much to are these words (in his video): "Every time you don't fit in, that's [your] gift." What he means is that you might feel awkward for not fitting in or being different from what your family and friends want you to be—we're all "the black sheep" of the family. Your willingness to see a different world and different possibilities from everybody else is your gift. Look at those people who inspire you and others. Are they like everyone else? Think about this: "We need more people who hear a different drummer[,] that dance to a different beat and not be constrained by the limitations that everyone finds so valuable [...] This difference that you've been making yourself wrong all your life [...] is your greatest gift to offer the world and if you actually allow yourself to have the willingness, the vulnerability, and the courage of choosing it, your world will become greater and our world become[s] greater."

Bear this in mind: "You have a whole new reality to discover and create! [...] It's different, just like you [...] Head in the direction of your reality[,]"[11] a reality that would inspire you, that would be joyful to you. "When you're truly being you, you are so amazing that if you were willing to see it, it would blow you away!" [11] Allowing yourself to be you, you will feel that you're extending your own space which will make you more joyful, despite the hard information you've received here. Remember, "You are crucial for the future of the world[;] there are things that only you know[...]" When you decide to be you, the world will change. Yes, you're that crucial. Lisa Nichols says that some gifts come wrapped up in sandpaper. Well, my gifts (and this awakening too) definitely came to me wrapped up in sandpaper. So, if you're anything like me, please allow yourself to be who you are with all your unique knowing and skills. And you're not alone. "There are others like us out there that desire the same peaceful, kind, contributory world that has a generosity of spirit to it, that has an innate kindness to it, and gentleness to it. You're not alone [...] please find other people like you that are the seekers of the world, that desire something different. It's time on our planet and in your life for things to change." [11]

I understand what he is saying. When you have this awakening, you want to bring as many people into their best selves as possible. As a group, that's our goal. The only "agenda" is to help people rediscover the wonderful "you" that is inside of them. You are reading this book for a very good reason. Actually, this book picked you out. (Things that resonate at the same vibration attract each other. It's basic physics, even if it sounds strange.) Your personal reaction and unique perspective, even the pain and shock that you may experience while reading this book, may be the catalyst that triggers awareness in others even if you don't speak with them. Your being is needed! You're one of the "hundredth" monkeys whose consciousness will subliminally educate others.

How to Cope with these Disclosures: Emotional Support

One of my favorite integrating techniques from Nelson's *A Guide to Energetic Healing* is the body-therapy of *focusing*. "What body workers will tell you, or you know if you've been practicing a body discipline like yoga or tai chi or even martial arts, is that the body has its own intelligence, which expresses itself in various ways, such as instinctual reactions that may account for the lightening quick actions and responses of martial arts experts [...] The human body is an amazing instrument in many ways with all the millions of cellular processes happening every second to oxygenate the blood, remove waste materials, build or replace cells and tissues, and at the micro DNA level synthesize hormones and enzymes responsible for much of the body's building and repair work. Now, as part of this ensemble, the energetic bodies [spiritual layers around the physical body] can coordinate with the physical body to release emotional blocks and to absorb and integrate the energy discharged. Dr. Eugene Gendlin was a psychiatrist who realized that only a small percentage of his patients were experiencing real psychological transformation and that they were all doing something similar. When feelings arose from the recall of past trauma, they didn't just think about its import, they focused on their feelings, let the feelings settle and didn't turn away from them and hide out in the mind. Eventually the body would shift the energy of those feelings and integrate them, to the patient's great relief [...]

"I bring this up here because while you may be undergoing an extensive period of [trauma recovery], the process will arouse your emotions even as you release the energy of particular experiences [like reading this book], and you need to deal with this heightened emotional atmosphere. What Gendlin also discovered is that after

195

your body shifts the feelings that arise over a present situation, you can ask yourself what underlies that emotional outburst or nuance, or may have precipitated it, and feel your way through what comes up until that shifts as well. I've gone down as many as twenty levels from something bothering me in the present to an experience that happened in my childhood." For instruction on this technique, read Gendlin's book *Focusing*, or go to his YouTube video and let him walk you through it. https://www.youtube.com/watch?v=j7PEC5Mh5FY

When I have been devastated by these revelations, I allowed myself to rest more, even take short naps during the day, which is very unusual for me, the "busy bee," as my closest friends call me. What also helped me a lot was listening to meditation music and beneficial tones at 432 & 528 hertz. (Most modern music is recorded at 440 hertz, which is not harmonious to the human body. You can read more here http://www.collective-evolution.com/2013/12/21/heres-why-you-should-convert-your-music-to-432hz/). Eating food that you feel is good for you, but realize that we're all different so we need different foods and different nutrition. I'm doing my utmost to eat as healthy as possible to sustain myself—especially during this stressful period of time with its shattering exposures, but sometimes I allow myself to have some comfort food (though not on a regular basis). You can use various modalities like **Ho'oponopono**, the Hawaiian practice of reconciliation and forgiveness, joining discussion groups on disclosures, or those focused on spiritual awakening. There is a resistance movement where you can find people that support each other during these challenging (historical) times. There are lots of videos that I listened, some of which say that you "are here" because you resonate with these contents and by sharing these feelings and experiences you feel less awkward and alone. You may also need a lot of time to be alone, as I do, and so if you work outside home as most people do, take short breaks, long lunches. Weekend excursion into the country is also very beneficial, leaving the city vibe behind you for a couple days.

I wanted to share with you coping strategies of other people who have experienced this process, and I got a wonderful response from one of the administrators of The Resistance Movement on Facebook that you may resonate with: "Well, at first I hid from it, I ran from it. Of course, that led to more darkness and anger. For me mindfulness was and is the key. I am a warrior by nature, and it is imperative that I act, so I began to act. Through this action I had to examine, re-examine and adjust; it was a truly maddening process. However, a day came when I realized that sometimes the truest form of control is giving up control, so I surrendered. On that day I began to truly learn to listen to things that are beyond my ability to reason and sometimes understand. While being who I am and being in control of the things I should control, I have learnt to allow things into my life and allow a flow of energy that is in harmony with creation. I still struggle at times, and I know this is my own limitation and my own emotional blockage. Awakening for me has been a process, not a moment. I no longer long to cope, I long to be." Steve Allen Hornback, retired US Army (He has been on a spiritual path his entire adult life and has researched this type of information for fourteen years).

Mental Support

During my awakening process (still ongoing) when my spirits were low because of so many worries and anxieties and financial hardships, I would remind myself of that Neale Donald Walsch and Eckhart Tolle, who are both best-selling authors and spiritual teachers, were homeless (Neale for 1 year and Eckhart for 2 years) and what happened to them afterwards. Eckhart Tolle had a type of instantaneous awakening into a state of joyful beingness, despite the harsh physical conditions he was experiencing as a homeless man in London. When asked at the time what he was doing, he answered that it's not about doing, but "it is more a state of being." He describes his spiritual awakening (which helped him cope with his negative experiences) in these words: "On that night there was a disidentification from this unpleasant dream of thinking and the painful emotions. The nightmare became unbearable and that triggered the separation of consciousness from its identification with form. I woke up and suddenly realized myself as the I Am and that was deeply peaceful." [12]

Neale Donald Walsch on the other hand didn't awaken "over night" and experienced all the range of emotions that you and I might experience in a long-term process. "Walsch, in the early 1990s, lost his health, his job and his marriage. Homeless at age 49, he relied on the kindness of people he met on the street." However, what changed everything for him was a spiritual breakthrough: "In February 1992, Walsch had a mystical experience that set his life on an extraordinary new path. That experience became the basis for his bestselling *Conversations with God* series, which established him as an international leader in the New Spirituality [...] To deal with the enormous response to his writings, Walsch created the Conversations with God Foundation, a non-profit educational organization dedicated to inspiring humanity to move from violence to peace, from confusion to clarity and from anger to love.

"Walsch is viewed as one of the world's leading authorities on change — not only on how to cope with it, but also on how to harness its life-changing power for good." [13, 14]

Walsch was confused and angry about what life has given him. You can see this in the movie based on his book, *Conversations with God*, that "he remains troubled and confused by what life has dealt him. One night, alone, angry and reeling at <u>God</u>, he hears his own voice speaking to him. 'Are you ready to talk?' The voice identifies itself as God. Confused and questioning his sanity, Walsch picks up a pen and records everything he hears. After filling multiple notepads, the words begin to <u>inspire</u> him and he realizes he has the material for a book – maybe more than one book. He is right." [15]

During my awakening process, I had to compassionately look at other people going through similar experiences and having an even tougher time than me because, as I kept reminding myself, I had lots of support from my parents who sent money, bought me clothes, and sent food. They helped me in so many ways. I was never left alone like most others. I was and still am so lucky and grateful for their material support, and I'm also grateful for my closest friends who stuck by me. This support system gave me so much hope. People who start this awakening process often join groups such as the Resistance Movement where they can talk and support each other during these challenging times, especially when few of our acquaintances could understand us.

While we may feel sad about Tolle and Walsch's periods of homelessness, it was during these times, "when the world is not too much with [them]," that they were able to examine their mental process, or what we call the monkey-mind. Those of us in the world usually get too caught up in our dramas to actually examine the emotional-laden content of minds on a daily basis. Meditation helps with that, but what really struck me in one of Tolle's books is him sitting on a park bench and just watching the world go by. What's helpful about "mindfulness" exercises is that you do it in the world and not while you're separate from it. A useful technique is wear a watch, or use your cell phone's clock (or the clock on your computer), to stop for 30 seconds at the top of every hour and just listen to what' going on in your mind. You'll be amazed. And as you watch it, you activate what's called in esoteric philosophy the "Watcher." (Similar to the "observer" in the movie *What the Bleep Do We Know*.) This is based on the concept that if you can watch the mind and its ramblings, then you're not the mind but what watches it. Nelson tells a funny story in his book about an author who programmed her runner's watch to beep every 10 minutes so she could "watch" what she was thinking. He tried it but couldn't hear the faint beeps go off.

Physical Support

I know that every culture is different, but hugging a real friend or someone who really loves you, can help relieve the tension and soothe you. I know it helped me during the worst of times and still helps (my holistic healer gives wonderful hugs). Hugging over 20 seconds helps release the neurotransmitter Oxytocin. Read about why this hormone is so helpful for you during the awakening or consciousness shift which is what should happen to you while reading this book and researching these topics (http://www. collective-evolution.com/2015/12/03/the-chemistry-of-hugging-11-benefits-of-hugging/). Physical contact with friends and lovers is another way to release the build-up of tension in the body.

But probably one of the best body/mind techniques is the ancient practice of yoga in all its varied forms. It's like hugging yourself as you stretch and twist your body and stop your mental chatter. To quote Nelson again, "While yoga has become a worldwide fad, its roots go back thousands of years in India. Its original meaning is to 'yoke' the body and mind, or realize that pure consciousness *(purusha)* is separate from matter *(prakrti)*, which includes our minds and their thoughts, and yoga helps to purify the lower half of this equation so pure consciousness can express itself through the vehicle of our minds and bodies. The practice was meant to help liberate oneself from our attachments, whether they be our pleasures or pain, but that starts, or at least it did for me and others seeking relief, with the physical asanas."

For most beginners, as many yoga sites will tell you, Hatha Yoga with its many physical asanas is the starting point to explore this practice. I learned a few postures from a masseuse to help my back pain and continue to do them on a daily basis, mostly in the morning to limber up my body. But, as Nelson has noted in his book, for those in recovery from substance abuse (or their reaction to these revelations), it's important to realize that while you may jump into emotional clearing exercises, that you need to approach the physical side of yoga slowly and by all means take classes and don't try to do this on your own. This is especially true for those older than thirty: our bodies have accumulated lots of toxins—the reason they're so stiff—and you need to gradually work out these kinks.

Nelson recommends an excellent book for those in recovery (aren't we all): Kyczy Hawk's *Yoga and the Twelve-Step Path*. While it's mainly written for those in 12-step programs, it applies to all of us in need of a practice to deal with our recovery from trauma in all its forms.

Meditation

As I've mentioned repeatedly in this chapter, the mind's restless ramblings is the source of much of our physical, mental, and spiritual "discomfort." In fact, there is evidence that our mental reaction to what's happening in the world is what triggers our emotional outbursts. Yoga and its physical postures were first created to not only "loosen-up" the body, but develop a one-pointed focus to observe the mind's activity in order to calm it. For those taking up yoga, most lessons end with meditation, but for those wanting to quick entry into this practice, there are any number meditation books out there. Nelson in his book outlines a simple beginner's practice: "You first exhale through your nose, pulling in your abdominal muscles and completely deflating your lungs; pause, and then inhale pushing out your abdominal muscles and then expanding your diaphragm and filling your lungs; pause, and repeat. You can play soft music in the background, But I've found that concentrating on your rhythmic breathing is the best approach. When a thought comes up, and it will quite often even for practiced meditators, you don't push it away or try to repress it, you just acknowledge it as part of the 'isness' of what's happening and return your focus to your breathing. Buddhist nun Pema Chodron suggests that you just label the thought as 'mind' during sitting meditation or your active mindfulness exercises while you're out in the world."

These are few of the healing modalities that have helped to balance and soothe me when feeling devastated by the revelations that I shared with you in this book. Other modalities, some of which I have not practiced myself, were presented here to help readers cope with their exposure to this hard information. Whatever you choose to do, I hope it helps you deal with the awakening to the truth.

FOOTNOTES

[1] https://www.ncbi.nlm.nih.gov/pmc/articles/PMC3249911/

[2] https://www.youtube.com/
watch?v=-1uQc3pZKe8&feature=em-subs_digest

[3] https://www.helpguide.org/articles/ptsd-trauma/traumatic-stress.
htm

[4] http://www.trauma-pages.com/s/t-facts.php

[5] http://www.personaltransformation.com/awakening.html

[6] http://www.innerworkspublishing.com/news/fall2010/story.htm

[7] https://www.goodreads.com/author/quotes/110742.Adyashanti

[8] https://zoepopper.wordpress.com/2016/09/06/
are-you-ready-to-be-consumed-in-a-fire-without-end/

[9] https://www.goodreads.com/book/show/2669192-the-end
-of-your-world

[10] https://en.wikipedia.org/wiki/Adyashanti

[11] https://www.youtube.com/watch?v=VxPazhmlZGU

[12] https://www.eckharttolle.com/article/
Spiritual-Awakening-Of-Eckhart-Tolle

[13] http://nealedonaldwalsch.presskit247.com/content/content-
article.asp?ArticleID=5339

[14] http://www.nealedonaldwalsch.com/cwgmovie/blog_text.html

[15] https://www.yogitimes.com/review/
conversations-with-god-movie-neale-donald-walsch

REFERENCES

1. http://foreverconscious.com/5-ways-to-deal-with-an-awakening

2. http://in5d.com/how-the-consciousness-shift-may-be-affecting-you/

3. https://lauramarietv.com/21-symptoms-of-spiritual-awakening/

4. http://upliftconnect.com/awakening-is-a-destructive-process/

5. http://www.theawakeningworkshop.com/Spiritual-Awakening-Journey.html

6. Spiritual Awakening & DEPRESSION - (& How to Cope)
   https://www.youtube.com/watch?v=Nn_WzUlsRgA

PART III

THE NEW EARTH IS HERE

CHAPTER NINE

THE EVENT

At this point you may feel as I once did at this stage in my awakening: that it cannot get any weirder than this. I used to tell people that I stopped reading science fiction novels and thrillers, after I became aware of what is really occurring in the world and our real reality. Well, buckle up, because this is leading to an amazing outcome. A spiritual war is being waged against us, and it will be won in the spiritual realm first and then be manifested on the physical level. We're in the process of liberating Earth from an evil Cabal, and are in the final phase of removing these bad entities, who were given many chances to redeem themselves but haven't, from our reality.

We're now living in "the darkest hour before the dawn" of this mass awakening, although there is no definite date for the culmination of this process in what is being called "The Event." This is characterized as an influx of energy that elevates consciousness worldwide. I first read about this "Event" a year after finding out about the "agenda" for decimating humanity. I was still immersed in my negative reactions. At the time I had no idea who Cobra-from the Resistance Movement-was, and wondered if he was a Cabal stooge/ CIA asset. Misinformation was proliferated, and so I suspected all unknown players and their pronouncements, but I started following the reports and intel about it.

I found it hard to believe, but then others, like David Wilcock, spoke about solar flashes that are responsible for evolutionary changes on earth. Nothing disappears, he says; it just goes through evolutionary leaps. Now I think that this "Event" may be real after following the intel in general-not just Cobra or the Portal 2012 blogspot. I also asked my friends, who've been following this topic for years and whom I consider reasonable, discerning, and highly intuitive.

They present a few perspectives about "The Event." Hector Guerra: "I believe I heard about [it] sometime in 2013-2014[…] My feelings about it are, well… to put it in a nutshell, now I know why I chose to come to Earth. To participate in this cosmic event." I asked Hector if he believes it's true and this was his response: "Oh my goodness, of course I believe it to be true, not just believe it but know it […] When I first heard about the Event, everything started making sense to me. I knew then why most of us have been imprisoned here and why we have all been in this recycling cycle. I also knew that we had to get out. Cobra and the Resistance Movement helped me see the bigger planetary picture."

I then asked my colleague, Daniel James: "I heard about it in May 2017. I think it may be a real experience but I don't think it will be as soon as is predicted, and I think the experience will be slightly different for everyone […] Honestly it[']s subjective. I think for some, yes and for others there won't be a flash event, but rather more of a subtle and gradual roll of global changes. It will be different for everyone based on their beliefs, as opposed to one experience for everyone. Reality is subjective like that."

There are many groups involved worldwide in bringing this changeover to fruition and setting the stage for The Event. "It will be a moment of breakthrough for the planet, which will be physical and nonphysical. On the nonphysical plane, there will be a *'big wave of flash of Divine energy and light coming from the Galactic Central sun going towards the surface of the planet.'* This energy will "permeate the earth and humanity, raising the frequencies of all living entities on the planet."[1]

About the Event cosmic event:

https://www.youtube.com/watch?v=rI0hQNHoTsw&feature=youtu.be
https://www.youtube.com/watch?v=9NO196KcU1g&feature=youtu.be

David Wilcock says that this solar flash is intelligent, and it does accelerate the elevation of human consciousness. "It will calm humanity in the light of love energy and end duality. It's a magnificent energy not seen or felt before on Earth. Everyone on Earth will feel and know something has happened. It will be a surprise as to when it will happen, even for us. It's never happened before. It will not be a major shock event, it will be a positive event." [1]

This elevation of consciousness will accelerate the changes already happening:

"On the physical plane there will be:

- The arrest of the Cabal (already started).
- The reset of the Financial Systems.
- Disclosure—the release of ET information.
- The beginning of a new, fairer financial system with prosperity funds for all humanity.
- NEW Political system, Education system, Healthcare system, etc.
- Awakening of humanity slowly and gradually to the existence of positive non-terrestrial races and our galactic connections.
- Introduction of new advanced technologies.
- The release of [energy for] spiritual growth and healing for every human being on the planet [...]
- And of course we have been gradually going toward the first contact, which is an actual official contact between the earth civilization and other positive ET races that exist throughout the galaxy. And the Event is a trigger point which begins that process [...]"[1]

We are all entitled to receive the prosperity funds. There will also be funds given to projects benefitting humanity like those involving free energy, and to end homelessness, poverty, hunger. It's all the money and gold that the Cabal has stolen from humanity. You'll probably be glad to know that other things are expected after the Event – financially speaking:

All currencies will still be alive.

- There will be a financial re-evaluation after the Event – gold, currencies, etc.
- There will be transparency accounting with banks that reopen.
- Interest charges will stop.
- Fractional banking will cease.
- The IRS will be dismantled immediately.
- All Banks with strong ties to The Cabal will be bankrupt.
- The Federal Reserve will be dismantled immediately.
- All debts will not be forgiven, meaning if you used credit cards to buy goods thinking your debts were forgiven, that will not happen.
- Food, shelter, and technology will be available for everyone.
- No gold will be traded on the open market.
- There will be no more stock market.
- Money in bank accounts will be frozen from reset to the new bank system (3-14 days). If funds were acquired legally, then the money will be kept.
- The Cabal's money is illegal and will be seized.

More Future Details to The Changes for The New Society:

- The only tax will be 14% on new items purchased.
- New technology will be released, but electrical grids will be operational during the conversion.
- Everyone will receive $100,000 from collateral accounts.

- Debts up to $100,000 will be forgiven. If over that amount, it will be analyzed. Real outstanding debt will be taken from that amount or if not enough, you will be advised to go into bankruptcy.
- All countries' debts will be forgiven.
- Mortgages will be cancelled out.
- Retirement accounts will be preserved.
- Social security/retirement/health care will be changed; free health insurance will be provided for a new, advanced medical system.
- The average work week will be 3-4 hours a day, 5 days a week.
- The police force will be restructured for protection, not money collectors.
- Common law will be respected – not distorted.
- Most credit card debt will be cancelled.
- Most of Congress (U.S.) will be disbanded.
- Congress and parliaments will close at reset.
- There will be new elections for Congress and parliaments (All governments worldwide) within 4 months of RESET.
- Monsanto, and the corrupt part of Microsoft, will be bankrupt immediately. Same for other corrupt companies.
- Most prisoners will be released and receive psychological counseling and training.
- CIA-operated drug trade will cease, and drastic restructuring will be needed.
- When we are all fully 'healed,' we will stop eating meat (animals will be appreciated for what they are).
- Most Companies will keep operating.
- Companies will buy back shares and give investors back their money.
- The Resistance will help and advise others about this changeover.

- The electrical grid will be intact; however, when The Cabal loses control, there may be blackouts.
- Financial life after the "EVENT" will be vastly improved now that the bonds of debt illegally imposed by The Cabal are removed. Every person on the planet will have funds available for improving their lives.
- Victory to the Light Is Near!" [2]

I want to share my appreciation with you for all the volunteers worldwide who made such an effort and translated vital information for the general population that isn't aware of these changes about the Event to many languages. Thanks for everyone who contributed this information. I'm sharing a few links for you.

Please read more in different languages here:
http://communityleadersbrief.org/

The event explained in English
https://www.youtube.com/watch?v=rI0hQNHoTsw&feature=share

The Event explained in French
https://www.youtube.com/watch?v=ZDDeWMl4lHg&t=257s

NESARA and GESARA Act

What is Nesara/Gesara? The acronym NESARA stands for National Economic Security and Reformation Act. "The Act was passed by the American Congress in the year 2000 and never proclaimed. It was designed to provide a new economic system for the world during the present time of transition [...] NESARA is designed to erase poverty and all its attendant ills from Earth during a transitional period preceding Ascension so that the planet's sovereign citizens can again focus their spiritual attention on planetary transformation." [3] Nesara is designed for the U.S., while

Gesara is designed for the rest of the world. Why is it so important? "NESARA is legislation of the United States government that was designed by high-light beings in conjunction with spiritual beings on the planet as the LEGAL means to usher in the era of peace, love and harmony on Earth." [4]While this is a political act, it is also a spiritual one at the same time. It reminds me of what Neale Donald Walsch discussed in his series *Conversations with God* about spiritual politics (although it sounds like an oxymoron).

The benefits that Nesara provides the Americans (and Gesara to the population of the world):

1. Forgiveness of credit card and mortgage debt as remedy for bank frauds;
2. Creates U.S. Treasury Bank system which absorbs the Federal Reserve and new precious metals backed U.S. Treasury currency;
3. Restores Constitutional Law;
4. Requires resignations of Bush and Cheney (circa 2000) to be replaced by Constitutionally acceptable NESARA President and Vice President Designates until new elections;
5. Requires the President Designate to declare "Peace" and ends U.S. aggressive military actions immediately;
6. Abolishes IRS; flat rate non-essential "new items only" sales tax revenue for government, and many more improvements. [5]

Tom Price has another perspective on "The Event," which he calls "Magic Day." (He's a chemical engineer, who had his own semiconductor manufacturing business for 15 years. At the same time, Tom's wisdom-quest was learning how the universe works from a positive thinking perspective.) The author of *Getting Aligned for The Planetary Transformation,* he writes that there "will be a 'Magic Day' in the very near future [...] The energy to this planet is increasing daily, and that is why people are waking up. However, A HUGE increase in energy will happen on The Magic Day, and many will not make it to the 5ᵗʰ dimension […] If you are ready on that Magic Day, you will stay on Earth and realize the incredible place it will become (once again) […] Each person is on their own, and must use their own free will to get through this transition."

Change is Already Happening

Full disclosure will expose some very upsetting truths on how the negative ETs were working with the Cabal to strip us of this knowledge, including super-advanced technologies which aren't harmful to us (unlike the technology we use today, including smartphones, Wi-Fi), and healing modalities. We will also learn of the benevolent ETs and their positive influence, which are the majority of advanced beings in the cosmos from what I gather. Here you can watch testimonies of people who know about and have had contact with aliens for 50 years: http://www.stillnessinthestorm. com/2016/11/full-ufo-disclosure-inevitable.html?spref=fb

Captain Randy Cramer USMC (mentioned in chapter six) recently disclosed this information from his personal experience in the SSP program which he benefitted from. This is a super-advanced healing technology that thanks to it he's alive and whole. It's called Holobed Regenerating Technology, "medical devices which restore injured persons health." Cramer claims that "this Holographic technology repairs not only limbs and wounds, but illnesses and diseases by mapping the DNA of the individual."[6] (this was discussed in The Goldfish Report No. 183 video published on Jan 20, 2018)

Alex Collier, former CEO of an accounting practice, according to his 1994 interview, is the author of several books, and lectures in the western states about the topic of bad ETs collaborating with the Cabal. [7] "(Born 1956 Collier is a United States citizen claiming to be a contactee with friendly human ETs from the Andromeda star system) […] Collier has described in detail the members of a dangerous and malevolent ET confederation consisting of Reptilian

ETs from Alpha Draconis, the Orion Group, and the Grey ETs from Zeta Reticuli 2. According to Collier the NSA (National Security Agency) in the USA is the secret government working with this dangerous ET confederation and running joint alien/human bases on the Earth and the Moon. According to Collier, the president of the USA is just a powerless puppet."[8]

After he started sharing and exposing his information about the Cabal and his meetings with other humans and ETs from Andromeda, his life was turned upside down including losing his family and position. His video lectures show him to be a very eloquent, intelligent, and sane person.

After becoming aware of this information, we need to continue this path to evolve and transform our world into a magnificent place. Diane Canfield, a cosmic contactee, ascension expert, and a psychic-medium, brilliantly explains how this awakening process must include the search for truth and also shares her own experiences of the awakening process: "The journey to enlightenment, MUST include the search for the TRUTH, if it does not include this at the VERY TOP of the search the person will be bogged down with so much untruths they will not be able to make the DIVINE CONNECTIONS needed to make progress. We ALL have an inner awareness of what is TRUTH and what is not [...] In my own journey[,] which started 17 years ago for the search for TRUTH, I knew immediately not to listen to any untruths and not to get bogged down with them, that they all lead the WRONG direction. I discarded all of the information that carried any unresonate[d] activity freeing myself to find only TRUTH. This is what leads one to evolve. How did I know this? Because I was already being led by the Divine Creator."[9] According to David Wilcock on December 7, 2017, these positive changes are already happening but peacefully, as we've started to enter a new phase of non-violence. As he says on his page on Facebook: "The biggest message I would give from that discussion is that everything we want to see has ALREADY STARTED HAPPENING. The main 'problem,' if you will, is that people want some sort of epic Hollywood action-movie climax. It's not happening that way. There will be efforts to ensure it is far more peaceful than that. Some of the next wave of things we will see will be very, very revealing and upsetting. This is all part of the great cleansing we have to go through, so I feel we should all embrace these changes." [10]

First Contact with Benevolent ETs

"Yes, there have been crashed craft, and bodies recovered… We are not alone in the universe[;] they have been coming here for a long time." – Apollo 14 Astronaut Dr. Edgar Mitchell ([http:// www.citizenhearing.org/](http://www.citizenhearing.org/))

The benevolent ETs (or as some call them "the Galactics", including benevolent Andromedans, Pleiadeans, Arcturians, and Sirians—from Sirius, not Syria) who watch over us, have foiled nuclear attacks as well as natural or Cabal-made disasters, as mentioned in Chapter Six. They are now making themselves more visible to us. Watch this video expose: [https://www.youtube.com/ watch?v=42dHJrO9-c4&t=53s](https://www.youtube.com/watch?v=42dHJrO9-c4&t=53s) Even an American friend, Dee Collier from the Resistance Movement, told me she watched one such ship hovering above her home and she could see all the lights and hear it. They want us to become aware of their presence and not be afraid of them; they are prepping us for first contact. Tom Price even says that Trump is probably freaking out [about what the Galactics are doing to prevent disasters and removing the bad guys along with white hats from the surface humanity]. Price goes on in the following video and remarks, "Trust me, Trump isn't in charge of this at all [laughing]. I imagine that he's freaking out and just eating popcorn." [11]

David Wilcock, who diligently and bravely brought forth Corey Goode's testimony on his encounters with extraterrestrials, is now introducing Emery Smith who has recently come forward. According to Wilcock, "Emery claims to have autopsied some three thousand different species of ET while working at Sandia Labs on

Kirtland Air Force Base [...] It turns out that our galaxy is literally bursting with Earth-like planets and intelligent civilizations. <u>NASA has publicly estimated there are over 40 billion Earth-like planets in our galaxy alone.</u> What you learn 'on the inside' is that intelligent civilizations invariably have bodies that are humanlike or at least hominid in appearance. Emery calls this 'the five-star formation'—the head, two arms and two legs. It isn't always this way, but it again is very common." [12]

There are mostly benevolent ETs. One of these good ET groups is the Andromeda Council, which is "an intergalactic, interstellar & interdimensional <u>governance</u> & <u>development</u> body of aligned benevolent star systems & planets of sentient intelligent life... for worlds in both the Milky Way and Andromeda galaxies[...] One of the original groups of the Andromeda Council is the **Galactic Federation** which is a long-standing federation of star systems & planets of benevolent beings based in the **Tau Ceti** star system [...] [who are] willing to help the people of planet Earth in its process of evolution. The time of Earth's evolution has come." [13] The twelve Andromeda Council Biospheres include six healthcare biospheres or hospital ships to take care of surface humans. You can see here the structure of these biospheres, including the hospitals and the detailed medical staff aboard one ship.[14]

First Contact with People from Inner Earth

When I talk about first contact, I'm not only talking about ETs coming from above the Earth. Surprise, surprise. For the full picture we need to look down and more specifically, inside the Earth. Perhaps Jules Verne's science fiction novel *Journey to the Center of the Earth* from 1864 wasn't just fiction after you read the following recent testimonies from former military and SSP members (including filmed on videos).

Corey Goode, who served for 20 years in an SSP, talks about his encounters with representatives of different races from the Agartha

Network (inner earth). "Secret Space Program whistleblower Corey Goode made an astonishing revelation in yesterday's episode of *Cosmic Disclosure* in which he described his extensive tour of a massive underground cavern system belonging to an Inner Earth Civilization dating back millions of years. These people of the Inner Earth had helped the Ancient Sumerians rebuild civilization after a minor cataclysm on the surface." [15]

There are also drawings (no photos) from the place he visited. Not only did he represent the SSP (Secret Space Program) in conventions with Dracos that scared him, but also with people from Agartha and it was done telepathically. Here you can see pictures with a representative of the Anshar community of inner earth dwellers https://divinecosmos.com/start-here/davids-blog/1225-abr-legacy?showall=&start=1. He describes their means of transportation, how it felt to be travelling there, the actual meetings, and even the accommodations. It's absolutely reasonable to doubt Goode's testimony. However Wilcock, who spoke with many insiders, says that "Corey's testimony about the hidden interstellar community around us has gone significantly beyond the clues I gathered from other insiders [...] At the same time, he knew many dozens of specific, highly classified data points I had already assembled, and never shared anywhere online [...] None of us could have possibly expected what happened in March 2015, when Corey had an SSP craft land in his yard and bring him up to the LOC [Lunar Operations Command, an alleged secret base on the moon] [...] As we have reported before, Corey was brought into a conference room filled with people of all different races from earth, wearing the usual space-program one-piece jumpsuits [...] They were key members of an alliance that had formed within the SSP, seeking to break the secrecy and return all of their technology and facilities to the people here." [16]. You can watch here Goode's interview about Hollow Earth vs Honeycomb Earth & Inner Earth Civilizations —Corey Goode https://www.youtube.com/watch?v=qfafEQ9n5Xw

Another testimonial from a former military about meeting

people from inner earth (a similar experience to those of Corey Goode) is that of Billie Faye Woodward, a USAF Colonel[17]; the transcript of this video can be read here:

https://www.facebook.com/permalink.php?story_fbid=2173625 21732021&id=217350795066527).

Here's a brief summary of his experiences: "The people of the interior were very free with showing me around, very articulate in showing you what is exactly going on - they do not hold anything back. They always ask permission when working with Nature, they ask the plants for permission before consuming them or cutting them down, they ask the Mother Earth before they build on it, and do so build with the lay of the land which best suits their environment, a practice similar to the American Indians; therefore seeking to preserve a harmonious state at all times; wanting to be one with Nature at all times; they are more spiritually advanced than surface dwellers and greatly respect Mother Earth. The atmosphere is crystal clear, as a rule there are at times clouds, but nothing like rain clouds. The temperature is a constant 73 degrees. The people in the interior speak directly with the animals, and the animals speak directly to the people of the interior.

"There is no need for hoarding, for everything is free, no need to create in abundance as everything is ample. A process of bartering is more common than trade in money. This is basically a utopian culture with no depression leading into violence. No parties seeking to make war and gain dominance over each other. There are none richer nor poorer."[18]

Woodward's account is amazing, but from all the testimonies that I've encountered, the most fascinating is the one given by Vice Admiral Richard E. Byrd and polar explorer who submitted his testimony to the relevant American military authorities. "The first public scientific evidence occurred in 1947 when Rear Admiral Richard E. Byrd of the United States Navy flew directly to the North Pole and instead of going over the pole, actually entered the Inner Earth. Agartha - The light cities within inner earth (600 km or miles inside the earth) that are inter-connected, including Telos beneath Mount Shasta in northern California." [19]

His account is highly detailed. [20] https://www.youtube.com/watch?v=NOBBqtxSP7Q He was also interviewed on TV and talked about it. This is rare interview (https://www.youtube.com/watch?v=OOUwBYjEaGI) and this is his flight log (February 19th, 1947) which he has written in secrecy with a short relevant excerpt from it: "This can be the only hope for Mankind. I have seen the truth and it has quickened my spirit and has set me free! I have done my duty toward the monstrous military industrial complex. Now, the long night begins to approach, but there shall be no end. Just as the long night of the Arctic ends, the brilliant sunshine of Truth shall come again....and those who are of darkness shall fall in its Light. FOR I HAVE SEEN THAT LAND BEYOND THE POLE, THAT CENTER OF THE GREAT UNKNOWN."

Admiral Richard E. Byrd
United States Navy
24 December 1956 [21]

Agartha is not a legend!

Where are these "light cities" of inner earth civilizations located? There are several (allegedly) locations worldwide. From Graham Hancock, "There is an ancient legend among the Hindus of India that tells of a civilisation of immense beauty beneath central Asia. Several underground cities are said to be located north of the Himalayan mountains, possibly in Afghanistan, or under the Hindu Kush. This subterranean Shangri-la is inhabited by a race of golden people who seldom communicate with the surface world [...] Tunnel entrances are said to be in Ellora and the Ajanta caverns in the Chandore Mountain range of India. Eric Norman [says] [the author of the book *The Hollow Earth*] [...] One tunnel in Brazil is near Ponte Grosse in the state of Parana. (Fruit orchards were seen here.) Another entrance in Brazil is near Rincon, state of Parana. Also, in the state of Santa Catarina, Brazil, near the city of Joinville there is a mountain containing an entrance to the tunnels." [22] There are more entrances to inner earth in Brazil than those mentioned above, as well entrances in Canada, China, England, Egypt, Turkey, and others in South America (other than Brazil).

In the book *Revelations of the New Lemuria* (Telos, Vol. 1) [23], Aurelia Louise Jones, who channeled spiritual messages from Telos, the "light city" beneath Mount Shasta in Northern California, says, "They are the survivors of the lost continent of Mu who perished beneath of waves of the Pacific Ocean over 12,000 years ago" [23] [and] who "have succeeded in creating a civilization of peace and abundance, with no sickness, aging or death. They have mastered immortality in physical expression and they wish to teach us to do the same." [23] In this book she shares with her readers their wish of unification with our civilization when we are ready to receive them among us and teach us to accomplish the same heavenly existence in the 5th dimension as they've achieved. These amazing revelations only show that we have much to look for in the near future. I feel that all of this coming ET contact will just reinforce the concept that we are spiritual beings and that the time has come for us to embrace our totality.

FOOTNOTES

[1] http://prepareforchange.net/the-event/

[2] https://he.prepareforchange.net/financial/

[3] http://www.feelmorethanfine.eu/nesara/

[4] http://goldenageofgaia.com/2010/09/30/what-is-nesara/

[5] http://members.iimetro.com.au/~hubbca/nesara.htm

[6] (Video) The GoldFish Report No. 183 -- Capt. Randy Cramer,
   USMC S.S. on Holobed Regenerating Technology
   Posted: 21 Jan 2018 02:16 PM PST
   Published on Jan 20, 2018
   https://www.youtube.com/watch?v=2YSYLRq6GL8&feature=
   share

[7] https://www.youtube.com/watch?v=oQZgAEA95s8

[8] http://www.abovetopsecret.com/forum/thread480397/pg1

[9] www.DianeCanfield.com October 20, 2017

[10] https://www.facebook.com/divinecosmos

[11] https://www.youtube.com/watch?v=42dHJrO9-c4&t=53s

[12] https://divinecosmos.com/start-here/
   davids-blog/1225-abr-legacy?showall=&limitstart=

[13] http://www.andromedacouncil.com/about.html

[14] http://www.andromedacouncil.com/Andromeda_Council_-_
   Biospheres.pdf

[15] https://www.gaia.com/video/
   inner-earth-grand-tour?fullplayer=preview

[16] https://divinecosmos.com/start-here/davids-blog/1225-abr-legacy

[17] https://www.youtube.com/watch?v=aztFGGaD8w8

[18] https://www.facebook.com/permalink.php?story_fbid=21736252
   1732021&id=217350795066527

[19] http://exonews.org/tag/corey-goode/page/5/

[20] https://www.youtube.com/watch?v=NOBBqtxSP7Q

[21] http://www.thetruthseeker.co.uk/?p=7822

[22] http://grahamhancock.com/phorum/read.php?1,212474,212521

[23] *Revelations of the New Lemuria* (Telos, Vol. 1) July 1, 2004 by Aurelia Louise Jones https://www.amazon.com/Revelations-New-Lemuria-TELOS-Vol/dp/0970090242

REFERENCES

1. Shift from lack to prosperity hour 1:28 Goldfish Report

   https://www.youtube.com/watch?v=q4UlObxhJPM&feature=share

2. Tom Price - Currency Reset & 2012 Significance

   https://www.youtube.com/watch?v=WQ4d0FKc58k

3. *Getting Aligned For the Planetary Transformation: Your Guide to What's Going on, Why, and Your Responsibility* by Tom Price, September 17, 2016.

4. New Financial System (from 2012) after "the Event" http://2012portal.blogspot.co.il/2012/04/normal-0-microsoftinternetexplorer4 28.html? sm au =iVVqZfR8Z58sFs2M

5. https://www.docdroid.net/Qp24Kzx/st-germaine-history-and-nesara-save-this.pdf#page=3

6. http://theplanetdailynews.com/

7. http://askingangels.com/articles/newearth/nesara.php

8. http://goldengaiadb.com/index.php?title=NESARA

9. http://harmonhouse.net/archive/fdl/skeptic.html

10. http://fromthetrenchesworldreport.com/what-is-nesara/214719

11. http://goldenageofgaia.com/2010/09/30/what-is-nesara/

12. http://goldenageofgaia.com/2016/07/13/judy-byington-history-nesara/

13. http://www.ascensionwithearth.com/p/prosperity-funds-gifting.html

14. http://galacticconnection.com/the-reality-of-ancient-atlantis-extraterrestrial-contact-a-discussion-thats-gaining-more-credibility/

15. http://galacticconnection.com/the-reality-of-ancient-atlantis-extraterrestrial-contact-a-discussion-thats-gaining-more-credibility/

16. Thrive documentary http://www.thrivemovement.com/

17. *Visitors to the Inner Earth* by Professor Solomon

True tales (or so it was claimed) of subterranean journeys

Free download of entire book (6 MB file):

http://www.professorsolomon.com/graphics/visitorstotheinnerearth.pdf

18. https://www.newdawnmagazine.com/articles/mystery-of-shambhala

19. Our Ancient History https://www.bibliotecapleyades.net/esp_galacticdiplomacy_11.htm

20. The map of Agartha including the entrances

https://www.pathwaytoascension.com/blog/2015/12/14/hollow-earth-agartha-complete/

CHAPTER TEN

CREATING HEAVEN ON EARTH

The Grand Vision – New Earth is Already Here

I'm so excited to share my vision of the coming New Earth. We are now living during a truly historical time. When we look back to this period, we may characterize it as "the best times and the worst times." Today It still appears messy, scary, and edgy, but on the other hand, those of us who have investigated these behind-the-scenes machinations, see the changes. People are awakening en mass worldwide and demanding their rights back, eager to know the truth and demanding it and holding the Black Hats accountable for their offenses. It's very exciting to see this awakening. We've been waiting for this exposure for years and now it is actually happening.

We will soon witness the realignment of the world's financial system, with allotments to everyone on earth; there will be global humanitarian projects intended to end homelessness and hunger worldwide. We are heading into an amazingly bright future of joy, love, unity, and abundance for all, with free energy and the cleansing of the earth, oceans, and air worldwide. We will also be introduced to our extended family from different places on earth, inside the earth and from the stars. Everything has been set in motion for this amazing future. All the technologies are already there (only suppressed but used for decades in the secret space programs and other places like DUMBs, (Deep Underground Military Bases). I'm very excited, and this is what we should bear in mind during these hard times of transition and of full disclosure that is fast approaching.

Matt Kahn, an author, empathic healer and a spiritual teacher, talks about "the Love Commandos," those people who are energetically sensitive and are here to anchor the new vibrations of love. So "here's the love commando at your service." This is his YouTube channel https://www.youtube.com/user/JulieMuse He claims we will shift our collective frequency from 3D to 4D, and then to a 5D consciousness of love and harmony. And no, we're not moving en mass to another planet, and please don't believe this nonsense about boarding spaceships to be rescued from a catastrophe on earth. We're staying right here in our bodies. The only thing that changes is our level of consciousness. We will move from a fear-based duality to love, unity and harmony. (Jordan Sather's Youtube channel, *Destroying the Illusion*, has a wonderful video explaining the rise in Schumann resonance, part of the earth's electromagnetic field, and how it correlates to brain waves[1]). This is an excellent explanation of the ascension process.

Before delving into these exciting developments, I would like to introduce this new phase of evolution on earth and of humanity with a famous Israeli song track called in Hebrew "Yahad." It translates in English as "Together," and is a song for love (as we shift from a fear-based reality and what goes with it) to a love-based one—a time of unity, harmony and peace. For me, this song perfectly captures the "feel and touch" of this new vibration of love, and I'd like to share it with you. I attached the lyrics in English with the YouTube video that also included the translation to English. https://www.youtube.com/watch?v=X9KckXcVzug

English translation

Together

As the heart opens up,
it embraces the world,
and with a great big shout
to sing for love.

Together, heart to heart
we'll open, and we'll see, the light in the sky.
Together, heart to heart
we'll open with hope - for love. [2]

How is This Amazing Transition Unfolding?

As difficult as it may seem to comprehend and much less believe, the New Earth or the Golden Age is coming (with the dark era still being played out until its final collapse). This chapter will provide a glimpse into the projects that reveal how we will usher in the new age of limitless prosperity, free energy, free healing devices (like tachyon chambers from our "galactic neighbors"), and much more to uplift and inspire us. No major cataclysm is going to occur, except to the devastating impact of full disclosure on the elite offenders.

As mentioned earlier, Michael Tellinger is a pioneer in implementing a revolutionary, simple and straightforward economical system that frees towns from the need of money and bringing them abundance and prosperity—one small town at a time as the creator of the Ubuntu Project says. It is still at the grassroots level but being implemented worldwide, which includes developed countries like the US, UK and Canada. Mayors from all over the world are reaching out for advice on how to implement this system in their communities. [3] This economical system will remove the use of money, the root source of crime and violence in our world and in our lives. The genius idea underlying this financial model is that money, which has been used to enslave humanity, can be and needs to be used as a tool to liberate us all. Tellinger explains this concept in this video from last year on how to build the New Earth now, remove global elite, and create wealth for everyone worldwide. https://www.youtube.com/watch?time_continue=94&v=6FtbSRLoPzM

Such new economic models like the Ubuntu Liberation movement are becoming more widespread worldwide. This model creates "a totally new system that turns competition into collaboration," a philosophy known as Contributionism. There is no use of money but of people "working together to create towns, cities, countries and lives overflowing with abundance, food, arts, music, sports, technology, health, leisure and infinite variety [...] The first stage of the 'One Small Town' initiative is to create food and income generating projects within a community, all run by the power of the community members. In the beginning stages these funds are funneled back into more produce and income generating projects, until eventually the town is self-sustaining & generating a sizable income through external sales.

"This money is then split between the further advancement of the town, the business owners, and the community members themselves. The members of the community are rewarded for their efforts with free products and services, and an ever-growing income as more and more money- generating projects are formed." [4]

How Will the Spiritual Transition to 5D Ascension Happen?

There are many theories that discuss these possibilities like the earth splitting into two dimensional worlds, one for the higher vibrational people and another one for the lower vibrational people—here's one rendition of that theory by the late Dolores Cannon: http://projectavalon.net/forum4/showthread.php?5348-Ascension-Dolores-Cannon-Splitting-of-Earth-into-two-Earths I feel it's more like a purge of the negative energy that allows the positive vibration to take root. Right now, the "evil ones" are being arrested (to be tried in military tribunals); while some are being killed, others are trying to escape their fate as detailed earlier. Those people who are solely in "service to self" are going to be removed from earth one way or another. Those who are "service to others", even if only 51%, according to David Wilcock, will remain on an earth which will become "heaven on earth".

I know that this may sound "too good to be true" and you're right. I felt the same way for a long time. Putting away the bad guys is only one aspect of this scenario. The cataclysms that Edgar Cayce and others have predicted are predicated on our negative fear vibrations affecting the earth. But, after "The Event" and the influx of higher energy and its transformational effects on humanity, that deleterious effect will be canceled out. In fact, instead of cataclysms the earth will reveal even more of its bountiful nature. This might be difficult to believe, or maybe not; Edgar Cayce once said that if there were 100 "righteous" people on earth at the time, World War I wouldn't have happened. By "righteous," I believe he meant self-realized. This might explain how the elevated energy from the galactic center flooding the planet will be enough to transform people, and their higher vibration will affect the world's eco system.

According to Wilcock, "In order to be ready to inhabit this new world, we must reach certain minimum requirements for what they call graduation. This minimum only involves having a *51% percent desire to be of service to others*, rather than manipulating and controlling others, or what they call 'service to self' in order for us to be ready for graduation. When the same source was asked what is the best way to serve others they said, '*To seek the heart of the self.*' Again I believe this refers to the fact that when you really understand your identity, it will not end at the boundary of your skin to the air. When you begin looking into the faces of others and seeing yourself, for that same reason – why would you want to manipulate or control them?

To serve others is to help yourself." [5]

Wilcock provides other interesting details about how this "awakening" is occurring: "Supremely high-level intelligence uses synchronicity to direct us to the sources of information that feed us this awakening [...] What appears to be happening is that the people who are ready for it [will Ascend] when this spring springs [...] When this energetic springboard takes off, you'll be able to levitate. You'll be able to have telekinesis [...] You'll have telepathic contact with other people – all the Jesus miracles [...] If there is even one person who has ascended, he's going to be able to drive away all of these bad guys. And they see it coming [...]" [6]

I don't believe that the cataclysms or negative events, which were predicted in many scriptures (different religions) and are also depicted in recent movies, is going to happen to those who are at least 51% in "service to others", but dark times are coming for the bad guys. Members of Team Dark (or the most evil ones) are going to experience a negative timeline, I believe—but here on earth. They are going to suffer the consequences of their offenses, while those who are positive in nature will experience a positive timeline. What do I mean by "service to others"? In general, to make it clearer, it's about how they treat other people. Are they loving and compassionate? You don't have to be a Mother Theresa. You may have negative thoughts like we all have, but it's important how you react to these thoughts.

There's a wonderful phrase in the movie *Peaceful Warrior*, which I really love. The movie is an adaptation of the classic *Way of the Peaceful Warrior: A Book that Changes Lives*[7] that is "you are not your thoughts". It's what you do with them that counts and that affects your vibration as the documentary, *The Secret*, so clearly depicts. Here spiritual teachers talk about the impact of your thoughts and words, your feelings and actions and how they affect your reality. I feel that one's ascension may occur more in line as what is shown in the movie *The Celestine Prophecy*, based on the novel by James Redfield. At one point in the movie, a group of people feel a strong bond (perhaps love for each other), while running away from the bad guys and become invisible to those chasing them, or raise their vibration to become undetectable in 3D. They just feel bliss, holding hands, and able to hold it for a short while, or until one of their friend is caught and lose this higher vibration and become visible again.[8]

At this moment you may think that this ascension concept is some kind of elaborate fantasy. I totally relate with this sentiment. I felt this way for years. When I first heard this term, I was so put out that I completely ignored it. But I came across in so many different contexts that I became curious and started reading and asking a lot of questions about it. I also joined two support groups on Facebook for people experiencing this process physically and mentally (I like this one https://www. facebook.com/Ascension-support-group-130638063665040/?hc ref=ARQCkg3J36iiQPgvbAzArKzYxktjRAPRqJu2R0YD3kfjm AkSnU60Vjix48SAqDpzeQQ). I felt some of the symptoms listed, which scared me. I had heart palpitations that felt like my heart was going to leap out of my chest and had to put my palm on it to calm it down. They say this happens when the heart chakra is expanding. Eventually it stopped after a year. The amazing thing was that people from all over the world were experiencing similar symptoms and sharing with the group. From what I know, these symptoms aren't triggered by common physical or mental maladies. So I started to believe it may be true, that something is really happening and that ascension is real.

Today I perceive this as a combination of awakening to the truth of our reality that allows us to expand our consciousness. Spiritually, I'm definitely not the same person as I was before this awakening five years ago, and physically I feel the change goes as deep as our DNA. I found out that our emotions and feelings affect everything in our physical body including the brain, cells and even our genes. [9] Of course, I love the idea of the supernatural abilities and powers that we will gain after the ascension, as described here:

"You will be able to communicate telepathically in the Golden Age, but speaking aloud still will be important and pleasurable. When telepathic conversations are commonplace again, you will be able to communicate telepathically with people whose languages are different because a translation process is an inherent aspect of telepathy." [10] This site has a list of the amazing new powers and abilities as a result of this ascension or DNA upgrades as others call it. [11]

According to Tom Price, despite denying this ascension process which may sound weird to you, "Our job is to continue the effort to promote this wonderful transition [to 5D]. This is an exciting time of change. It seems surreal, and it is, but it is also very real. Everyone needs to wake up [...] Please help in getting the word out. The sooner everyone becomes aware, the sooner we progress into the 5th dimension, and the sooner Mother Earth becomes the beautiful planet we envision [...] When people hear this information for the first time, their first reaction is understandably barriers of denial and resistance [...] With that awareness comes the realization of how much we have been mind-controlled by the bad-guys [...] [And our] need to wake up and get aligned. We need to visualize our future and the beautiful Earth [...] We will be the ones creating these apparent miracles. To do so, we have to act and behave as if they have already happened. This is faith, with clear goals and unity consciousness at work." [12]

Apparently, the ascension process has a scientific basis according to Wilcock's research and his discussion with scientists. This awakening is supposed to happen of a mass scale, which I interpret as the entire humanity and living things on earth. It will be a cosmic event. This idea is not restricted to Christianity alone in what is described as the "rapture". Other religions prophesized this too. Wilcock says, "What also happens is that this energy 'zaps' all the creatures that are on the Earth, because the increase in the wavelength of the planetary spiral is accompanied by a spontaneous burst of energy from the Sun — a burst that has qualities of both radiation and intelligence [resembling what is told about the coming "Event"]. It's important to note that nothing disappears but only shifts according to this theory: there is no 'missing link' between Neanderthal man and Cro-Magnon (modern man) because what happened was that Neanderthal got "zapped" and spontaneously evolved. They grew much larger brains and lost the clumsiness of their bodies." [13]

The basis for Wilcock's theory and the idea that this ascension is imminent is based on changes in our solar system which are measurable and suggest that this leap in evolution is near. This unusual solar activity includes increased proton and radiation emissions, as well as other unusual bursts of energy. Another indication of this approaching shift is the changes in the sun's magnetic field, which has spiked 230 percent since 1901! This is according to a study conducted by Dr. Mike Lockwood, who has been investigating the Sun from Rutherford Appleton National Laboratories in California. This type of research is taking place in Russia by the Russian National Academy of Sciences in Novosibirsk, Siberia. They've reached the conclusion that this energetic shift is happening as planet earth is moving into an area with higher energy. They've also found out that, "The glowing plasma at the leading edge of our Solar System has recently increased 1000 percent [...] This plasma energy used to be 10 astronomical units deep (an astronomical unit is the distance from the Earth to the Sun, 93,000,000 miles). So ten astronomical units represents the normal thickness of this glowing energy that we used to see at the front end of the Solar System. Today, the glowing plasma has gone to 100 astronomical units deep. Although Dr. Dmitriev's paper [the esteemed Russian space physicist working in Akademgorodok, a clandestine scientific research city outside of Novosibirsk, Siberia] [14] does not give an exact timeline, we can assume that this increase happened in the same 1963 to 1993 period as the increase he found in natural disaster. Whenever it happened, that's a 1,000 percent increase in the overall brightness of the energy at the front end of the Solar System." [15]

This energy, which is conscious and intelligent as mentioned earlier, is the real cause in creating the previous spontaneous mass evolutionary changes. And this is supposedly what is going to happen in our time as well. Wilcock explains that, "When this new energy comes out of the Sun, we will naturally be transported into a higher level of our own being. Our physical body becomes irrelevant at that point. We are much more than that [...] The dinosaurs got blasted. Their souls turned into mammal souls. So nobody goes anywhere, nobody is actually extinguished. We can find the bodies and it looks cataclysmic, it looks horrible – but all they really do is just bump up another notch and start to inhabit different bodies [...] The Sun's energy can cause matter to just physically transmute [...] Each of us has the choice to create our lives so that we may participate in the Utopian world that will manifest on Earth after this Ascension process has completed – a world without poverty, hunger or pain; a world where full-body levitation, spontaneous healings, instant telepathic communication, and abundant Love are the law of the land [...] And then you realize that the only thing that ever mattered was how much love you were willing to share while you were incarnated on Earth." [13]

Corey Goode also repeats the notion of becoming more "service to others" to evolve and go through this process: "Every day focus on becoming more [in] "Service to Others" oriented. Focus on being more "Loving" and "Focus on raising your Vibrational and Consciousness Level" and learn to "Forgive Yourself and Others" (Thus "Releasing Karma"). This will change the Vibration of the Planet. The "Shared Consciousness of Humanity" and "Change Humanity One Person at a Time" (Even if that "One Person" is yourself.)." [16]

When I first encountered these ideas, I was so moved because I totally resonated with the idea of becoming more in "service to others," and it raised my vibration and consciousness level. I have my flaws like everyone else, but I'm much more aware today of my behavior, thoughts, and words and am also aware that I have to be more forgiving not only to others, but myself. I'm definitely more compassionate and started to love animals, which wasn't as natural to me until recently (the last 3 to 4 years). I find it difficult to see that I'm failing from time to time, but I tell myself that I'm not perfect and none of us need to be or can be perfect. We came here to experience and evolve. Perfect doesn't evolve. I'm just thinking and being grateful that every day I become better and better.

I dedicate the following text—that moved me to share it with others—to those who are doing their utmost to awaken others to this evolutionary shift (sometimes called "the great shift"), which isn't an easy task: "This is the rise of the emotion warriors [service to others]. Leading humanity into the golden age. These souls are courageous and unique of strength, taking upon them the task to walk through the depth of their pain, bravely and without swords, but with compassion and understanding facing what they had long believed to be their enemy – the most sacred, wisest, playful, innocent and hurt child within themselves. From there on, they embark on a life-long journey of expression, healing and connecting once again with their magical child. By doing so they are the fearless catalysers of the shift in consciousness sending clarion calls throughout all galaxies and to their human family who will begin to remember what it feels like to feel, love and be all again." [17]

You can watch here a popular TV series that hides, as many other TV series and films, the truth about our coming shift from 3D to 5D in plain sight in the Star Trek TV series.

See here http://in5d.com/moving-into-5d-hidden-in-plain-sight/

Want to know if you're going through this shift? Check here 14 Signs You're Going Through THE SHIFT - (The Ascension Process)

https://www.youtube.com/watch?v=bklSzXvkztQ

I want to inspire the readers to step forward and embrace this great changeover, to understand what is transpiring while providing a grand vision of the upcoming Golden Age, and to provide strength and to encourage you not to be afraid of what's coming. Yes, it's difficult to believe . . . I know. I had a hard time believing some of this myself. I'm not a natural optimist; the opposite is true. But as I mentioned earlier, I can't ignore the evidence coming from soft disclosures and recent events. I needed a lot of hard evidence to believe this myself.

Jordan Sather provides more sources on the science of ascension—a quantum solar shift, including Terrence McKenna's findings, the Montauk project – remote view into the future... the CIA – they couldn't see anything beyond 2012 (David Wilcock and Corey Goode also mention this...) Chapter 8 of "The Divine Cosmos" by David Wilcock: "The Transformation of the Solar System" - **https://goo.gl/WLMvGI** Dr. Paul LaVoilette's Starburst Foundation - **https://goo.gl/ObO94G**
https://www.youtube.com/watch?v=Ig7fshISKmk

Tom Price, mentioned earlier, says that you need to "be in the heart" and in complete unity consciousness. It seems that people from all walks of life, age groups and from all over the world are awakening to their own roles in this mass awakening happening now. [18]

Manifestations of New Earth

I would like to share with you a project that for me represents the new earth today in our world. "Humanity is the first ever Universally Owned Corporation - the first company in the history of our species owned equally by every single human being alive. Every person you see outside is no longer a stranger - they are a fellow partner: working on the same team, with the same goals. Humanity was created as a result of the emergence of the global collective human consciousness - a result of our species growing up and coming together as one.[...] A universal, collective consciousness, sees every human as equal, and all humans as one. It changes the focus of our entire species: to service to others, instead of service to self. Ours is now the first known species in the history of Earth to have reached this level of evolutionary development.[...] After over 4 years and 15,000 hours of effort, Humanity, the first Universal Company, is ready to present the first fruits of this global collective human effort: The New Internet.[...]

"Owned by the people, Humanity is the New Internet you'll come to love. Gorgeous, ad-free, and super-advanced, it is also secure and open source. Humanity will connect every human and business alive. The New Internet will offer a range of dozens of global online services, from social networking to food delivery, and almost everything in between. And it is owned by you.[...] It will soon be unfathomable that your internet connection once came with nothing, and you had to scour the net to find basic services like email and crowd-funding! In addition to the New Internet, Humanity is also working on a range of electronic devices: from virtual reality headsets, to phones, smart-watches and televisions. And even wireless headphones! The money from ALL of our products and services is pooled together, used to grow Humanity, and to support wonderful charitable projects around the world. Such as educating kids. Or saving dolphins." [19]

AFTERWORD

We have had a thrilling journey reading this book from the Cabal's dark agenda to our ascension. These are historical times that we live in. Look around you carefully and say goodbye to the old social and political structures in place, because our lives are about to transform completely worldwide (or perhaps the shift already occurred when this book has been published). Yes, these are challenging times, but we're here in this together and we need to support each other because despite all our differences; at our core we're one, and if you don't believe that, please watch the fascinating and very moving video called *the DNA Journey*: https://www.youtube.com/watch?v=tyaEQEmt5ls

We create our world by consciousness. Every thought, every word, every action brings it into being. You can watch here the trailer of the documentary entitled *The Field* https://www.youtube.com/watch?v=vIWTJiQQPfE, which is going to be released in 2018 and is based on a series of experiments on consciousness and how it affects our reality. The idea behind these experiments is that "consciousness is energy and energy is physics"; namely, you can measure it, with rules. According to the scientists featured in this movie (including Gregg Braden), consciousness has enormous power to change things. One such experiment was to check whether the consciousness of a man in the U.S. can affect the energy field of a man in Russia? The answer is yes. There is no limitation to distance as this isn't about that but how an energy field "communicates." We affect it and it affects us in return. It was proven scientifically (minute 3:54 mark).[20] Think about the implications of this single discovery on our reality and ability to change it. Another experiment showed how consciousness can affect cancer cells (Gregg Braden has an amazing presentation on curing cancer by consciousness in China watch here https://www.youtube.com/watch?v=VLPahLakP_Q).

The Ascension process is fed by individual choices: listen to your body about dietary options. Quiet your mind and use mindfulness practices through the day to keep centered and prepare yourself. How do you prepare yourself? By becoming more in "service to others," which means treating people in a more loving and compassionate manner. You don't have to be a saint. No one is. You may entertain negative thoughts like we all have, but it's important how you react to these thoughts. Do you act upon your negative thoughts or not? That's the major difference.

No one knows how it will unfold entirely as each shift and its response brings new options. But we're in this together. We ascend as One. Yes, it's challenging, but we'll come terms with it. We must help each other, especially those faltering, go through this process. Victor Oddo talks about moving to 4th Density Ascension: 10-Signs You Are Moving Into 4th Density.[21]

Cobra says about what James Gilliland, a bestseller author, counselor, minister, an international lecturer, and the founder of ECETI (http://www.eceti.org/) says, "I would completely agree with James that the change that is happening is so huge, **beyond everything that you could probably imagine**. That when this is over – when it's really over – we can have such a wonderful time so it's worth it to keep pushing – KEEP PUSHING – and you will get there. **Hold the Light and we will get there**, because **when this is finally over it will be the best times of our lives ever.** If you want confirmation that all this is real[,] you can visit James ECETI ranch if he agrees of course, because then you will get that evidence that there is a real contact happening there. There is a real underground base under that mountain. There is a real Confederation portal opening there and ships from our star friends are showing themselves to people that would need that confirmation." [22]

LET'S MAKE THIS EARTH GREAT AGAIN!

FOOTNOTES

[1] Jordan Sather's Youtube channel, *Destroying the Illusion*, video explaining the rise in Schumann resonance, part of the earth's electromagnetic field, and how it correlates to brain waves https://www.youtube.com/watch?v=RLczNzWBbpE

[2] http://lyricstranslate.com/en/Yachad-Together.html

[3] http://themindunleashed.com/2017/09/mayor-one-small-town-canada-aims-provide-free-food-electricity.html

[4] https://ubuntuplanet.org/

[5] http://www.mazzastick.com/david-wilcock-personal-spiritual-development/

[6] https://divinecosmos.com/start-here/davids-blog/1180-ssp-revealed

[7] *Way of the Peaceful Warrior: A Book that Changes Lives* by Dan Millman https://www.amazon.com/Way-Peaceful-Warrior-Changes-Lives/dp/1932073205

[8] http://www.imdb.com/title/tt0398842/

[9] https://www.huffingtonpost.com/debbie-hampton/how-your-thoughts-change-your-brain-cells-and-genes_b_9516176.html https://www.scientificamerican.com/article/changing-our-dna-through-mind-control/

[10] http://goldenageofgaia.com/2012/11/29/after-ascension-well-acquire-new-spiritual-abilities/

[11] http://howtoexitthematrix.com/2015/08/06/new-powers-abilities-dna-upgrades-the-upcoming-wave-x/

[12] *Getting Aligned for the Planetary Transformation: Your Guide to What's Going on, Why, and Your Responsibility* by Tom Price, September 17, 2016 https://www.amazon.com/Getting-Aligned-Planetary-Transformation-Happening-ebook/dp/B01GXY9D7C

[13] http://www.spiritofmaat.com/archive/sep2/wilcock.htm

[14] https://www.huffingtonpost.com/lawrence-e-joseph/passing-into-the-energy-c_b_405086.html

15 http://www.awaken.cc/awaken/pagesE/library/ePlanetChanges.html

16 https://spherebeingalliance.com/introduction

17 http://www.thenewempath.com/blog/the-emotion-warriors-are-rising

18 https://www.youtube.com/watch?v=WQ4d0FKc58k

19 https://www.facebook.com/thisishuman/videos/898604580189559/

20 *The Field* documentary https://www.youtube.com/watch?v=vIWTJiQQPfE

21 Victor Oddo talks about moving to 4th Density Ascension: 10-Signs You Are Moving Into 4th Density https://www.youtube.com/watch?v=hwqsSm1KHr8

22 https://prepareforchange.net/2018/01/25/everything-going-fine-no-everything-will-amazingly-unbelievably-fine-clarification-repetition-re-cobra-update-16-jan-2018-goldfish-report-interview/

REFERENCES

1. http://mattbelair.com/michaeltellinger/

   #100 | MICHAEL TELLINGER 2017: HOW TO BUILD THE NEW EARTH NOW, REMOVE GLOBAL ELITE & CREATE WEALTH

2. http://2012portal.blogspot.co.il/

3. **http://in5d.com/end-world-know/**

4. 10 Signs You're Going Through An "Ascension Upgrade"

   https://www.youtube.com/watch?v=kQZ7UJqLuro&feature=share

5. The Science of Ascension - A Quantum Solar Shift

   https://www.youtube.com/watch?v=Ig7fshISKmk

6. http://www.stillnessinthestorm.com/2016/02/david-wilcock-and-corey-goode-history.html including ascension by solar flare…

7. More about the ascension prophecy https://divinecosmos.com/start-here/davids-blog/1225-abr-legacy

8. Victor Oddo on Youtube – guiding people through their ascension process / Energy Updates

   https://www.youtube.com/watch?v=VgxDs1pYGTA

9. https://raymaor.com/about-ray/ master of awakening

BIBLIOGRAPHY

1. Anderson, Christopher Alan, *Psychotherapy As Life Really Mattered*, Sarasota Florida, First Edition Design Publishing, Inc., September 2012,

2. Ganser, Daniele, *NATO's Secret Armies: Operation GLADIO and Terrorism in Western Europe*, London, Frank Cass Publishers, December 22nd 2004.

3. Hennessey, Andrew, *Harvesting the Disconnected: The Alien Agenda for Mankind*, Edinburgh, Scotland, Lulu.com publishing, December 2010.

4. Koire, Rosa, *Behind the Green Mask: U.N. Agenda 21*, Santa Rosa, The Post Sustainability Institute Press, December 19, 2011.

5. Meier, Suzanne, Briggs, Mike, *Becoming human again From Sheeple to People*, Amazon Digital Services LLC as the publisher, September 2, 2010

6. Middelkoop, Willem, *The Big Reset Revised Edition: War on Gold and the Financial Endgame*, Amsterdam, Amsterdam University Press, March 23, 2016.

7. Milman, Dan, *Way of the Peaceful Warrior: A Book that Changes Lives*, Novato CA, HJ Kramer, April 13, 2006.

8. Price, Tom, *Getting Aligned for the Planetary Transformation: Your Guide to What's Going on, Why, and Your Responsibility*, Salem OR, Silvercreek Co Publishing, LLC, June 10, 2016.

9. Dr. Pruett, Jack, *The Grandest Deception*, Bloomington Indiana, Xlibris Corp., April 7, 2011.

10. Thomson Iserbyt, Charlotte, *The Deliberate Dumbing Down of America*, Ravenna, Ohio, Conscience Press; Revised edition (1788), 1999.

11. United Nations, Agenda 21 Earth Summit The United Nations Programme of Action from Rio, New York, Createspace Independent Publishing Platform, 2013.

12. Welton, Ken, *CAP-COM the Economics of Balance: Capitalism and Communalism in the Unfranchised Society*, Dana Point, Pandit Press, August 1, 2001.

13. Wilcock, David, *The Ascension Mysteries: Revealing the Cosmic Battle Between Good and Evil*, New York, Dutton, August 30, 2016.

14. Wood, Peter, Stotsky, Sandra, Milgram, R. James, Wurman, Ze'ev, and 8 more co-authors, *Drilling through the Core: Why Common Core Is Bad for American Education*, Boston, Pioneer Institute Public Policy Research, September 28, 2015.

ABOUT THE AUTHOR

Shoshi has an MBA degree from the University of Humberside in Hull, England (today it's https://www.lincoln.ac.uk/home/), and is a graduate (BA degree in English linguistics and special education) of Hebrew University in Jerusalem, Israel. She has worked as a journalist for PCON magazine (http://pcon.co.il/v5/home.asp), which is an IT magazine for CIOs and CTOs in major companies and organizations in Israel. In this position, she wrote in-depth articles on a wide array of advanced technologies, such as encryption, the Dark Net, analytic tools, protecting the corporate website. She also interviewed opinion leaders in the Israeli hi-tech arena. Shoshi has also worked as the content manager of IsraelAgri.com, the international Israeli agriculture portal, where she wrote articles on Israeli agriculture and carried out interviews with opinion leaders in this field.

Made in the USA
Las Vegas, NV
30 October 2021